MATCH
OF THE
DAY

MATCH OF THE DAY
VIDEOS

On 22 August 1964 when the BBC launched *Match of the Day* football entered a new world. Watched initially by only 20,000 people, who would have thought that it would run for over a quarter of a century?

BBC Video celebrates this success with three titles:

with the highlights and heroes of each decade

Or, follow the history of your club with a special *Match of the Day* compilation, which include:

DERBY COUNTY ● MIDDLESBROUGH

NEWCASTLE UNITED ● NOTTINGHAM FOREST

SHEFFIELD UNITED ● SHEFFIELD WEDNESDAY

SOUTHAMPTON ● SUNDERLAND ● WEST HAM UNITED

MATCH
OF THE
DAY

THE COMPLETE
RECORD SINCE 1964

Compiled by JOHN MOTSON
Foreword by GRAHAM TAYLOR

BBC BOOKS

Published by BBC Books,
a division of BBC Enterprises Limited,
Woodlands, 80 Wood Lane,
London W12 0TT

First Published 1992

The moral right of the author has been asserted

Reprinted 1992 (twice)

ISBN 0 563 36406 8

Typesetting by Goodfellow & Egan Ltd, Cambridge
Printed and bound in Great Britain by Clays Ltd, St Ives plc
Colour separation by DOT Gradations, Chelmsford
Jacket printed by Belmont Press, Northampton

The author would like to thank Heather Holden-Brown and
Julian Flanders of BBC Books for their support during the
writing of this book. Thanks are also due to Karen Williamson
and Robert Foster for their help with the research of statistics

PICTURE CREDITS

Black and white

Action Images 89 (lower), 220; Associated Sports Photography 15, 117, 209; ©
BBC 14, 75 (top), 108; Neville Chadwick Photography 89 (top), 155; Colorsport
11, 27 (lower), 28, 39, 41, 45, 64, 73, 81, 91, 98, 100, 106, 107, 125, 127, 149, 156,
193, 205, 221; Courtesy Crystal Palace F.C. 147; Steve Hale 175, 183; Jack Hickes
Photographers 35, 63; Hulton Picture Company 48; Jim Hutchison 186; Liverpool
Daily Post & Echo 27 (top), 72, 97, 124, 134, 197, 214, 216; North London News
Ltd 80; Mike Pierce 164; Popperfoto 33 (lower), 55; Press Association 33 (top),
145; Professional sport 192, 215; Raymonds Press Agency 54 (top); David Smith
191; Sport & General 20, 116, 135, 167; Sporting Pictures UK 146, 203 (lower);
George Sturrock 208; Syndication International 17, 21, 23, 38, 46, 54 (lower), 57,
66, 75 (lower), 110, 165, 172, 181, 187, 203 (top), 211; Bob Thomas Sports
Photography 83, 119, 137, 158, 173, 189, 195, 198, 200; York & County Press 80.

Colour

John Motson & Kenneth Wolstenholme: © Ray Pickard Photography; Jimmy
Greaves: Allsport; Denis Law: Syndication International; Roger Hunt: Colorsport;
Geoff Hurst: Colorsport; Spurs v Man Utd: Syndication International; Man Utd v
West Ham: Bob Thomas Sports; Radford goal & Fashanu goal © BBC; George
Graham: Sporting Pics UK; Kenny Dalglish: Allsport; Dave Beasant save: Allsport;
Dave Beasant with cup: Action Images; Stuart Pearce: Bob Thomas Sports;
Gascoigne & Lineker: Allsport/David Cannon, Bryan Robson & Bobby Robson:
Allsport/Radford.

MATCH OF THE DAY

CONTENTS

FOREWORD
— 6 —

INTRODUCTION
— 7 —

AUTHOR'S NOTE
— 9 —

THE SEASONS
1964—65 to **1991—92**
— 10 —

APPEARANCES
1964—1992
— 222 —

INDEX
— 223 —

FOREWORD

NOWADAYS WHEN IT seems possible to watch any football match from any part of the world, it is hard to imagine that less than thirty years ago there was only ONE programme for the football connoisseur, namely BBC's *Match of the Day*.

Saturday evenings were planned according to the time of the programme. Video recording and other television companies showing football was for the future. Life was simple – Saturday was football day. Match in the afternoon – match on the telly at night. Smashing!

By 1964 I had been a professional footballer for two years and therefore by second nature I became a compulsive viewer. I was 'in at the start' – the black and white picture era with no instant replays, and have remained a supporter of the programme ever since.

My career has meant that I have been involved with several editions of the programme and consequently have experienced the professionalism of all those involved in order for the viewer to be presented with the best possible showing of the game or games involved.

This foreword does not give me the space to detail the importance *Match of the Day* has played in so many people's lives within the professional game but every photograph, every result, every scorer has a story – and the very presence of the television cameras along with the production of this book means those stories will long continue to be part of football's history.

There can be no greater compliment than that.

Best wishes,

GRAHAM TAYLOR, ENGLAND TEAM MANAGER

INTRODUCTION

F OR TWO DECADES and more, it was something between a ritual and an institution. It persuaded Saturday night drinkers to leave the pub before 10 o'clock, only to return the following day to discuss what they had seen when they got home. It kept the children up and sometimes sent Mum to bed. It made perfectly normal people start to hum a tune under their breath and its appeal crossed the social spectrum from royalty to railwaymen, from episcopates to engineers. It was a quintessential part of English life called *Match of the Day*.

From the moment the BBC launched a new Saturday night programme on BBC2 in August 1964, before an estimated audience of a mere 22,000, to the heady days of the 70s when the BBC1 peak-time version attracted an average of more than 10 million viewers, *Match of the Day* was a weekly fix for the armchair football addict.

Regular televised football had started a decade earlier, in the 50s with *Sports Special*. But then coverage was courtesy of old-fashioned film cameras, with the footage rushed by motor cycle to the nearest regional studio, and edited by hand to produce flickering black-and-white pictures belonging to the era of the newsreel.

Then, in the 60s, the advent of the electronic camera, its pictures beamed directly to base on to huge reels of videotape, changed the name of the game in television Outside Broadcasts and, together with new toys like the action-replay machine, changed with it the viewing habits of a nation. By the late 60s, two matches which had finished just a few hours earlier could be shown in colour, sensitively edited, even before the cocoa had cooled. There was no such thing as a Saturday night without *Match of the Day*. Until the late 70s, that is, when an audacious attempt to 'snatch' the coveted sport by ITV led to a compromise between the two terrestrial channels. In alternate years, *Match of the Day* moved from Saturday night to Sunday afternoon.

Next, in the early 80s, came the thirst for 'live' football. For a short time there was *Match of the Day* on Friday nights – then it was back to Sunday afternoons – and in 1988, when ITV secured the Football League rights exclusively, the show adopted a new image and title in keeping with the BBC's FA Cup contract. Now, it was *Match of the Day – The Road to Wembley*.

What had not changed, however, was the identity between the programme and its adherents. How often football supporters would wallow in nostalgia by reminding each other of the time their team had been seen in a memorable game on *Match of the Day*. As time went by, recalling the exact date and match details took on the mantle of a football quiz in itself.

Hopefully, this book will settle a few of those arguments and serve as a memory jogger for Saturdays gone by. It does not set out to be a technical tribute to the programme, more a football lover's guide to three decades of gripping action, as seen through the magic eye of the longest-running football programme on television.

And long may it continue. This book was almost completed and approaching the production stage when, in May 1992, the BBC in partnership with the satellite channel BSkyB secured the rights to screen matches from the new Premier League for the five years from August 1992 to the end of the 1996–7 season.

The decision meant an immediate return of *Match of the Day* on a Saturday night. While BSkyB, who paid the greater share of the £304 million contract, had exclusive rights to 'live' Premier League action, the BBC were able to restore edited highlights of two matches to their original slot.

Times and tastes may have changed, but the nation was able to welcome back an old friend.

AUTHOR'S NOTE

WHAT FOLLOWS is a complete review of the 28 seasons of *Match of the Day*, from its inception in 1964/5 to the end of the 1991/2 season. Each season is dealt with separately in chronological order, with a short account of the highlights, followed by a week-by-week guide to the matches shown on *Match of the Day*, together with results and goal-scorers.

The author has made a personal selection of one outstanding match and one outstanding player from each season. Although the choice is loosely based on the football shown by *Match of the Day* in the year in question, the matches covered by the BBC would, in any event, be a fair and general reflection of the English game at the said time.

It should be stressed that this is in no way intended to be a complete list of every match shown on television. It does not cover the midweek games shown in the BBC's *Sportsnight* programme; nor does it include regional highlights shown in Scotland, Wales or elsewhere. And, needless to say, it does not reflect the considerable amount of football screened on other channels.

In short it is a straightforward tribute to the managers, players, television professionals and most of all the football audience, who helped turn *Match of the Day* from a nervous experiment into a market leader.

IT COST JUST 4 SHILLINGS, 20p in today's currency, to stand on the terraces in the mid-60s. The most expensive seats at Anfield, where *Match of the Day* started in August 1964, were 8 shillings (40p). Even the annual tv licence was only £5. It was even better value when they threw in Saturday night football.

Liverpool, the defending champions, staged the first *Match of the Day* on the opening Saturday of the season when they beat Arsenal, and on the last Saturday the cameras covered their game at Old Trafford, when Liverpool lost, both match and league, to Manchester United. These two clubs would dominate the small screen more than any others over the next quarter of a century.

But back in 1964, talk of a Premier League was a long way off. You could watch First Division football at Craven Cottage, where the cameras captured a hat-trick by Blackpool's 19-year-old prodigy Alan Ball against Fulham, just a few weeks after *Match of the Day* had made its debut at 6.30 p.m. on BBC 2.

Tommy Docherty's Chelsea team of freshlings included two managers of the future. Terry Venables and George Graham were among the scorers on *Match of the Day* that first season, and when Chelsea crashed 4–0 at Old Trafford in March, so too was an 18-year-old Irishman called George Best. His hero status would be much enhanced by television. But it wasn't all about superstars. The democracy of the programme was established by visits to Northampton – then poised for a meteoric rise to the First Division – and to Fourth Division Oxford, where a certain Ron Atkinson was right-half and captain.

Not that television had things all its own way in these embryonic times. Their contract with the Football League did not entitle the BBC to extensive FA Cup coverage, and on one Saturday night in January there was no football at all. As one pundit observed at the time: 'It took Winston Churchill's funeral to stop *Match of the Day*'.

At the age of 18 George Best became a role model to millions, thanks partly to the photo opportunities offered by *Match of the Day*

a.e.t. = after extra time   **o.g.** = own goal   **pen.** = penalty

---

22/8/64	**Liverpool** ....3 Hunt Wallace (2)	**Arsenal** ....2 Strong Baker	*Division One*

29/8/64	**Chelsea** ....3 Murray Graham Shellito	**Sunderland** ....1 Herd	*Division One*

5/9/64	**Fulham** ....2 Stiles (o.g.) Haynes	**Manchester United** ....1 Connelly	*Division One*

12/9/64	**West Ham United** ....3 Byrne (3)	**Tottenham Hotspur** ....2 Greaves (2) (1 pen.)	*Division One*

19/9/64	**Chelsea** ....2 Venables Hollins	**Leeds United** 0	*Division One*

26/9/64	**Manchester United** ....4 Crerand (2) Law (2)	**Tottenham Hotspur** ....1 Robertson	*Division One*

3/10/64	**Chelsea** ....5 Bridges (3) Tambling R. Harris	**Blackburn Rovers** ....1 McEvoy	*Division One*

10/10/64	**Tottenham Hotspur** ....3 Robertson Greaves Saul	**Arsenal** ....1 Baker	*Division One*

17/10/64	**Leicester City** ....3 Hodgson Appleton (pen.) Stringfellow	**Nottingham Forest** ....2 Crowe Wignall	*Division One*

24/10/64	**Tottenham Hotspur** ....1 Jones	**Chelsea** ....1 Graham	*Division One*

31/10/64	**Arsenal** ....3 Baker (2) Anderson	**Everton** ....1 Pickering	*Division One*

7/11/64	**West Ham United** ....1 Sissons	**Blackburn Rovers** ....1 Byrom	*Division One*

14/11/64	**Wolverhampton Wanderers** ....3 Wharton Crawford Le Flem	**Tottenham Hotspur** ....1 Brown	*Division One*

21/11/64	**Fulham** ....3 Earle Chamberlain Howfield	**Blackpool** ....3 Ball (3)	*Division One*

RESULTS
1964-5

28/11/64	**Arsenal** ....2 Anderson Eastham	**Manchester United** ....3 Law (2) Connelly	*Division One*
5/12/64	**West Ham United** 0	**Leicester City** 0	*Division One*
12/12/64	**Chelsea** ....2 Bridges (2)	**Wolverhampton Wanderers** ....1 Crawford	*Division One*
19/12/64	**Aston Villa** ....3 A. Baker (2) MacLeod	**Arsenal** ....1 J. Baker	*Division One*
26/12/64	**Nottingham Forest**...............1 Chapman	**Tottenham Hotspur**...............2 Gilzean Jones	*Division One*
28/12/64	**West Ham United** ....2 Byrne Kirkup	**Birmingham City** ....1 Sharples	*Division One*
2/1/65	**Stoke City**...........................1 Viollet	**West Ham United** 0	*Division One*
9/1/65	**Everton** ....2 Pickering Burgin (o.g.)	**Sheffield Wednesday** ....2 Fantham Quinn	*FA Cup 3rd round*
	Oxford United ....1 Beavon (pen.)	**Tranmere Rovers**.................0	*Division Four*
16/1/65	**Nottingham Forest**...............2 Hinton (2)	**Manchester United** ....2 Law (2)	*Division One*
23/1/65	**West Bromwich Albion** ....2 Cram Clark	**Tottenham Hotspur**...............0	*Division One*
30/1/65	**No programme: Winston Churchill's funeral**		
6/2/65	**Tottenham Hotspur**...............1 Henry	**Manchester United** 0	*Division One*
13/2/65	**Arsenal** ....1 Eastham	**Leeds United** ....2 Giles Weston	*Division One*
20/2/65	**Leyton Orient**......................2 Elwood (2)	**Newcastle United** ....1 McGarry (pen.)	*Division Two*
27/2/65	**West Ham United** ....2 Hurst Presland	**Liverpool** ....1 Hunt	*Division One*
6/3/65	**Charlton Athletic** ....1 Kenning	**Bolton Wanderers** ....3 Lee (pen.) Bromley Butler	*Division Two*
13/3/65	**Manchester United** ....4 Herd (2) Best Law	**Chelsea** 0	*Division One*

Date	Home		Away		Division
20/3/65	**Leeds United** ....4 Johanneson (2) Bremner Peacock		Everton ....1 Temple		*Division One*
27/3/65	**West Ham United** ....2 Hurst Byrne		Arsenal ....1 Baker		*Division One*
3/4/65	**Aston Villa** ....1 Baker		Tottenham Hotspur...............0		*Division One*
10/4/65	**Northampton Town** ....2 Martin Brown		Derby County.......................2 Durban (2)		*Division Two*
17/4/65	**Leeds United** 0		Manchester United...............1 Connelly		*Division One*
24/4/65	**Manchester United** ....3 Law (2) Connelly		Liverpool 0		*Division One*

MATCH OF THE SEASON

Liverpool 3   Arsenal 2
at Anfield,
Saturday 22 August 1964

Kenneth Wolstenholme's words were mildly prophetic: 'Welcome to *Match of the Day*, the first of a weekly series on BBC 2. This afternoon we are in Beatleville . . .' It wasn't only John, Paul, George and Ringo who were putting Merseyside on the map. The Kop at Anfield, witty and refreshing, were signalling the arrival of a new force in the English game – Bill Shankly's Liverpool.

The champions opened their programme against Billy Wright's Arsenal, and if the game was memorable for the BBC, it certainly wasn't for Don Howe, the England full-back making his Arsenal debut. Howe was up against Peter Thompson, Liverpool's flying left-winger, who helped set up the opening goals for Roger

They didn't know what they'd started! A TV image of Roger Hunt (left) celebrating the first goal ever shown on *Match of the Day*. Ron Yeats and Ian Callaghan share Hunt's delight

Hunt with a splendid volley, and Gordon Wallace, deputising for the injured Ian St John.

But Arsenal retaliated. Geoff Strong, who ironically joined Liverpool soon afterwards, pulled a goal back, and then Joe Baker headed the equaliser. Every new production needs a fitting climax, and the armchair viewers got one when Wallace struck the winner three minutes from time.

In the second half, a black cat delayed the taking of a corner by running across the Liverpool goalmouth. The BBC had got lucky with their first *Match of the Day*.

Liverpool: Lawrence, Byrne, Moran, Milne, Yeats, Stevenson, Callaghan, Hunt, Chisnall, Wallace, Thompson. Scorers: Hunt, Wallace (2)

Arsenal: Furnell, Howe, McCullough, Snedden, Ure, Simpson, Armstrong, Strong, Baker, Eastham, Anderson. Scorers: Strong, Baker

PLAYER OF THE SEASON
Denis Law
(Manchester United)

It was Manchester United's championship, and it was Denis Law's season. He scored 28 goals in 36 First Division matches, and also read the producer's script for *Match of the Day*, scoring 9 goals in 8 televised appearances, including doubles against Tottenham, Arsenal, Nottingham Forest and Liverpool.

The sight of Law, in his long-sleeved shirt with his right arm raised pugnaciously to celebrate another deadly strike, was a salute to the 60s. He wasn't the steadfast figure that Bobby Charlton was, or the fashionable idol that George Best became, but he was one of three great players that Manchester United had contrived to combine in one thrilling attack.

Denis collected goals like others collected cigarette cards – easily, greedily, always able to say at the end of the season that his set were the best. He cut a dashing style and had a heroic nerve to go with it.

He was shy off the pitch, refusing to take part in television interviews, even on his finest days. But he later became a radio personality – and on the pitch that championship season personality might easily have been his middle name.

THIS WOULD PROVE the most momentous season in the history of English football, climaxed by the winning of the World Cup on home soil. Those whose goals would prove invaluable to England set their stall out on *Match of the Day* in the preceding months. Geoff Hurst and Martin Peters were on target for West Ham, Roger Hunt for Liverpool, Bobby Charlton for Manchester United and there was even a televised goal by little Nobby Stiles.

Manchester United gave way in their League Championship power battle with Liverpool, who were applauded on to the pitch by their opponents when *Match of the Day* covered their last home game against Chelsea. Not that Tommy Docherty's team were too worried about a 2–1 defeat that day. They had already won at Anfield in front of cameras in the third round of the FA Cup, and the first extended coverage of the competition by *Match of the Day* also captured a titanic Chelsea victory over Don Revie's Leeds in the fourth round.

Sheffield Wednesday ended Chelsea's hopes in the semi-final at Villa Park, but BBC cameras brought no luck at all to the other Sheffield club. United were on the wrong end of a 6–2 scoreline at Arsenal, and then crashed 4–0 at West Ham.

But in a season when BBC 2 viewers were swamped with goals, the Hammers were also on the receiving end. Nottingham Forest put five past them, and there were four apiece for Fulham against Sheffield Wednesday, with future England manager Bobby Robson among the scorers, and for Tottenham against Blackburn Rovers.

This match, at White Hart Lane at the end of January, marked the return to action of Jimmy Greaves, who had been out for three months with hepatitis. He scored, of course, but his draining illness was felt by many to be a contributory factor to his disappointment in the World Cup.

The BBC's blanket coverage of the big event in the summer of 1966 does not come under the *Match of the Day* title. But the new technology that sent crisp, pertinent pictures flashing around the world was to precipitate a major revolution in BBC football in the season to follow.

Never again would *Match of the Day* be tucked away on the second channel.

Bobby Robson of Fulham, later to manage England for eight years, steers a left-foot shot across an anxious Bobby Charlton. Fulham were in the First Division during the first four seasons of *Match of the Day*

2/10/65	**West Bromwich Albion** ....1 Fraser	**Chelsea** ....2 Bridges Graham	*Division One*
9/10/65	**Nottingham Forest**.................5 Hinton Wignall Storey-Moore Addison Wilson	**West Ham United** 0	*Division One*
16/10/65	**Tottenham Hotspur**...............5 Johnson Clayton Greaves Gilzean Robertson	**Manchester United**...............1 Charlton	*Division One*
23/10/65	**Chelsea** 0	**Leicester City** ....2 Sjoberg Dougan	*Division One*
30/10/65	**Wolverhampton Wanderers** ....1 Knowles	**Crystal Palace** 0	*Division Two*
6/11/65	**Arsenal** ....6 Baker (2) Skirton (2) Armstrong (2)	**Sheffield United**...................2 Reece Jones	*Division One*
13/11/65	**Leicester City** 0	**Manchester United**...............5 Connelly Herd (2) Charlton Best	*Division One*
20/11/65	**Sheffield Wednesday** ....1 Ford	**Fulham** 0	*Division One*
27/11/65	**Tottenham Hotspur**...............2 Gilzean Robertson	**Stoke City**............................2 Vernon (pen.) Dobing	*Division One*
4/12/65	**Chelsea** 0	**Liverpool** ....1 Hunt	*Division One*
11/12/65	**Leeds United** ....4 Giles (2) O'Grady Storrie	**West Bromwich Albion** 0	*Division One*
18/12/65	**Manchester United**...............5 Law (2) Charlton Herd Beal (o.g.)	**Tottenham Hotspur**...............1 Jones	*Division One*
1/1/66	**Sheffield United**...................2 Jones (2)	**Northampton Town** ....2 Lines Martin	*Division One*

8/1/66	**Arsenal** 0	**Liverpool** ....1 Yeats		*Division One*

8/1/66   **Arsenal** 0   **Liverpool** 1   *Division One*
Yeats

15/1/66   **Fulham** 0   **Manchester United** 1   *Division One*
Charlton

22/1/66   **Liverpool** 1   **Chelsea** 2   *FA Cup 3rd round*
Hunt   Osgood
Tambling

29/1/66   **Tottenham Hotspur** 4   **Blackburn Rovers** 0   *Division One*
Greaves (pen.)
Saul
Gilzean (2)

5/2/66   **Bristol City** 1   **Manchester City** 1   *Division Two*
Clark   Young

12/2/66   **Chelsea** 1   **Leeds United** 0   *FA Cup 4th round*
Tambling

19/2/66   **West Ham United** 4   **Sheffield United** 0   *Division One*
Hurst
Peters
Brabrook
Matthewson (o.g.)

26/2/66   **Fulham** 2   **Liverpool** 0   *Division One*
Earle (2)

5/3/66   **Wolverhampton Wanderers** 2   **Manchester United** 4   *FA Cup 5th round*
Wharton (2)   Law (2)
Best
Herd

12/3/66   **Liverpool** 1   **Tottenham Hotspur** 0   *Division One*
Hunt

19/3/66   **Manchester United** 2   **Arsenal** 1   *Division One*
Law   Walley
Stiles

26/3/66   **Preston North End** 1   **Manchester United** 1   *FA Cup 6th round*
Dawson   Herd

2/4/66   **Scotland** 3   **England** 4   *Home International Championship*
Law   Hurst
Johnston (2)   Hunt (2)
Charlton

Liverpool v. Sheffield United was cancelled due to snow

9/4/66   **Arsenal v. Leeds United was cancelled due to snow**

16/4/66   **Fulham** 4   **Sheffield Wednesday** 2   *Division One*
Barrett   Ford
Leggat   McCalliog
Earle
Robson (pen.)

Date	Home		Away		Competition
23/4/66	**Chelsea**	0	**Sheffield Wednesday**	2	*FA Cup semi-final*
			Pugh		
			McCalliog		
30/4/66	**Liverpool**	2	**Chelsea**	1	*Division One*
	Hunt (2)		Murray		
7/5/66	**Huddersfield Town**	0	**Coventry City**	2	*Division Two*
			Gould		
			Pointer		
14/5/66	**Everton**	3	**Sheffield Wednesday**	2	*FA Cup final*
	Trebilcock (2)		McCalliog		
	Temple		Ford		
21/5/66	**Oldham Athletic**	3	**Oxford United**	0	*Division Three*
	Towers				
	Dearden				
	Frizzell				
28/5/66	**Brentford**	0	**Gillingham**	2	*Division Three*
			Weston		
			Rackstraw		

MATCHES OF THE SEASON

Tottenham Hotspur 5
Manchester United 1
at White Hart Lane,
Saturday 16 October 1965
and Manchester United 5
Tottenham Hotspur 1
at Old Trafford,
Saturday 18 December 1965

This was probably *Match of the Day*'s best double bill. The matches were played two months apart, but the cavalier spirit of the times, personified by two clubs who always put the accent on entertainment, produced 12 goals and filled both grounds.

In their black and white transmission on BBC 2, *Match of the Day* listed the teams in

Goal of the Season? Tottenham's Jimmy Greaves leaves the Manchester United defence spreadeagled. He was then laid low by hepatitis and missed three months of the World Cup season

the old 2–3–5 formation. And that's how they played, in a fixture that was to take on a classic status over the years.

Spurs went 4–0 up at White Hart Lane, with Jimmy Greaves beating four defenders and the goalkeeper with a stroke of genius for the third goal. He missed the return match through illness, but this was United's day. Law scored two and Bobby Charlton beat Jennings from distance, as he had in their first encounter.

Tottenham: Jennings, Norman, Knowles, Mullery, Brown, Mackay, Johnson, Clayton, Gilzean, Greaves, Robertson. Scorers: Gilzean, Johnson, Greaves, Clayton, Robertson (For the second match, Beal, Jones and Saul replaced Norman, Johnson and Greaves. Jones was Spurs scorer.)

Manchester United: P. Dunne, Brennan, A. Dunne, Crerand, Foulkes, Stiles, Connelly, Best, Charlton, Law, Aston. Scorer: Charlton (At Old Trafford, Gregg, Cantwell and Herd replaced P. Dunne, Brennan and Aston. United's scorers were Law (2), Charlton, Herd and an own goal by Beal.)

PLAYER OF THE SEASON
Bobby Charlton
(Manchester United)

The BBC hadn't started their 'Goal of the Season' competition in the 60s. If they had, they would have been spoiled for choice. The likes of Law, Greaves and Charlton were producing little masterpieces nearly every week.

Charlton's two goals against Spurs in the matches already covered were typical. Dynamic shots rifled in from outside the penalty area, with the left foot at White Hart Lane, and on the volley with the right at Old Trafford. Neither gave Pat Jennings an earthly.

But shooting was just the most spectacular part of his game. His goals against Mexico and Portugal apart, he harnessed the attacking side of England's game from a central midfield position, to turn a promising World Cup team into a successful one.

Fittingly, he was voted Footballer of the Year in England and Europe in 1966, and went on to set what were, at the time, England records of 106 caps and 49 goals.

If Stanley Matthews was the first gentleman of football in the 50s, Bobby Charlton assumed that mantle in the 60s. His impeccable manners, on and off the field, made him every schoolboy's hero, but those who never saw Matthews play because television was in its infancy, were treated to a store of Charlton memories thanks to *Match of the Day*.

J UST THREE SHORT WEEKS after English football had enjoyed its finest hour with England's 4–2 victory over West Germany in the World Cup final *Match of the Day* opened the new domestic season at Upton Park, home of West Ham United. Come to think of it, there was nowhere else to start. Listen to how Ken Wolstenholme introduced the programme:

'Welcome to those who have followed us from BBC 2 to BBC 1, but a special welcome to those new viewers who have been won over by the World Cup. We hope you will go along and watch your local team as well as watch *Match of the Day*. And in response to your many requests, I will explain some of the more technical points of the game as we go along . . .'

This last undertaking was a direct reference to the number of women and children who had suddenly been infected with the football virus during the World Cup plague which swept through the country that summer. Suddenly, the national game had a brand new audience, and a much larger one too, which the BBC promptly acknowledged by switching the Saturday night output to its major channel.

No sooner had Wolstenholme got his opening words out, than three West Ham players took the field. Yes, just three. Bobby Moore, Geoff Hurst and Martin Peters, joint architects of England's triumph, went down the tunnel ahead of their team-mates to receive a fantastic ovation. The stadiums of England were still bathed in euphoria.

This was dampened a little at Upton Park by Chelsea, who beat West Ham 2–1. Docherty's exuberant team then scored six goals in front of the cameras at Villa Park, and later put four past Manchester City.

Chelsea maintained their momentum up to the FA Cup semi-final, where they beat Leeds United 1–0. One of the first televised controversies flared when the referee disallowed Peter Lorimer's effort from a last-minute free-kick, taken before he had signalled.

Also hotly disputed was a quickly taken free-kick by Jimmy Greaves for Spurs against Liverpool at White Hart Lane. Here, the champions claimed the wall was not ready. The referee allowed the goal and Liverpool eventually conceded the title to Manchester United.

United's chief contribution to *Match of the Day* was a 4–3 win over West Brom at The Hawthorns, all the goals coming in the first half. David Herd got a hat-trick, and Busby's team won what would be their last championship for at least 26 years.

The swinging sixties. Tommy Docherty cuts a sharp image as his young Chelsea players relax on the greyhound track at Stamford Bridge

20/8/66	**West Ham United** ....1 Boyce	**Chelsea** ....2 Hollins Cooke	*Division One*
27/8/66	**Leeds United** ....3 Lorimer Reaney Madeley	**Manchester United** ....1 Best	*Division One*
3/9/66	**Sheffield Wednesday** ....1 Pugh	**Leicester City** ....1 Dougan	*Division One*
10/9/66	**Tottenham Hotspur** ....2 Gilzean Greaves	**Manchester United** ....1 Law	*Division One*
17/9/66	**Aston Villa** ....2 MacLeod Hateley	**Chelsea** ....6 Tambling (5) Boyle	*Division One*
24/9/66	**Manchester United** ....4 Crerand Herd Law Sadler	**Burnley** ....1 Lochhead	*Division One*
1/10/66	**Chelsea** ....4 Tambling Baldwin Kirkup Osgood	**Manchester City** ....1 Young	*Division One*
8/10/66	**Arsenal** ....2 Boot Clark (o.g.)	**Newcastle United** 0	*Division One*
15/10/66	**Manchester United** ....1 Law	**Chelsea** ....1 Crerand (o.g.)	*Division One*
22/10/66	**Wales** ....1 R. Davies	**Scotland** ....1 Law	*Home International Championship and European Championship Qualifier*
29/10/66	**Leeds United** 0	**Southampton** ....1 Davies	*Division One*
5/11/66	**Leicester City** ....5 Rodrigues Sinclair (2) Gibson Stringfellow	**Burnley** ....1 Elder	*Division One*
19/11/66	**Sheffield Wednesday** ....1 Ford	**Tottenham Hotspur** 0	*Division One*
26/11/66	**Stoke City** ....1 Dobing	**Chelsea** ....1 Hateley	*Division One*
3/12/66	**Chelsea** ....1 Hateley	**Everton** ....1 Young	*Division One*

10/12/66	**Tottenham Hotspur**...............2 Greaves Rodrigues (o.g.)	**Leicester City** 0	*Division One*
17/12/66	**West Bromwich Albion** ....3 Astle (2) Kaye	**Manchester United** ....4 Herd (3) Law	*Division One*
24/12/66	**Chelsea** ....1 Boyle	**Liverpool** ....2 Hinton (o.g.) Strong	*Division One*
31/12/66	**Fulham** ....4 Leggat (2) Clarke Skeels (o.g.)	**Stoke City**...........................1 Vernon	*Division One*
7/1/67	**Liverpool** ....2 Thompson (2)	**West Ham United** 0	*Division One*
14/1/67	**Manchester United** ....1 Herd	**Tottenham Hotspur**................0	*Division One*
21/1/67	**West Ham United** ....3 Dear Hurst Sissons	**Sheffield Wednesday** 0	*Division One*
28/1/67	**Manchester United** ....2 Law Herd	**Stoke City**............................0	*FA Cup 3rd round*
	Millwall..............................0	**Tottenham Hotspur**...............0	*FA Cup 3rd round*
4/2/67	**Nottingham Forest**................1 Hennessey (pen.)	**Tottenham Hotspur**...............1 Greaves	*Division One*
11/2/67	**Leeds United** ....3 Bell Lorimer Belfitt	**Stoke City**...........................0	*Division One*
18/2/67	**Wolverhampton Wanderers** ....1 Wharton	**Everton** ....1 Ball (pen.)	*FA Cup 4th round*
	Fulham ....1 Clarke	**Sheffield United** ....1 Jones	*FA Cup 4th round*
25/2/67	**Portsmouth**.........................2 Portwood (2)	**Wolverhampton Wanderers** ....3 Bailey Hunt Knowles	*Division Two*
4/3/67	**Queens Park Rangers** ....3 R. Morgan Marsh Lazarus	**West Bromwich Albion** ....2 Clark (2)	*Football League Cup final*

11/3/67	**Sunderland** ....1 Martin	**Leeds United** ....1 Charlton	*FA Cup 5th round*
	Norwich City ....1 Bryceland	**Sheffield Wednesday** ....3 Quinn Ford Fantham	*FA Cup 5th round*
18/3/67	**Coventry City** ....1 Gould	**Bolton Wanderers** ....1 Phillips	*Division Two*
25/3/67	**Wolverhampton Wanderers** ....4 Dougan (3) Knowles	**Hull City** 0	*Division Two*
1/4/67	**Tottenham Hotspur** ....2 Greaves (2)	**Liverpool** ....1 Thompson	*Division One*
8/4/67	**Nottingham Forest** ....3 Storey-Moore (3)	**Everton** ....2 Husband (2)	*FA Cup 6th round*
	Birmingham City 0	**Tottenham Hotspur** 0	*FA Cup 6th round*
15/4/67	**Coventry City** ....1 Gould	**Huddersfield Town** 0	*Division Two*
22/4/67	**West Ham United** 0	**Leeds United** ....1 Lorimer	*Division One*
29/4/67	**Leeds United** 0	**Chelsea** ....1 Hateley	*FA Cup semi-final*
6/5/67	**Southampton** ....2 Chivers Paine (pen.)	**Nottingham Forest** ....1 Barnwell	*Division One*
13/5/67	**Manchester United** 0	**Stoke City** 0	*Division One*
20/5/67	**Chelsea** ....1 Tambling	**Tottenham Hotspur** ....2 Saul Robertson	*FA Cup final*
27/5/67	**Austria** 0	**England** ....1 Ball	*Friendly*

MATCH OF THE SEASON

Nottingham Forest 3
Everton 2
(*FA Cup 6th round*)
at the City Ground,
Saturday 8 April 1967

In any other season, perhaps, the pick of the *Match of the Day* offerings would have been the Football League Cup final – played for the first time at Wembley – in which Third Division Queens Park Rangers came from 2–0 down to beat West Bromwich Albion. But a month later, this FA Cup quarter-final topped it. Forest were chasing the League and Cup double, Everton were the cup holders, and they produced a game that was talked about by the Trent for many years to come.

Certainly, Jimmy Husband of Everton and Ian Storey-Moore of Forest won't forget it. Each scored twice before Storey-Moore brought the afternoon to a terrific crescendo with the winning goal.

It took him four attempts to score it. His first shot struck a defender, his second struck the goalkeeper, his third effort came back off the crossbar, then he threw himself forward to head the ball over the line.

Forest lost the semi-final to Spurs and came second in the league to Manchester United. But drama like this boosted the *Match of the Day* audience to some five million. Not bad for a three-year-old!

Nottingham Forest: Grummitt, Hindley, Winfield, Hennessey, McKinlay, Newton, Lyons, Barnwell, Baker, Wignall, Storey-Moore.
Scorer: Storey-Moore (3)

Everton: Rankin, Wright, Wilson, Hurst, Labone, Harvey, Young, Ball, Husband, Brown, Morrissey.
Scorer: Husband (2)

'Get in there'. Ian Storey-Moore completes a hat-trick as he heads the winning goal against Everton. Scenes of Forest jubilation followed, but they finished the season empty-handed

PLAYER OF THE SEASON
Bobby Tambling (Chelsea)

Chelsea played a formative part in the growth of *Match of the Day*. The programme started and grew during the Docherty years at Stamford Bridge, where brash young men like Peter Osgood, Terry Venables, Charlie Cooke and George Graham cocked a snook at the northern giants.

Bobby Tambling was the quiet man of the side, yet he set a Chelsea goalscoring record that outstripped notable predecessors like Roy Bentley and Jimmy Greaves. His career total of 202 included a haul of 5 collected in just one afternoon – and the *Match of the Day* cameras were there to capture it.

The setting was Villa Park in mid September, and Chelsea, in a natty change strip of white shirts and black shorts, simply took Villa apart. They won 6–2, and Tambling's five goals in one match remain a record for *Match of the Day*.

But his season did not end there. With 28 goals in 46 League and Cup games, he was largely responsible for Chelsea reaching their first Wembley FA Cup final – and he scored their goal in the 2–1 defeat for Spurs.

Nearly 25 years later, just short of his 50th birthday, Tambling was his old friend Venables's guest when Spurs played near his home at Portsmouth in the FA Cup. Modern players in the hotel hardly knew who he was. But defenders of the 60s will never forget him. Neither will Chelsea supporters.

T HE BURGEONING POPULARITY of *Match of the Day* was now having major side-effects. Footballers hitherto unknown outside their own town or city were suddenly catapulted into the national limelight. The programme was still in black and white, and still covered just one match each week, but its impact on millions of people was rising steadily.

The League season opened with an Everton victory over

A relaxed Joe Mercer and his radical coach Malcolm Allison brought the League Championship to Maine Road with some glittering football champions Manchester United. A Goodison crowd of 61,452 was bigger than the starting audience of *Match of the Day* three years earlier, but now around 5 million saw 22-year-old Alan Ball score two goals for the club he had joined for a record fee just after the World Cup.

The young players coming fresh into the game were not to know it, but the new generation would find themselves courted by agents, marketeers, sponsors and potential business partners. For better or worse, televised football had opened up new horizons.

Two young 'graduates', 18-year-old Peter Shilton and 19-year-old Trevor Brooking, came face to face when their clubs Leicester and West Ham met in front of the cameras just after Christmas. Brooking put West Ham's first goal past Shilton in a 4–2 win.

Twenty-four years and many England games later, the pair were still contributing to football on the screen, Shilton playing in goal for Derby and Plymouth at the age of 42, Brooking as the BBC's chief summariser in the commentary box.

Talking of famous goalkeepers, Tottenham's Pat Jennings, then just 22 years old, put himself into *Match of the Day* history by scoring direct from his own penalty area in the Charity Shield match against champions Manchester United at Old Trafford. He launched a huge kick into the United half, the ball bouncing just outside the penalty area and over the head of Jennings's opposite number, Alex Stepney. Jennings's joy was tempered by two scorching left-foot shots from Bobby Charlton, which enabled the champions to fight back to 3–3.

This was another in the long line of classic matches between Spurs and Manchester United (*see* Matches of the Season, page 20).

12/8/67	**Manchester United** ....3 Law Charlton (2)	**Tottenham Hotspur** ....3 Jennings Saul Robertson	*FA Charity Shield*
19/8/67	**Everton** ....3 Ball (2) Young	**Manchester United** ....1 Charlton	*Division One*
26/8/67	**Queens Park Rangers** ....2 Keen (pen.) I. Morgan	**Norwich City**........................0	*Division Two*
2/9/67	**West Ham United** ....1 Peters	**Manchester United** ....3 Kidd Ryan Sadler	*Division One*
9/9/67	**Liverpool** ....3 Smith (pen.) Hateley (2)	**Chelsea** ....1 Houseman	*Division One*
16/9/67	**Bristol City** ....2 Quigley Derrick	**Blackpool** ....4 Ingram (2) Skirton (2)	*Division Two*
23/9/67	**Arsenal** ....1 Radford	**Manchester City**..................0	*Division One*
30/9/67	**Sheffield Wednesday** ....2 Mobley Ritchie	**Wolverhampton Wanderers** ....2 Knowles Evans	*Division One*
7/10/67	**Manchester United** ....1 Aston	**Arsenal** 0	*Division One*
14/10/67	**Chelsea** ....1 Baldwin	**Everton** ....1 Ball	*Division One*
21/10/67	**Ireland** ....1 Clements	**Scotland** 0	*Home International Championship and European Championship Qualifier*
28/10/67	**Coventry City** ....2 Tudor Lewis (pen.)	**Sunderland** ....2 Martin (2 pens)	*Division One*
4/11/67	**Tottenham Hotspur**...............1 Jones	**Liverpool** ....1 Hunt	*Division One*
11/11/67	**Arsenal** ....2 Sammels Johnston	**Everton** ....2 Husband Hurst	*Division One*
18/11/67	**Fulham** ....2 Clarke (2)	**Nottingham Forest**...............0	*Division One*
25/11/67	**Chelsea** ....1 Baldwin	**Manchester United** ....1 Kidd	*Division One*
2/12/67	**Burnley** ....1 Harris	**Arsenal** 0	*Division One*

9/12/67	**Manchester City**.................4	**Tottenham Hotspur**...............1	*Division One*
	Bell	Greaves	
	Summerbee		
	Coleman		
	Young		

16/12/67	**Queens Park Rangers** 2	**Portsmouth**..........................0	*Division Two*
	I. Morgan		
	Keen		

23/12/67	**Newcastle United**.................1	**Liverpool** 1	*Division One*
	Scott	St John	

30/12/67	**Leicester City** 2	**West Ham United** 4	*Division One*
	Svarc	Brooking	
	Large	Dear (2)	
		Sissons	

6/1/68	**Ipswich Town** 2	**Birmingham City** 1	*Division Two*
	Wigg (2)	Vowden	

13/1/68	**Arsenal** 1	**Sheffield United** 1	*Division One*
	Graham	Addison	

20/1/68	**Leeds United** 2	**Everton** 0	*Division One*
	Jones		
	Giles (pen.)		

27/1/68	**Fulham** 4	**Macclesfield Town** 2	*FA Cup 3rd round*
	Clarke (2) (1 pen.)	Taberner	
	Gilroy	Fidler	
	Haynes		

	AFC Bournemouth 0	**Liverpool** 0	*FA Cup 3rd round*

	Chelsea 3	**Ipswich Town** 0	*FA Cup 3rd round*
	Tambling		
	Birchenall (2)		

3/2/68	**Leicester City** 2	**Leeds United** 2	*Division One*
	Large	Giles	
	Stringfellow	Madeley	

10/2/68	**Arsenal** 0	**Newcastle United** 0	*Division One*

17/2/68	**Tottenham Hotspur**...............3	**Preston North End** 1	*FA Cup 4th round*
	Greaves (2)	Charnley	
	Chivers		

	Leeds United 2	**Nottingham Forest**...............1	*FA Cup 4th round*
	Jones	Baker	
	Giles (pen.)		

24/2/68	**Scotland** 1	**England** 1	*Home International Championship and European Championship Qualifier*
	Hughes	Peters	

2/3/68	**Wolverhampton Wanderers** ....1 Dougan	**Liverpool** ....1 Hunt	*Division One*
	Manchester United ....1 Kidd	**Chelsea** ....3 Tambling Osgood Baldwin	*Division One*
9/3/68	**Sheffield Wednesday** ....2 D. Megson Ritchie	**Chelsea** ....2 Tambling Baldwin	*FA Cup 5th round*
	Rotherham United ....1 Downes	**Leicester City** ....1 Nish (pen.)	*FA Cup 5th round*
16/3/68	**Torquay United** ....3 J. Smith Scott Baxter	**Bury** 0	*Division Three*
23/3/68	**Leeds United** ....2 Giles Charlton	**Manchester City**...................0	*Division One*
30/3/68	**Leicester City** ....1 Nish	**Everton** ....3 Husband (2) Kendall	*FA Cup 6th round*
	Birmingham City ....1 Pickering	**Chelsea** 0	*FA Cup 6th round*
6/4/68	**Manchester United** ....1 Best	**Liverpool** ....2 Yeats Hunt	*Division One*
13/4/68	**Swindon Town** ....3 Rogers (2) Smart	**Southport** ....3 Redrobe Harkin Andrews	*Division Three*
20/4/68	**Queens Park Rangers** ....3 Marsh (2) Legg (o.g.)	**Huddersfield Town**...............0	*Division Two*
27/4/68	**Birmingham City** 0	**West Bromwich Albion** ....2 Astle T. Brown	*FA Cup semi-final*
4/5/68	**Leeds United** ....1 Jones	**Liverpool** ....2 Lawler Graham	*Division One*
11/5/68	**Manchester United** ....1 Best	**Sunderland** ....2 Suggett Mulhall	*Division One*
18/5/68	**Everton** 0	**West Bromwich Albion** ....1 Astle	*FA Cup final*

MATCH OF THE SEASON
Manchester City 4
Tottenham Hotspur 1
at Maine Road,
Saturday 9 December 1967

Genial Joe Mercer and his radical coach, Malcolm Allison, were two of television's first soccer pundits as the profile of the manager grew in the 60s. Their Manchester City team came out of the Second Division to win the Championship within two years.

One of the exuberant performances produced by their star-studded forward line came against Spurs on a frozen pitch. Francis Lee, Colin Bell, Mike Summerbee, Neil Young and Tony Coleman made light of the conditions to perform a football ballet on ice.

After Jimmy Greaves had put Spurs ahead, City tiptoed through the Tottenham defence time and again. Bell,

More like a Christmas card than a First Division match, as City's Colin Bell shoots past a young Pat Jennings. Dave Mackay (right) can only admire the view

Summerbee, Coleman and Young scored in that order, but such was their mastery of the conditions there could have been many more goals.

Such a winter's scene could only have happened before City installed their superb under-soil heating, which was later laid 9 inches under the surface. But even on better pitches, it is arguable whether Maine Road fans have ever seen a better exhibition.

It gave City a platform for

only their second Championship, which they clinched at Newcastle on the last day of the season, while United abdicated the throne in front of the cameras by losing to Sunderland.

Manchester City: Mulhearn, Book, Pardoe, Doyle, Heslop, Oakes, Lee, Bell, Summerbee, Young, Coleman.
Scorers: Bell, Summerbee, Coleman, Young

Spurs: Jennings, Kinnear, Knowles, Mullery, Hoy, Mackay, Saul, Greaves, Gilzean, Venables, Jones.
Scorer: Greaves

PLAYER OF THE SEASON
Rodney Marsh
(Queens Park Rangers)

Sometimes when the weather interfered with the selected *Match of the Day*, the BBC would whisk their cameras round the corner from Television Centre into the compact stadium in the shadow of the A40.

QPR were the local team, and they played at Loftus Road in west London. At this time, under the shrewd Alec Stock, they were on their way from the Third Division to the First

in successive seasons.

A conjurer called Rodney Marsh was one of the reasons why. In an era of entertainers, Rodney was a one-off. He could make the ball do everything but talk. His individual approach to the game, which sometimes included irreverent treatment of opponents and referees, made him a huge crowd-pleaser.

Rodney's two goals against Huddersfield in front of the cameras in April virtually ensured that Rangers would play First Division football for

the first time. That meant his baffling box of tricks would be on show in the best company – which is where he belonged.

OVER THE PREVIOUS four years, *Match of the Day* had established a virtually unchallenged position in the television football arena. Now, there was suddenly another player in the game. ITV's London Weekend region launched an ambitious Sunday afternoon show known as *The Big Match*.

Two heavyweights were signed to give it a powerful presence. Jimmy Hill, fresh from football management with Coventry City, brought a new and pungent approach to match analysis; Brian Moore, BBC Radio's football correspondent, switched to television to take on the double role of presenter and commentator.

The intensified competition reflected the growing demand for televised football. Both channels now had a Saturday lunchtime preview programme – the late Sam Leitch's *Football Preview* at the start of BBC *Grandstand* (this later became Bob Wilson's *Football Focus*) and Moore's *On The Ball*, which was networked across all the ITV regions.

While the BBC felt the competition most in the London area, where Moore and Hill used the extra editing time to provoke some lively Sunday afternoon debate, the other ITV regions showed highlights from their own area. It was a particularly good season in Yorkshire, where Don Revie's Leeds United, having won the Football League Cup the year before, now stormed to their first Championship with a record 67 points. They lost just 2 of their 42 First Division matches. *Match of the Day* picked them up early, a diving header by Mike O'Grady and a Jack Charlton goal accounting for Arsenal at Elland Road in September; then Johnny Giles and Eddie Gray were the scorers when Leeds beat high-flying Everton in late November. Gray scored again when Revie's team drew at West Ham – his dribbling prowess added to the television entertainment of the time. When he and Mick Jones scored the goals that beat Leicester in April, the *Match of the Day* cameras saw Leeds virtually sew up the title.

Elsewhere, European champions Manchester United went into gradual decline, but still entertained liberally (*see* 'Match of the Season', page 38), and Ron Greenwood's West Ham stuck to their principles as the decade drew to a close with the stark demand for success starting to take over from the free-wheeling football that had survived for much of the 60s.

Mick Jones heads past Leicester's Peter Shilton in Leeds United's Championship season. Revie's team lost only two First Division matches and collected a (then) record 67 points

10/8/68	**Queens Park Rangers** ....1 Allen	**Leicester City** ....1 Clarke	*Division One*
17/8/68	**Manchester City**..................0	**Manchester United** 0	*Division One*
24/8/68	**Tottenham Hotspur**...............1 England	**Sheffield Wednesday** ....2 McCalliog Whitham	*Division One*
31/8/68	**West Ham United** ....4 Peters (3) Redknapp	**West Bromwich Albion** 0	*Division One*
7/9/68	**Chelsea** ....1 Osgood (pen.)	**Everton** ....1 Morrissey	*Division One*
14/9/68	**Sheffield United**..................1 Woodward	**Oxford United** ....2 G. Atkinson Shuker	*Division Two*
21/9/68	**Leeds United** ....2 O'Grady Charlton	**Arsenal** 0	*Division One*
28/9/68	**Fulham** ....1 Macdonald	**Blackburn Rovers** ....1 Martin	*Division Two*
5/10/68	**Manchester United** 0	**Arsenal** 0	*Division One*
12/10/68	**Wolverhampton Wanderers** ....1 Knowles	**Chelsea** ....1 Tambling	*Division One*
19/10/68	**Tottenham Hotspur**...............2 Greaves (2)	**Liverpool** ....1 Hunt	*Division One*
26/10/68	**Arsenal** 0	**West Ham United** 0	*Division One*
2/11/68	**Chelsea** ....2 Baldwin Osgood	**Manchester City**..................0	*Division One*
9/11/68	**Sunderland** ....1 Harris	**Manchester United** ....1 Hurley (o.g.)	*Division One*
16/11/68	**Charlton Athletic**..................1 Tees	**Hull City** ....1 Wagstaff	*Division Two*
23/11/68	**Leeds United** ....2 Giles (pen.) Gray	**Everton** ....1 Royle	*Division One*
30/11/68	**West Ham United** ....2 Peters Hurst	**Manchester City**..................1 Lee (pen.)	*Division One*
7/12/68	**Blackpool** ....1 James	**Middlesbrough** ....1 Rooks	*Division Two*
14/12/68	**West Ham United** ....1 Peters	**Leeds United** ....1 Gray	*Division One*

21/12/68	**Liverpool** ....1 Hughes	**Tottenham Hotspur** 0	*Division One*
4/1/69	**Everton** ....2 Royle Hurst	**Ipswich Town** ....1 O'Rourke	*FA Cup 3rd round*
	Exeter City ....1 Banks	**Manchester United** ....3 Fitzpatrick Kidd Newman (o.g.)	*FA Cup 3rd round*
	Cardiff City..........................0	**Arsenal** 0	*FA Cup 3rd round*
11/1/69	**Stoke City**...........................1 Conroy	**Tottenham Hotspur**...............1 Jenkins	*Division One*
18/1/69	**Swindon Town** 0	**Luton Town** 0	*Division Three*
25/1/69	**Liverpool** ....2 Smith (pen.) Hughes	**Burnley** ....1 Latcham	*FA Cup 4th round*
1/2/69	**Leicester City** ....1 Clarke	**West Ham United** ....1 Dear	*Division One*
8/2/69	**Cardiff City**..........................5 Bird Clark (2) Toshack (2)	**Oxford United** 0	*Division Two*
15/2/69	**Leeds United** ....1 Lorimer	**Chelsea** 0	*Division One*
22/2/69	**Tottenham Hotspur**...............1 Morgan	**Wolverhampton Wanderers** ....1 Curran	*Division One*
1/3/69	**Chelsea** ....1 Webb	**West Bromwich Albion** ....2 Brown Astle	*FA Cup 6th round*
8/3/69	**Blackpool** ....2 Brown Craven	**Derby County**......................3 McFarland O'Hare Hinton (pen.)	*Division Two*
	Mansfield Town 0	**Leicester City** ....1 Fern	*FA Cup 6th round*
15/3/69	**Chelsea** ....3 Webb Hutchinson Tambling	**Manchester United** ....2 James Law (pen.)	*Division One*
22/3/69	**Nottingham Forest**...............3 Hall Hennessey Hilley	**West Bromwich Albion** 0	*Division One*
29/3/69	**Manchester City**...................3 Bell Doyle (pen.) Owen	**Stoke City**...........................1 Marsh	*Division One*

5/4/69	**Liverpool** ....**1** Hunt	**Wolverhampton Wanderers** **0**	*Division One*
12/4/69	**Newcastle United** ....**2** B. Robson (pen.) Foggon	**Manchester United** **0**	*Division One*
19/4/69	**Leeds United** ....**2** Jones Gray	**Leicester City** **0**	*Division One*
26/4/69	**Manchester City**..................**1** Young	**Leicester City** **0**	*FA Cup final*

Match of the Day viewers probably saw more of Ian Hutchinson's goal for Chelsea than some of the 60 000 at Stamford Bridge. Note those perched on the hoardings, and also the absence of perimeter advertising.

MATCH OF THE SEASON

Chelsea 3
Manchester United 2
at Stamford Bridge,
Saturday 15 March 1969

The arrival of Dave Sexton as Chelsea's manager did nothing to dull the artistry of a side that painted on a broad canvas. In the next two years, they joined the privileged English masters in the European winners' academy.

The style and free spirit of their football was matched by that of the European champions Manchester United when a crowd of 60 000 saw the teams walk out side by side in front of BBC cameras.

Bobby Charlton was injured, but George Best was there, so was Denis Law, and Peter Osgood was back for Chelsea. The match was a thriller.

David Webb put Chelsea ahead in the first minute, Ian Hutchinson made it 2–0, then Steve James pulled one back for United.

In the second half, Bobby Tambling ran half the length of the pitch for Chelsea's third, and Law scored from a penalty.

But there was still time for humour in the game of the 60s.

The cameras caught referee George McCabe calming down an incensed Nobby Stiles by ruffling his hair.

Chelsea: Bonetti, Webb, McCreadie, Hollins, Dempsey, Harris, Boyle, Tambling, Hutchinson, Osgood, Houseman.
Scorers: Webb, Hutchinson, Tambling

Manchester United: Stepney, Fitzpatrick, A. Dunne, Crerand, James, Stiles, Morgan, Kidd, Sadler, Law, Best.
Scorers: James, Law (pen.)

PLAYER OF THE SEASON
Martin Peters
(West Ham United)

One of the most notable interviews screened in the early years of *Match of the Day* was with West Ham's articulate manager, Ron Greenwood, after they had beaten Manchester City at Upton Park in November 1968.

Greenwood talked lucidly about the telepathic understanding between his England World Cup forwards Geoff Hurst and Martin Peters. Each had made an identical goal for the other with near-post crosses that day.

For Peters, now 25, but with arguably his best years still to come at Tottenham and Norwich, this was an excellent season in front of the cameras. He emerged from the shadow of Hurst and Bobby Moore to be a modern star in his own right.

On the last day of August, Peters collected what was to be the only hat-trick seen on *Match of the Day* that season. West Brom's defence had no answer to the timing of his runs from deep positions.

Peters scored against the champions-elect, Leeds United, at Upton Park in December. His stealthy strikes on goal may have come as a surprise to opponents and viewers alike, but his immaculate reading of the play as attacks built up was an initutive quality few others could match.

To amend Alf Ramsey's opinion slightly, Peters was very much a player of his time.

THE WEEKEND COMPETITION from the regional ITV companies now persuaded *Match of the Day* to expand, a little gingerly at first, but in a manner that was a signpost to the future. In this season, viewers still saw one main match nationwide, but each BBC region covered a second match to be shown just in their area.

Thus it was, that on the last Saturday in August, after the nation had seen Fairs Cup holders Newcastle beat Arsenal at St James's Park, those watching in the south and west of the country were treated to an exceptional one-man show from Swindon.

Don Rogers was a direct, well-built winger with craft and pace. Only a few months earlier, he had powered Third Division Swindon to an extraordinary League Cup triumph over Arsenal at Wembley. They also won promotion and now, as a Second Division outfit, took Charlton apart at their County Ground. Swindon won 5–0, Peter Noble scored a hat-trick, and Rogers made all five goals.[*]

In November 1969 came another *Match of the Day* landmark, when the first match was transmitted in colour. Viewers saw the red shirts of Bill Shankly's Liverpool overcome West Ham at Anfield with goals by Chris Lawler and Bobby Graham.

The following month, Graham scored again in the Merseyside derby at Goodison Park, but it was an own goal by Everton full-back Sandy Brown, who sent a flying header into his own net, that is best remembered from Liverpool's 3–0 victory.

Just seven days later, Liverpool were on the receiving end. Manchester United crushed them 4–1 at Anfield, with Bobby

---

[*] Details of the Swindon v. Charlton match will not be found in the statistics section for this season. It was one of many matches shown only in one or more BBC regions, but not necessarily screened nationwide. As has been made clear in the preface, various regional 'opt outs' down the years, especially in Scotland and Wales, have not been included. Neither have short 'goal clips' that may from time to time have been shown at the end of the programme from matches not afforded full camera coverage.

The triumphant trio. Colin Harvey,
Alan Ball and Howard Kendall
celebrate an Everton goal en route to
the Championship. Behind them,
Johnny Morrissey congratulates Joe
Royle

Charlton, inevitably, serving up another televised blockbuster.
That defeat, together with an embarrassing FA Cup exit at
Watford, also seen on *Match of the Day*, provoked Shankly into
wholesale rebuilding.

In the meantime, a thrusting young manager called Brian
Clough was forcing himself into the nation's consciousness. His
clean-cut Derby County side finished fourth in their first season in
Division One.

But as the 70s dawned, one of the rebels of the 60s bowed out.
Tearaway Wolves forward Peter Knowles left football to become
a Jehovah's Witness. He never came back to the game.

During this season the BBC experimented with a second match for *Match of the Day* viewers. But the game shown varied from region to region, so that viewers in the south-east, for example, saw a different second feature to those in the north. To avoid confusion the only matches listed here were the main network games shown nationally.

2/8/69	**Leeds United** ...... 2 Gray Charlton	**Manchester City** ...... 1 Bell	*FA Charity Shield*
9/8/69	**Crystal Palace** ...... 2 Blyth Queen	**Manchester United** ...... 2 Charlton Morgan	*Division One*
16/8/69	**Tottenham Hotspur** 0	**Liverpool** ...... 2 Hughes Lawler	*Division One*
23/8/69	**Manchester City** ...... 1 Bowyer	**Everton** ...... 1 Morrissey	*Division One*
30/8/69	**Newcastle United** ...... 3 Davies Foggon Robson	**Arsenal** ...... 1 Robertson	*Division One*
6/9/69	**Derby County** ...... 2 O'Hare Hector	**Everton** ...... 1 Kendall	*Division One*
13/9/69	**Cardiff City** ...... 1 Toshack	**Leicester City** ...... 1 Carver (o.g.)	*Division Two*
20/9/69	**Leeds United** ...... 2 Giles (pen.) Lorimer	**Chelsea** 0	*Division One*
27/9/69	**Manchester United** ...... 5 Burns Best (2) Charlton Kidd	**West Ham United** ...... 2 Hurst (2)	*Division One*
4/10/69	**Wolverhampton Wanderers** .... 2 Curran (2) (1 pen.)	**Everton** ...... 3 Royle (pen.) Morrissey Harvey	*Division One*
11/10/69	**Chelsea** ...... 2 Houseman Hollins	**Derby County** ...... 2 Hector O'Hare	*Division One*
18/10/69	**Tottenham Hotspur** ...... 2 Greaves (2)	**Newcastle United** ...... 1 Robson	*Division One*
25/10/69	**Leeds United** ...... 2 Clarke (2)	**Derby County** 0	*Division One*
1/11/69	**Manchester United** ...... 1 Charlton	**Stoke City** ...... 1 Burrows	*Division One*

8/11/69	**Queens Park Rangers** ....2 Bridges Clarke	**Sheffield United** ....1 Woodward	*Division Two*
15/11/69	**Liverpool** ....2 Lawler Graham	**West Ham United** 0	*Division One* *first BBC colour transmission*
22/11/69	**Arsenal** ....1 Neill (pen.)	**Manchester City**...................1 Bowyer	*Division One*
29/11/69	**Derby County** 0	**Nottingham Forest**...............2 Storey-Moore Lyons	*Division One*
6/12/69	**Everton** 0	**Liverpool** ....3 Hughes Brown (o.g.) Graham	*Division One*
13/12/69	**Liverpool** ....1 Hughes	**Manchester United** ....4 Yeats (o.g.) Ure Morgan Charlton	*Division One*
20/12/69	**Chelsea** ....3 Webb (2) Hutchinson	**Manchester City**...................1 Summerbee	*Division One*
27/12/69	**Leeds United** ....2 Jones (2)	**Everton** ....1 Whittle	*Division One*
3/1/70	**Bradford City** ....2 England (o.g.) Stowell	**Tottenham Hotspur**...............2 Greaves Morgan	*FA Cup 3rd round*
	Hull City 0	**Manchester City**...................1 Young	*FA Cup 3rd round*
	Sheffield Wednesday ....2 Whitham (2)	**West Bromwich Albion** ....1 Brown	*FA Cup 3rd round*
10/1/70	**Chelsea** ....2 Hollins Osgood	**Leeds United** ....5 Clarke Cooper Giles (pen.) Lorimer Jones	*Division One*
17/1/70	**Luton Town** 0	**Plymouth Argyle**...................2 Rickard Bickle	*Division Three*
24/1/70	**Chelsea** ....2 Osgood Hollins	**Burnley** ....2 Dobson (2)	*FA Cup 4th round*
	Sutton United 0	**Leeds United** ....6 Clarke (4) Lorimer (2)	*FA Cup 4th round*
	Watford...........................1 Franks	**Stoke City**...........................0	*FA Cup 4th round*

31/1/70	**Huddersfield Town** ....1 Smith	**Carlisle United** 0	*Division Two*
7/2/70	**Queens Park Rangers** ....1 Mackay (o.g.)	**Derby County** 0	*FA Cup 5th round*
	Liverpool 0	**Leicester City** 0	*FA Cup 5th round*
	Leeds United ....2 Giles Clarke	**Mansfield Town** 0	*FA Cup 5th round*
14/2/70	**Manchester United** ....1 Kidd	**Crystal Palace** ....1 Sewell (pen.)	*Division One*
21/2/70	**Watford** ....1 Endean	**Liverpool** 0	*FA Cup 6th round*
	Swindon Town 0	**Leeds United** ....2 Clarke (2)	*FA Cup 6th round*
28/2/70	**Blackburn Rovers** ....1 Martin (pen.)	**Sheffield United** ....2 Woodward Currie	*Division Two*
7/3/70	**Liverpool** 0	**Leeds United** 0	*Division One*
14/3/70	**Manchester United** 0	**Leeds United** 0	*FA Cup semi-final*
21/3/70	**Manchester City** ....1 Lee	**West Ham United** ....5 Greaves (2) Hurst (2) Boyce	*Division One*
28/3/70	**Leeds United** ....1 Lorimer	**Southampton** ....3 Charlton (o.g.) Davies (pen.) Yorath (o.g.)	*Division One*
4/4/70	**Sheffield Wednesday** 0	**Everton** ....1 Morrissey	*Division One*
11/4/70	**Leeds United** ....2 Jones Charlton (Chelsea won the replay 2–1)	**Chelsea** ....2 Hutchinson Houseman	*FA Cup final*
18/4/70	**Wales** ....1 Kryzwicki	**England** ....1 Lee	*Home International Championship*
21/4/70	**England** ....3 Peters Hurst Charlton	**Northern Ireland** ....1 Best	*Home International Championship*
25/4/70	**Scotland** 0	**England** 0	*Home International Championship*
	Wales ....1 Rees	**Northern Ireland** 0	*Home International Championship*

MATCH OF THE SEASON

Chelsea 2 Leeds United 5
at Stamford Bridge,
Saturday 10 January 1970

The FA Cup final replay between Chelsea and Leeds at Old Trafford later this season was watched by over 32 million people – the highest British tv audience ever for a football match. This league meeting did not attract quite that many, but the growing *Match of the Day* figures were due in part to awesome football such as that served up by Leeds in the second half at Stamford Bridge.

From 2–1 down, they piled four goals past Chelsea's reserve goalkeeper Tommy Hughes, and drew rave reviews that put them in the frame for the treble of League, League Cup and European Cup.

In the first half, John Hollins and the flamboyant Peter Osgood had replied to an early Leeds goal from Allan Clarke. But after the break, Terry Cooper equalised with a curling shot, Johnny Giles stroked in a penalty, Peter Lorimer bundled in the fouth and Mick Jones completed a miserable afternoon for the Chelsea faithful.

Chelsea would have their revenge in May, by which time Leeds had lost their Championship to Everton and been waylaid in the European Cup by Celtic. They finished the season empty-handed.

Chelsea: Hughes, Webb, McCreadie, Hollins, Dempsey, Harris, Cooke, Hudson, Osgood, Hutchinson, Houseman.
Scorers: Hollins, Osgood

Leeds: Sprake, Reaney, Cooper, Bremner, Charlton, Hunter, Lorimer, Clarke (sub. Bates), Jones, Giles, Madeley.
Scorers: Clarke, Cooper, Giles (pen.), Lorimer, Jones

A crushing victory for Allan Clarke and Leeds. But David Webb and Chelsea had their revenge at the end of the season in the FA Cup final replay in which Webb scored the winning goal

PLAYER OF THE SEASON
Jimmy Greaves
(Tottenham Hotspur,
West Ham)

Jimmy Greaves scored 357 goals in 517 First Division matches. Not to mention 54 in major Cup ties and a further 44 for England. Yet in this season when he reached his 30th birthday, he was fast approaching the point when he would give up the game.

That was far from his mind when he produced two goals against Newcastle at White Hart Lane, the second one a gem. When he received the ball from 17-year-old Steve Perryman, Greaves was in his own half of the field.

It took him just five touches of the ball to run 60 yards, cut inside defender Ollie Burton, round keeper Willie McFaul, and prod the ball into the net. The crowd were mesmerised, then rose to acclaim sheer genius.

Yet, four months later, Greaves was making his debut for West Ham against Manchester City at Maine Road, after being transferred in part exchange for Martin Peters. When he scored after 10 minutes, commentator Barry Davies pointed out that Greaves had scored on his debuts for Chelsea Juniors, Chelsea Reserves, England Youth, Chelsea's League side, England U23s, the full England

England U23s, the full England side, AC Milan, Spurs Reserves, Tottenham and now West Ham.* He did more than that. He lit up the formative years of *Match of the Day* with a unique amalgam of a goalscorers' sixth sense, instinct and opportunism. We would never see his like again.

---

* This match was also notable for an amazing goal by West Ham's Ronnie Boyce. He volleyed a clearance by Joe Corrigan straight back over the City goalkeeper's head from 45 yards.

THE LEEDS CONTROVERSY apart (see page 55), it was, without question, Arsenal's year. They emulated the achievement of their north London rivals Spurs 10 years earlier by winning the League and Cup 'double', clinching the Championship, just to rub their neighbours' noses in it, at White Hart Lane.

Ironically, the deciding match was not seen on television. It was played on the Monday evening before the Cup final, and Ray Kennedy's headed goal was shown only in news programmes. But Kennedy and his striking partner, John Radford, got their share on *Match of the Day*. Radford hit a hat-trick against Manchester United early in the season, a match which also included a superb save by Bob Wilson at the feet of George Best.

A 5–0 defeat at Stoke apart, Arsenal were virtually unstoppable. George Graham, later to win two Championships as their manager, was among the scorers, Wilson and captain Frank McLintock two others whose profile would stay on the screen for years to come.

Arsenal completed the double with an extra-time victory over Liverpool at Wembley, but it was the earlier rounds which gave *Match of the Day* viewers a keyhole appetite for the magic of the FA Cup.

In the third round, inside-forward Tony Green inspired Blackpool to a 4–0 win over West Ham, after which four of the Hammers' team were fined for staying up late at a Blackpool nightclub. An early night did Leeds no good in the fifth round. They went three goals down to Fourth Division Colchester, for whom Ray Crawford scored twice, before losing 3–2.

The cheekiest goal of this season was scored by Ernie Hunt for Coventry against Everton. Willie Carr jumped with the ball between his legs to set up Hunt's volley from a free-kick. Seen by millions on *Match of the Day*, it became known as the 'donkey kick'. But was it legal? Just another spicy subject for television debate!

Arsenal's double act. John Radford at the forefront, his partner Ray Kennedy out of the picture, and scorer Peter Storey on the ground as his header beats the Blackpool defence

The two-match experiment of the previous season was deemed to be a success. So, from the start of this season, *Match of the Day* screened two games nationally, giving the programme its most successful format which continued for the next 15 years.

It was at the start of the league season 1970-1 that the now familiar *Match of the Day* theme tune was adopted. It was written specifically for the programme by Barry Stroller and is simply called 'Match of the Day'. The *original* signature tune, used from the first programme in August 1964 until August 1970, was 'Drum Majorette' by Arnold Stock.

8/8/70	**Chelsea** ...... 1 Hutchinson	**Everton** ...... 2 Whittle Kendall	*FA Charity Shield*
15/8/70	**Manchester United** 0	**Leeds** ...... 1 Jones	*Division One*
	Chelsea ...... 2 Hutchinson (2)	**Derby County** ...... 1 O'Hare	*Division One*
22/8/70	**Arsenal** ...... 4 Radford (3) Graham	**Manchester United** 0	*Division One*
	Wolverhampton Wanderers 0	**Tottenham Hotspur** ...... 3 Morgan Chivers Mullery	*Division One*
29/8/70	**Everton** 0	**Manchester City** ...... 1 Bell	*Division One*
	Tottenham Hotspur ...... 1 Chivers	**Coventry City** 0	*Division One*
5/9/70	**Liverpool** ...... 1 Evans	**Manchester United** ...... 1 Kidd	*Division One*
	Arsenal ...... 2 Armstrong (2)	**Tottenham Hotspur** 0	*Division One*
12/9/70	**Sheffield Wednesday** ...... 1 Wilcockson	**Queens Park Rangers** 0	*Division Two*
	West Bromwich Albion ...... 2 Suggett (2)	**West Ham United** ...... 1 Howe	*Division One*
19/9/70	**West Ham United** 0	**Newcastle United** ...... 2 Robson (2)	*Division One*
	Derby County ...... 1 Hinton	**Burnley** 0	*Division One*
26/9/70	**Stoke City** ...... 5 Ritchie (2) Conroy Greenhoff Bloor	**Arsenal** 0	*Division One*
	Nottingham Forest 0	**Leeds United** 0	*Division One*

3/10/70	**Coventry City** **3**	**Everton** **1**	*Division One*
	Hunt (2)	Hurst	
	Martin		
	Liverpool **1**	**Chelsea** **0**	*Division One*
	Evans		
10/10/70	**Chelsea** **1**	**Manchester City**..................**1**	*Division One*
	Weller	Bell	
	Birmingham City **0**	**Sheffield United** **1**	*Division Two*
		Tudor	
17/10/70	**Arsenal** **4**	**Everton** **0**	*Division One*
	Kennedy (2)		
	Kelly		
	Storey (pen.)		
	Cardiff City..........................**2**	**Leicester City** **2**	*Division Two*
	Gibson (pen.)	Farrington	
	Carver	Sjoberg	
24/10/70	**Derby County** **0**	**Leeds United** **2**	*Division One*
		Clarke	
		Lorimer	
	Ipswich Town **1**	**Liverpool** **0**	*Division One*
	Hill		
31/10/70	**Newcastle United** **1**	**Manchester United** **0**	*Division One*
	Davies		
	Torquay United **3**	**Fulham** **1**	*Division Three*
	Rudge	Johnston	
	Mitchinson (2)		
7/11/70	**Hull City** **0**	**Luton Town** **2**	*Division Two*
		Givens	
		Macdonald	
	Tottenham Hotspur...............**4**	**Burnley** **0**	*Division One*
	Chivers (2)		
	Perryman		
	Gilzean		
14/11/70	**Manchester City**...................**1**	**Derby County** **1**	*Division One*
	Bell	O'Hare	
	West Bromwich Albion **1**	**Southampton** **0**	*Division One*
	Hartford		
21/11/70	**Wolverhampton Wanderers** **2**	**Leeds United** **3**	*Division One*
	Gould	Holsgrove (o.g.)	
	Curran	Clarke	
		Madeley	
	Oxford United **0**	**Swindon Town** **0**	*Division Two*
28/11/70	**Fulham** **0**	**Aston Villa** **2**	*Division Three*
		Hamilton	
		McMahon	
	Everton **0**	**Tottenham Hotspur**...............**0**	*Division One*

5/12/70	**Liverpool** ....1 Toshack	**Leeds United** ....1 Madeley	*Division One*
	Chelsea ....1 Weller	**Newcastle United** 0	*Division One*
12/12/70	**Arsenal** ....2 Graham Radford	**Wolverhampton Wanderers** ....1 Dougan	*Division One*
	Cardiff City..........................3 Pitt (o.g.) Phillips Gibson	**Sunderland** ....1 Baker	*Division Two*
19/12/70	**Manchester United** ....1 Sartori	**Arsenal** ....3 McLintock Graham Kennedy	*Division One*
	Leicester City 0	**Queens Park Rangers** 0	*Division Two*
26/12/70	**Derby County**.......................4 Mackay Wignall Hector Gemmill	**Manchester United** ....4 Law (2) Best Kidd	*Division One*
	Cardiff City..........................1 Sutton	**Swindon Town** ....1 Rogers	*Division Two*
2/1/71	**Blackpool** ....4 Green (2) Craven Mowbray	**West Ham United** 0	*FA Cup 3rd round*
	Manchester City...................1 Bell	**Wigan Athletic** 0	*FA Cup 3rd round*
	Nottingham Forest...............1 McIntosh	**Luton Town** ....1 Macdonald	*FA Cup 3rd round*
9/1/71	**Leeds United** ....1 Clarke	**Tottenham Hotspur**...............2 Chivers (2)	*Division One*
	Manchester City...................1 Book	**Crystal Palace** 0	*Division One*
16/1/71	**Huddersfield Town**................2 Chapman Worthington (pen.)	**Arsenal** ....1 Kennedy	*Division One*
	Manchester United ....1 Aston	**Burnley** ....1 Dobson	*Division One*

23/1/71	**Derby County**.............2 Hinton (pen.) O'Hare	**Wolverhampton Wanderers** ....1 Richards	*FA Cup 4th round*
	Portsmouth.................1 Trebilcock	**Arsenal** ....1 Storey (pen.)	*FA Cup 4th round*
	Everton ....3 Newton Harvey Royle	**Middlesbrough** 0	*FA Cup 4th round*
30/1/71	**Chelsea** ....4 Hollins (2) (1 pen.) Hutchinson Smethurst	**West Bromwich Albion** ....1 Astle	*Division One*
	Wolverhampton Wanderers ....2 Dougan (2)	**Crystal Palace** ....1 Birchenall	*Division One*
6/2/71	**Leeds United** 0	**Liverpool** ....1 Toshack	*Division One*
	Manchester United ....2 Best Morgan (pen.)	**Tottenham Hotspur**..............1 Peters	*Division One*
13/2/71	**Colchester United**................3 Crawford (2) Simmons	**Leeds United** ....2 Hunter Giles	*FA Cup 5th round*
	Liverpool ....1 Lawler	**Southampton** 0	*FA Cup 5th round*
	Leicester City ....1 Partridge	**Oxford United** ....1 Lucas	*FA Cup 5th round*
20/2/71	**Portsmouth**...................0	**Luton Town** ....1 Givens	*Division Two*
	West Ham United 0	**Manchester City**...................0	*Division One*
27/2/71	**Derby County**....................2 McFarland Hector	**Arsenal** 0	*Division One*
	Crystal Palace 0	**Burnley** ....2 Coates Dobson	*Division One*
6/3/71	**Everton** ....5 Kendall (2) Royle Ball Husband	**Colchester** 0	*FA Cup 6th round*
	Leicester City 0	**Arsenal** 0	*FA Cup 6th round*
13/3/71	**Blackpool** ....1 Craven	**Leeds United** ....1 Lorimer	*Division One*
	Coventry City ....1 O'Rourke	**Liverpool** 0	*Division One*

20/3/71	**Luton Town** ....3 Moore Busby Macdonald	**Hull City** ....**1** Houghton		*Division Two*
	Nottingham Forest...............3 Cormack (2) Storey-Moore	**Everton** ....**2** Hurst M. Lyons		*Division One*
27/3/71	**Everton** ....1 Ball	**Liverpool** ....**2** Evans Hall		*FA Cup semi-final*
3/4/71	**Bristol Rovers** 0	**Preston North End** **0**		*Division Three*
10/4/71	**Leicester City** 0	**Sheffield United** **0**		*Division Two*
	Burnley ....1 Fletcher	**Blackpool** **0**		*Division One*
17/4/71	**Leeds United** ....1 Clarke	**West Bromwich Albion** ....**2** T. Brown Astle		*Division One*
	Arsenal ....1 George	**Newcastle United** **0**		*Division One*
24/4/71	**Southampton** 0	**Leeds United** ....**3** Hollywood (o.g.) Jones (2)		*Division One*
	Millwall.............................4 Possee Cripps (pen.) Bridges Kitchener	**Hull City** **0**		*Division Two*
1/5/71	**Liverpool** ....1 Hughes	**Southampton** **0**		*Division One*
	Fulham 0	**Preston North End** ....**1** Heppolette		*Division Three*
8/5/71	**Arsenal** ....2 Kelly George	**Liverpool** ....**1 (a.e.t.)** Heighway		*FA Cup final*
15/5/71	**Northern Ireland**..................0	**England** ....**1** Clarke		*Home International Championship*
	Wales 0	**Scotland** **0**		*Home International Championship*
22/5/71	**England** ....3 Peters Chivers (2)	**Scotland** ....**1** Curran		*Home International Championship*
	Northern Ireland..................1 Hamilton	**Wales**.................................**0**		*Home International Championship*
29/5/71	**Crystal Palace** ....1 Birchenall	**Inter Milan**.........................**1** Boninsegna		*Anglo-Italian Tournament*

MATCH OF THE SEASON

**Derby County 4
Manchester United 4
at the Baseball Ground,
Saturday 26 December 1970**

If the *Match of the Day* team had to miss their Christmas dinner to set up the cameras for the following day, the feast of football served up on a frozen pitch at Derby brought seasonal cheer for the viewers.

Brian Clough and Peter Taylor's team were making strong waves in the First Division. Captain Dave Mackay put them ahead, then Frank Wignall made it 2–0.

Early in the second half, United scored three times in four minutes. Two were diving headers by Denis Law, sandwiched between them was a scrambled effort by George Best.

Derby's Archie Gemmill then took a hand. He made the equaliser for Kevin Hector,

then scored himself to edge Derby in front 4–3. Finally Brian Kidd headed in to complete an eight-goal thriller.

But all was not well in the United camp. Two days later, Wilf McGuinness was relieved of the manager's job he had held for 18 months. Sir Matt Busby, whose act he and others found so hard to follow, temporarily resumed control.

Derby County: Green, Webster, Daniel, Hennessey, McFarland, Mackay, Durban,

A day for forwards at the Baseball Ground. Denis Law joins in the Christmas festivities under the scrutiny of the *Match of the Day* cameras now sited on permanent, purpose-built gantries

Wignall, O'Hare, Hector, Gemmill.
Scorers: Mackay, Wignall, Hector, Gemmill

Manchester United: Rimmer, Fitzpatrick, A. Dunne, Crerand, Ure, Sadler, Morgan, Best, Charlton, Kidd, Law.
Scorers: Law (2), Best, Kidd

PLAYER OF THE SEASON
Dave Mackay (Derby County)

In the 1970/1 season, Dave Mackay played a full complement of 42 First Division games in his 37th year. But by then, they had run out of adjectives to describe one of the game's great competitors. It is doubtful whether any post-war player possessed such inner strength as the craggy Scot with the mud-splattered shirt.

At Tottenham, Bill Nicholson said Mackay changed the whole face of the club on the first day he turned

up for training. Here he was in the team that won the 'double' and the FA Cup three times. He

twice came back from a badly broken leg.

He was nearly 34 when Brian Clough persuaded him to become captain of Derby. In his first season, Mackay led them to the Second Division title. The next year they were fourth in the First Division.

Mackay left to manage Swindon and Nottingham Forest, returning to Derby when Clough resigned in stormy circumstances. With typical tenacity, Mackay quelled a players' revolt and managed the Derby side that won the Championship for the second time in 1975.

The Leeds Controversy

'That decision, or non-decision, will be talked about for years,' said Barry Davies as irate Leeds fans invaded the Elland Road pitch on 17 April 1971. He was right. But was referee Ray Tinkler *as wrong* as Leeds maintained?

A television toy called the 'video disc' was now developed to its full potential. It enabled key incidents to be replayed, usually in slow motion and sometimes from a different angle, and led to accusations that referees were being 'pilloried' by television.

Before we lay that debate to rest, consider Leeds's position before that controversial West Bromwich goal that kept the nation arguing for weeks. They were about to squander a seven-point lead over Arsenal in the championship race, and

20 minutes from the end against Albion, they were already a goal down.

Then Norman Hunter drove a misplaced pass against Tony Brown and the ball rebounded into the Leeds half, where Colin Suggett was standing in an offside position. Yet Suggett was to play no part in what took place next.

While the Leeds defenders stood still seeing the linesman's flag, Brown carried the ball unchallenged towards the Leeds goal, looked up to find the referee waving play on, then squared the ball for Astle to score.

What happened next was sheer mayhem. 'And Leeds will go mad. Don Revie is a sickened man,' exclaimed commentator Davies as the Leeds manager walked on to the pitch to restrain players and spectators who were

surrounding the referee and linesman.

When police had cleared the field, play restarted with Leeds two goals down. Allan Clarke scored five minutes from the end, but they lost the game and the Championship. It is certain that most referees would have stopped the play and awarded Leeds a free-kick. But looking at the videotape again 20 years later, Tinkler was technically correct according to the laws of the game.

Suggett was not interfering with play, nor was he seeking to gain an advantage by being in an offside position. Leeds were guilty of not playing to the whistle. They were also found guilty by an FA hearing of crowd misbehaviour. Elland Road was closed for the first four home games of the following season, and Leeds were forced to play on neutral grounds.

The whole incident was given a much higher profile because it was televised and replayed. A few years earlier, nobody outside Leeds would have seen it. But it is misleading to blame 'trial by television'. Over the years which followed, the 'replay' machine proved referees right a comforting 98 per cent of the time.

What was perhaps rather more questionable was the fact that television made some of them into personalities in their own right!

Anarchy! Referee Ray Tinkler surrounded by affronted Leeds players after allowing Astle's goal. Albion men try to act as peacemakers

THE CHELSEA PROGRAMME this season reported: 'Up, up, up go the viewing figures for football on television. The combined weekend audiences have averaged 20 million. BBC claim 12 million for *Match of the Day*, ITV up to 8 million for *The Big Match*.'

No wonder the 10 o'clock spot on Saturday nights on BBC 1 was sacrosanct. Football was doing business like never before at peak viewing times, and looking at some of the personalities and performances that season, it is not hard to see why.

On the opening Saturday of the season, *Match of the Day* was a launching pad for the career of a superstar who would bustle busily through the decade. Twenty-year-old Kevin Keegan made his debut for Liverpool, and scored after just 12 minutes against Nottingham Forest.

A more expensive purchase, Newcastle's £180,000 Malcolm Macdonald, also made an impact. With his long sideburns and unfettered style, he prolonged the career of the original centre-forward before they all became known as strikers.

Under new manager Frank O'Farrell, Manchester United dominated the first half of the season, losing only two of their 23 First Division matches before the turn of the year. Then their form collapsed, but not before the nation had witnessed some epic matches (*see* 'Player of the Season', below).

After Christmas, *Match of the Day* screened two unforgettable Cup ties. In a third round replay, Southern League Hereford United beat First Division Newcastle, Macdonald's goal being wiped out by a 40-yard shot from building worker Ronnie Radford. Viewers voted it 'Goal of the Season'. In extra-time, Hereford substitute Ricky George came up with the winner. The night before, he had been chastised by the great Newcastle cup hero, the late Jackie Milburn, for staying up too late!

In the fifth round, Second Division Orient produced the

comeback of the season. Two goals down to Chelsea, then the best Cup team around, they replied through Phil Hoadley from 35 yards, Mickey Bullock and Barrie Fairbrother.

The pitch invasions that met these two memorable giant-killing moments were spontaneous and good-natured. We did not know then that the age of the hooligan was but two years away.

Supercharged Supermac. Malcolm Macdonald, all strength and sideburns, followed in the line of legends to wear the number nine shirt for Newcastle United

31/7/71	**Halifax Town** ....2 Atkins Wallace (pen.)	**Manchester United** ....1 Best (pen.)	*Watney Cup*
	Colchester United................1 Lewis (pen.)	**Luton Town** 0	*Watney Cup*
7/8/71	**West Bromwich Albion** ....4 Astle (2) Cantello Suggett (Colchester won 4–3 on penalties)	**Colchester** ....4 Mahon (2) Simmons Lewis	*Watney Cup final*
14/8/71	**Arsenal** ....3 Radford Kennedy McLintock	**Chelsea** 0	*Division One*
	Liverpool ....3 Keegan Smith (pen.) Hughes	**Nottingham Forest**................1 Storey-Moore (pen.)	*Division One*
21/8/71	**Birmingham City** ....3 Bowker Summerill Campbell	**Carlisle United**....................2 Webb Hatton	*Division Two*
	Burnley ....2 Casper Kindon	**Luton Town** ....1 Busby	*Division Two*
28/8/71	**Manchester City**...................4 Bell Lee Davies Summerbee	**Tottenham Hotspur**...............0	*Division One*
	Derby County......................2 McGovern Hector	**Southampton** ....2 Stokes Gabriel (pen.)	*Division One*
4/9/71	**Tottenham Hotspur**...............2 Peters Chivers	**Liverpool** 0	*Division One*
	Swindon Town 0	**Queens Park Rangers** 0	*Division Two*
11/9/71	**Crystal Palace** ....1 Blyth	**Manchester United** ....3 Kidd Law (2)	*Division One*
	Aston Villa ....2 Graydon Hamilton	**Brighton & Hove Albion**..........0	*Division Three*
19/9/71	**Everton** ....2 Royle Johnson	**Arsenal** ....1 Kennedy	*Division One*
	Leicester City 0	**Sheffield United** ....1 Woodward	*Division One*

25/9/71	**Liverpool** ....2 Graham Hall	**Manchester United** ....2 Law Charlton		*Division One*
	West Ham United ....2 Best Smith (o.g.)	**Stoke City**...........................1 Ritchie		*Division One*
2/10/71	**Manchester United** ....2 Best Gowling	**Sheffield United** 0		*Division One*
	Southampton 0	**Arsenal** ....1 Simpson		*Division One*
9/10/71	**Derby County** ....2 Todd McFarland	**Tottenham Hotspur**..............2 Chivers Pearce		*Division One*
	Liverpool 0	**Chelsea** 0		*Division One*
16/10/71	**Leeds United** ....3 Clarke Jones Lorimer	**Manchester City**..................0		*Division One*
	Millwall...........................3 Merrick (o.g.) Rooks (o.g.) Bolland	**Bristol City** ....1 Spiring		*Division Two*
23/10/71	**Derby County** ....2 O'Hare Hinton (pen.)	**Arsenal** ....1 Graham		*Division One*
	Blackpool ....1 Lennard	**Queens Park Rangers** ....1 Marsh		*Division Two*
30/10/71	**Manchester United** 0	**Leeds United** ....1 Lorimer		*Division One*
	Wolverhampton Wanderers ....1 Munro	**Coventry City** ....1 Carr		*Division One*
6/11/71	**Hull City** ....1 Knighton	**Norwich City**........................2 Cross Silvester		*Division Two*
	West Ham United ....1 Robson	**Sheffield United** ....2 Reece (2)		*Division One*
13/11/71	**Manchester United** ....3 McIlroy Law (2)	**Tottenham Hotspur**..............1 Chivers		*Division One*
	Aston Villa ....1 Graydon	**Notts County** 0		*Division Three*

| 20/11/71 | **Wolverhampton Wanderers** 5
Wagstaffe
Hibbitt
Dougan (2)
McCalliog (pen.) | **Arsenal** 1
Kennedy | *Division One* |

| | **West Ham United** ....0 | **Manchester City**...................2
Lee (pen.)
Davies | *Division One* |

| 27/11/71 | **Southampton** 2
Gabriel
Davies | **Manchester United** 5
Best (3)
Kidd
McIlroy | *Division One* |

| | **Burnley** 1
Dobson | **Swindon Town** 2
Jones
Noble | *Division Two* |

| 4/12/71 | **Derby County**......................3
Hinton (pen.)
Webster
Durban | **Manchester City**...................1
Lee (pen.) | *Division One* |

| | **Crystal Palace** 5
Taylor
Hughes (2)
Badger (o.g.)
McCormick | **Sheffield United** 1
Dearden | *Division One* |

| 11/12/71 | **Southampton** 3
Gabriel (pen.)
Channon
Paine | **West Ham United** 3
Bonds
Best
Brooking | *Division One* |

| | **Chelsea** ....0 | **Leeds United** ....0 | *Division One* |

| 18/12/71 | **Arsenal** 2
Roberts (2) | **West Bromwich Albion** ....0 | *Division One* |

| | **Liverpool** ....0 | **Tottenham Hotspur**...............0 | *Division One* |

| 1/1/72 | **Queens Park Rangers** 3
Leach (2)
Marsh (pen.) | **Burnley** 1
Fletcher | *Division Two* |

| | **Arsenal** 1
Simpson | **Everton** 1
Kendall | *Division One* |

| 15/1/72 | **Swindon Town** ....0 | **Arsenal** 2
Ball
Armstrong | *FA Cup 3rd round* |

| | **Wolverhampton Wanderers** 1
McCalliog | **Leicester City** 1
Farrington | *FA Cup 3rd round* |

| | **Blackpool** ....0 | **Chelsea** 1
Dempsey | *FA Cup 3rd round* |

22/1/72	**Sheffield Wednesday** ....1 Craig (pen.)	**Millwall** ....1 Allder	Division Two
	Wolverhampton Wanderers 0	**Liverpool** 0	Division One
29/1/72	**Tottenham Hotspur** ....1 Chivers	**Leeds United** 0	Division One
	West Bromwich Albion ....2 Gould Astle	**Manchester United** ....1 Kidd	Division One
5/2/72	**Hereford United** ....2 Radford George	**Newcastle United** ....1 (a.e.t.) Macdonald	FA Cup 3rd round replay
	Liverpool 0	**Leeds United** 0	FA Cup 4th round
	Preston North End 0	**Manchester United** ....2 Gowling (2)	FA Cup 4th round
12/2/72	**Aston Villa** ....2 Vowden Lochhead	**AFC Bournemouth** ....1 MacDougall	Division Three
	Sheffield United ....3 Dearden Woodward (pen.) Currie	**Manchester City** ....3 Lee (2) (1 pen.) Bell	Division One
19/2/72	**Leeds United** ....5 Jones (3) Clarke Lorimer	**Manchester United** ....1 Burns	Division One
	Coventry 0	**Wolverhampton Wanderers** 0	Division One
26/2/72	**Leyton Orient** ....3 Hoadley Bullock Fairbrother	**Chelsea** ....2 Webb Osgood	FA Cup 5th round
	Cardiff City 0	**Leeds United** ....2 Giles (2)	FA Cup 5th round
	Manchester United 0	**Middlesbrough** 0	FA Cup 5th round
4/3/72	**Leeds United** ....7 Clarke (2) Lorimer (3) Charlton Jones	**Southampton** 0	Division One
	Tottenham Hotspur ....2 Chivers Perryman	**Manchester United** 0	Division One
11/3/72	**Norwich City** ....1 Bone	**Sunderland** ....1 Harvey	Division Two
	Newcastle United ....2 Macdonald Smith	**Arsenal** 0	Division One

18/3/72	**Leeds United** 2	**Tottenham Hotspur** 1	*FA Cup 6th round*
	Clarke	Pratt	
	Charlton		
	Manchester United 1	**Stoke City** 1	*FA Cup 6th round*
	Best	Greenhoff	
25/3/72	**Brighton & Hove Albion** 2	**Aston Villa** 1	*Division Three*
	Irvine	B. Rioch	
	K. Napier		
	Newcastle United 0	**Manchester City** 0	*Division One*
1/4/72	**Derby County** 2	**Leeds United** 0	*Division One*
	O'Hare		
	Hunter (o.g.)		
	Fulham 1	**Millwall** 0	*Division Two*
	Barrett		
8/4/72	**Manchester City** 3	**West Ham United** 1	*Division One*
	Marsh (2)	Hurst	
	Bell		
	Arsenal 2	**Wolverhampton Wanderers** 1	*Division One*
	Graham (2)	Richards	
15/4/72	**Birmingham City** 0	**Leeds United** 3	*FA Cup semi-final*
		Jones (2)	
		Lorimer	
22/4/72	**Manchester City** 2	**Derby County** 0	*Division One*
	Marsh		
	Lee (pen.)		
	Birmingham City 1	**Middlesbrough** 1	*Division Two*
	Francis	Hickton	
29/4/72	**England** 1	**West Germany** 3	*European Championship*
	Lee	Hoeness	*quarter-final first leg*
		Netzer (pen.)	
		Muller	
6/5/72	**Arsenal** 0	**Leeds United** 1	*FA Cup final*
		Clarke	
13/5/72	**West Germany** 0	**England** 0	*European Championship*
			quarter-final second leg
20/5/72	**Wales** 0	**England** 3	*Home International Championship*
		Hughes	
		Marsh	
		Bell	
	Scotland 2	**Northern Ireland** 0	*Home International Championship*
	Law		
	Lorimer		
27/5/72	**Scotland** 0	**England** 1	*Home International Championship*
		Ball	

Leeds United 7*
Southampton 0
at Elland Road,
Saturday 4 March 1972

If Southampton's players had been watching *Match of the Day* every week, they should really have known they were in for a hiding. Although this was to be another season when Leeds failed to deliver the championship, the fluency of their football had the nation enthralled.

They had done the double over early-season pacemakers Manchester United, beating them 5–1 at Elland Road just

'It was almost cruel'. Leeds stars Jones (in net), Lorimer and Gray leave Southampton in disarray. Mike Channon (hands on hips) is speechless

* Leeds' seven-goal total was then a record for *Match of the Day*, beating the six scored by Arsenal against Sheffield United in November 1965. It would be beaten by Spurs in the 1977/8 season.

two weeks prior to Southampton's visit. Ominously, outside-right Peter Lorimer had scored in both games, as well as volleying a breathtaking shot over Joe Corrigan's head from 30 yards against Manchester City.

But it wasn't Lorimer's hat-trick, nor Allan Clarke's two goals, for which this Leeds performance is enshrined in the archives. Twenty years later, *Match of the Day* regulars still remember the way they toyed with poor Southampton – in one movement putting together 25 passes without their opponents touching the ball. Each pass was greeted with a triumphant cheer from the 34,000 crowd as Leeds turned on an exhibition at the expense of their hapless opponents.

At the heart of the Leeds exploitation of mature skills over bewildered stooges were those midfield maestros, Billy Bremner and Johnny Giles. They produced back heels, outrageous flicks and stunning reverse passes. As commentator Barry Davies remarked: 'It was almost cruel.'

Leeds United: Sprake, Reaney, Madeley, Bremner, Charlton, Hunter, Lorimer, Clarke, Jones, Giles, Gray. Scorers: Lorimer (3), Clarke (2), Charlton, Jones

Southampton: Martin, McCarthy, Fry, Stokes, Gabriel, Steele, Paine (sub. Byrne), Channon, Davies, O'Neill, Jenkins

---

PLAYER OF THE SEASON
George Best
(Manchester United)

It remains one of the daftest acts of self-destruction in modern sport that George Best stopped playing football when he was 26 years old. All right, there were countless comebacks over the next 10 years, but this was to be the last chance the nation had to savour skills unimpaired by what was to happen next to the most gifted product of post-war football.

The legacy he left has been the topic of hundreds of articles, books and conversations. The reasons why he let it slip away have been the subject of thousands more. But *Match of the Day* viewers were left with a lasting memory of his genius.

In October, promoted Sheffield United went to Old Trafford at the top of the First Division and unbeaten in 10 matches. With only six minutes of the match left there was no score. The 15,000 fans who had been locked out had not missed much.

Then Best picked up a Brian Kidd flick half-way inside the Sheffield half. With the ball apparently glued to the outside of his right foot, he cut an unwavering diagonal line from left to right, accelerating across the path of four United defenders. As goalkeeper John Hope advanced, Best was still running away from goal towards the corner flag.

How he cut the ball back inside the far post with his right foot has never been satisfactorily explained – rather like what happened to the rest of his life.

THIS WAS THE SEASON when Bobby Charlton and the old Manchester United bowed out, while the John Toshack–Kevin Keegan combination ushered in the new Liverpool. A United team who had led the First Division only a year earlier were eclipsed by a Liverpool side who would lead it, more often than not, for the next 17 years.

Frank O'Farrell's brief tenure as boss at Old Trafford was effectively ended by England's Martin Peters, who scored all four goals when Spurs won 4–1 before a stunned crowd of 52,000 and the *Match of the Day* cameras at the end of October 1972.

Tommy Docherty took over, his arrival at Old Trafford also closely monitored by the BBC just two days before Christmas, when United started their revival with a draw against Leeds.

By the time Charlton played his 754th and last game for United at Stamford Bridge on the last day of the season, their survival in the First Division was assured. But only for one year more. The cameras focused on a fitting presentation to Charlton in the centre circle, but it was Chelsea's Peter Osgood who scored the only goal of Bobby's last First Division match, and Osgood too who volleyed one of the best televised goals of the season in the sixth round of the FA Cup against Arsenal.

Running that one close for the popular 'Goal of the Season' award, was a spectacular strike by Arsenal's George Graham against Ipswich, and two from Liverpool's Emlyn Hughes in the Merseyside derby at Goodison Park.

Hughes led Shankly's Liverpool to a 'double' of League Championship and UEFA Cup – their first European trophy, and their first League title for seven years.

The understanding between the rangy Toshack and the energetic Keegan brought many goals, at home and abroad. Over the next generation, Liverpool would be the most televised team in Britain.

A titan and his trophy. Bill Shankly with Liverpool's first European prize. They won the UEFA Cup and the First Division title to start 20 years of unparalleled success

29/7/72	**Bristol Rovers** ....**2** Bannister (pen.) Stephens	**Wolverhampton Wanderers** **0**	*Watney Cup*
	Notts County **0**	**Sheffield United** ....**3** Currie (2) Woodward	*Watney Cup*
5/8/72	**Bristol Rovers** ....**0** (Bristol Rovers won 7–6 on penalties)	**Sheffield United** **0**	*Watney Cup final*
12/8/72	**Leicester City** **0**	**Arsenal** ....**1** Ball (pen.)	*Division One*
	Liverpool ....**2** Hall Callaghan	**Manchester City**..................**0**	*Division One*
19/8/72	**Sheffield United** ....**1** Salmons	**Newcastle United** ....**2** Macdonald Tudor	*Division One*
	Derby County ....**1** Hector	**Chelsea** ....**2** Harris Garland	*Division One*
26/8/72	**Norwich City**........................**1** Paddon	**Derby County**......................**0**	*Division One*
	Tottenham Hotspur...............**0**	**Leeds United** **0**	*Division One*
2/9/72	**Blackpool** ....**2** Burns Dyson	**Millwall**............................**1** B. Brown	*Division Two*
	Arsenal ....**1** Webb (o.g.)	**Chelsea** ....**1** Cooke	*Division One*
9/9/72	**Leicester City** ....**1** Sammels	**Everton** ....**2** Connolly Cross (o.g.)	*Division One*
	Manchester United **0**	**Coventry City** ....**1** Carr	*Division One*
16/9/72	**Manchester City**...................**2** Marsh (2)	**Tottenham Hotspur**...............**1** Peters	*Division One*
	Ipswich Town ....**2** Belfitt (2)	**Stoke City**..........................**0**	*Division One*
23/9/72	**Newcastle United** ....**3** Tudor Smith Macdonald	**Leeds United** ....**2** Jones Clarke	*Division One*
	Watford............................**1** Farley	**Notts County** **0**	*Division Three*

30/9/72	**Luton Town** ....2 Aston (pen.) Halom	**Burnley** ....2 James (2)		Division Two
	Derby County ....2 Hector Hinton (pen.)	**Tottenham Hotspur** ....1 Perryman		Division One
7/10/72	**Liverpool** ....1 Cormack	**Everton** 0		Division One
	Fulham ....2 Mullery Mitchell	**Aston Villa** 0		Division Two
14/10/72	**Sheffield Wednesday** 0	**Burnley** ....1 James		Division Two
	Arsenal ....1 Graham	**Ipswich Town** 0		Division One
21/10/72	**Leeds United** ....1 Charlton	**Coventry City** ....1 Carr		Division One
	Tottenham Hotspur 0	**Chelsea** ....1 Hollins		Division One
28/10/72	**Manchester United** ....1 Charlton	**Tottenham Hotspur** ....4 Peters (4)		Division One
	Chelsea ....1 McCreadie	**Newcastle United** ....1 Smith		Division One
4/11/72	**Crystal Palace** ....1 Rogers	**Everton** 0		Division One
	Southampton ....1 McCarthy	**Norwich City** 0		Division One
11/11/72	**Manchester United** ....2 MacDougall Davies	**Liverpool** 0		Division One
	Aston Villa 0	**Blackpool** 0		Division Two
18/11/72	**West Ham United** ....1 Robson	**Derby County** ....2 Hector (2)		Division One
	Wolverhampton Wanderers 0	**Ipswich Town** ....1 Whymark		Division One
25/11/72	**Leeds United** ....3 Cherry Lorimer Clarke	**Manchester City** 0		Division One
	West Bromwich Albion ....2 T. Brown (2) (1 pen.)	**Stoke City** ....1 Hurst		Division One
	Cardiff City ....3 McCulloch (2) Woodruff	**Fulham** ....1 Mullery		Division Two

2/12/72	**Liverpool** ....4 Lindsay (2) Cormack Toshack	**Birmingham City** ....3 Taylor Latchford Hope	*Division One*
	Coventry City ....1 Alderson	**Everton** 0	*Division One*
9/12/72	**Derby County** ....2 Hinton (pen.) Gemmill	**Coventry City** 0	*Division One*
	Luton Town ....2 Butlin Halom	**Queens Park Rangers** ....2 Givens Clement	*Division Two*
16/12/72	**West Ham United** ....3 Robson (2) Best	**Stoke City**............................2 Hurst Ritchie	*Division One*
	Wolverhampton Wanderers ....1 Sunderland	**Chelsea** 0	*Division One*
23/12/72	**Manchester United** ....1 MacDougall	**Leeds United** ....1 Clarke	*Division One*
	West Bromwich Albion ....2 Glover Hartford	**Ipswich Town** 0	*Division One*
30/12/72	**Tottenham Hotspur**...............2 Peters Chivers	**Wolverhampton Wanderers** ....2 Naylor (o.g.) Richards	*League Cup semi-final*
	Liverpool ....1 Cormack	**Crystal Palace** 0	*Division One*
6/1/73	**Arsenal** ....3 Ball Armstrong Kennedy	**Manchester United** ....1 Kidd	*Division One*
	Derby County ....1 Hinton (pen.)	**Norwich City**.........................0	*Division One*
13/1/73	**Arsenal** ....2 Kennedy Armstrong	**Leicester City** ....2 Worthington Farrington	*FA Cup 3rd round*
	Norwich City.........................1 Cross	**Leeds United** ....1 Lorimer	*FA Cup 3rd round*
	Leyton Orient.......................1 Arber (pen.)	**Coventry City** ....4 Alderson (2) Carr Hutchison	*FA Cup 3rd round*
20/1/73	**Manchester United** ....2 Charlton (pen.) Macari	**West Ham United** ....2 Best Robson	*Division One*
	Norwich City.........................1 Cross	**Leeds United** ....2 Jordan Clarke	*Division One*

27/1/73	**Queens Park Rangers** .... 2 Leach Givens	**Burnley** 0	*Division Two*
	Leeds United .... 1 Clarke	**Stoke City** 0	*Division One*
3/2/73	**Newcastle United** 0	**Luton Town** .... 2 Aston (2)	*FA Cup 4th round*
	Liverpool 0	**Manchester City** 0	*FA Cup 4th round*
	Sheffield Wednesday .... 1 Craig (pen.)	**Crystal Palace** .... 1 Craven	*FA Cup 4th round*
10/2/73	**Liverpool** 0	**Arsenal** .... 2 Ball (pen.) Radford	*Division One*
	Tottenham Hotspur .... 2 Chivers (2)	**Manchester City** .... 3 Marsh Lee (2)	*Division One*
17/2/73	**AFC Bournemouth** .... 2 Boyer Cave	**Bolton Wanderers** 0	*Division Three*
	Ipswich Town .... 4 Harper Viljoen Hamilton (2)	**Manchester United** .... 1 Macari	*Division One*
24/2/73	**Carlisle United** .... 1 Martin	**Arsenal** .... 2 Ball McLintock	*FA Cup 5th round*
	Wolverhampton Wanderers .... 1 Richards	**Millwall** 0	*FA Cup 5th round*
	Derby County .... 4 Davies Hector (3)	**Queens Park Rangers** .... 2 Leach Givens	*FA Cup 5th round*
3/3/73	**Derby County** .... 2 Durban Hector	**Leeds United** .... 3 Lorimer (2 pens) Clarke	*Division One*
	Everton 0	**Liverpool** .... 2 Hughes (2)	*Division One*
10/3/73	**Queens Park Rangers** .... 1 Leach	**Aston Villa** 0	*Division Two*
	Birmingham City .... 3 Latchford Hatton Campbell (pen.)	**Manchester United** .... 1 Macari	*Division One*

17/3/73	**Chelsea** 2	**Arsenal** 2	*FA Cup 6th round*
	Osgood	Ball	
	Hollins	George	
	Sunderland 2	**Luton Town** 0	*FA Cup 6th round*
	Watson		
	Guthrie		
24/3/73	**AFC Bournemouth** 1	**Grimsby Town** 1	*Division Three*
	Aimson	Brace	
	West Bromwich Albion 1	**Southampton** 1	*Division One*
	T. Brown	Gilchrist	
31/3/73	**Arsenal** 0	**Derby County** 1	*Division One*
		Powell	
	Nottingham Forest...............3	**Burnley** 0	*Division Two*
	McKenzie		
	O'Neill		
	Lyons		
7/4/73	**Leeds United** 1	**Wolverhampton Wanderers** 0	*FA Cup semi-final*
	Bremner		
14/4/73	**West Ham United** 1	**Leeds United** 1	*Division One*
	Holland	Clarke	
	Liverpool 1	**West Bromwich Albion** 0	*Division One*
	Keegan (pen.)		
21/4/73	**Newcastle United** 2	**Liverpool** 1	*Division One*
	Tudor (2)	Keegan	
	Everton 0	**Arsenal** 0	*Division One*
28/4/73	**Chelsea** 1	**Manchester United** 0	*Division One*
	Osgood		
	Southampton 3	**Leeds United** 1	*Division One*
	O'Neil	Hunter	
	Stokes		
	Channon		
5/5/73	**Leeds United** 0	**Sunderland** 1	*FA Cup final*
		Porterfield	
12/5/73	**Northern Ireland**..................1	**England** 2	*Home International Championship*
	Clements (pen.)	Chivers (2)	
	Wales 0	**Scotland** 2	*Home International Championship*
		Graham (2)	
19/5/73	**England** 1	**Scotland** 0	*Home International Championship*
	Peters		
	Northern Ireland..................1	**Wales** 0	*Home International Championship*
	Hamilton		

MATCH OF THE SEASON

Liverpool 4
Birmingham City 3
at Anfield,
Saturday 2 December 1972

Gordon Taylor, later to become the high-profile secretary of the PFA, the players' union, was a chunky, cheerful outside-left with a thunderous shot. He never had a better game in front of the cameras than this one.

Birmingham City, under Freddie Goodwin, were on a rare high. They had won promotion and reached the semi-final of the FA Cup the previous season, and their forward line of Trevor Francis, Bob Latchford and Bob Hatton propelled them into the top half of the First Division.

But it was Taylor, wide on the left, who gave Liverpool trouble that winter's afternoon at Anfield. First, his right-foot shot flew off the heels of defender Trevor Storton and wide of Ray Clemence, then Taylor and Latchford set up Birmingham's second for Bobby Hope.

Alec Lindsay pulled one back for Liverpool from a free-kick, only for Latchford, with his 50th goal in League football, to make it 3–1 after combining with Hatton.

Liverpool's fabled powers of recovery now came to their aid. Keegan made a goal for Cormack just before half-time, and in the second half another set piece enabled Lindsay to square the match at 3–3.

After Toshack had scored the winner from a flick by Keegan, *Match of the Day*

viewers were left with a lasting image of sheer misery on the face of Birmingham's unlucky goalkeeper, Mike Kelly. His team had twice been two goals in front, but still lost!

Liverpool: Clemence, Lawler, Lindsay, Storton, Lloyd, Hughes, Keegan, Cormack, Heighway, Toshack, Callaghan.
Scorers: Lindsay (2), Cormack, Toshack

Birmingham City: Kelly, Martin, Want, Pendrey, Hynd, Harland, Hope, Calderwood, Latchford, Hatton, Taylor.
Scorers: Taylor, Hope, Latchford

PLAYER OF THE SEASON
Alan Ball (Arsenal)

Not many football personalities have figured on *Match of the Day* in four separate decades. But Alan Ball, scorer of a hat-trick for Blackpool in front of the cameras only three months after the programme started, has proved to be one of the game's enduring characters.

In the 60s, a red-haired World Cup hero at the age of 21, he figured in a record transfer to Everton, where he played in the FA Cup final and won a League Championship medal in Harry Catterick's cultured team of 1970.

In the 70s, after pushing the transfer barrier past £200,000 with a move to Arsenal, he had five years in London, taking his total of international caps to 72 and captaining both Arsenal and England.

His years under Lawrie McMenemy at Southampton took him into the 80s, and on 30 January 1981 Ball was part of the Southampton side that led the First Division for the first time in the club's 97-year history.

In 1987, as manager of Portsmouth, he led the club back into the First Division. And in the 90s, he was still on the small screen, managing first Stoke City and then Exeter City as these Third Division clubs featured in *Match of the Day – The Road to Wembley*.

Back in 1972/3, viewers saw Ball score against Leicester, Manchester United, Liverpool (at Anfield), and in the FA Cup against Carlisle and Chelsea. But Arsenal lost in the semi-final to Sunderland, and 'Bally' never won an FA Cup-winners' medal.

THIS WAS A SEASON of change. Jimmy Hill was the new presenter of *Match of the Day*; Denis Law was playing in the sky blue of Manchester City, while his old club United plunged to relegation; Sir Alf Ramsey lost his job when England were knocked out of the World Cup by Poland; and Bob Wilson announced his retirement as Arsenal's goalkeeper.

But it was also a season of achievement. Especially by Leeds United, who went 29 First Division matches unbeaten from the start of the season until they lost at Stoke. They won their second championship, whereupon Don Revie left to manage England.

Ramsey's nadir was the crazy 1–1 draw at home to Poland that October. While Jan Tomaszewski performed miracles at one end, Peter Shilton was beaten by Jan Domarski at the other. Thus, England failed to appear in the World Cup Finals for the first time since the Second World War.

Shilton was also on the other end of the BBC's 'Goal of the Season', when Fulham's Alan Mullery beat him with a ferocious volley in the fourth round of the FA Cup.

Match of the Day now also mounted a special evening programme from the banquet hotel of the FA Cup winners. Jimmy Hill, dark hair and beard neatly cropped after his transfer from London Weekend Television, produced hilarious interviews with Bill Shankly and Kevin Keegan after Liverpool had taken Newcastle apart at Wembley.

The anachronistic Home International Championship meant the *Match of the Day* season now extended beyond the Cup final. Joe Mercer had a caretaker spell in charge of England, bridging the gap between Ramsey and Revie, and taking the team on tour to Eastern Europe, while the rest of the world, including Scotland, prepared for the World Cup finals in West Germany.

A new partnership for *Match of the Day*. Jimmy Hill is signed from ITV and Bob Wilson from Arsenal. Both would be part of the BBC team for the next two decades

11/8/73	**Bristol Rovers** 1	**West Ham United** 1	*Watney Cup*
	Bannister	MacDougall	

(Bristol Rovers won 6–5 on penalties)

	Plymouth Argyle 0	**Stoke City** 1	*Watney Cup*
		Hurst	

18/8/73 **Stoke City** ...... 2 **Hull City** ...... 0 *Watney Cup final*
Greenhoff (2)

25/8/73 **Derby County** ...... 1 **Chelsea** ...... 0 *Division One*
McGovern

Manchester City ...... 3 **Birmingham City** ...... 1 *Division One*
Law (2) Hatton
Bell

1/9/73 **Tottenham Hotspur** ...... 0 **Leeds United** ...... 3 *Division One*
Bremner (2)
Clarke

Everton ...... 3 **Ipswich Town** ...... 0 *Division One*
Connolly
Hurst
Harper

8/9/73 **Liverpool** ...... 1 **Chelsea** ...... 0 *Division One*
Keegan

Coventry City ...... 2 **Southampton** ...... 0 *Division One*
Coop (pen.)
Green

15/9/73 **Manchester United** ...... 3 **West Ham United** ...... 1 *Division One*
Kidd (2) Bonds (pen.)
Storey-Moore

Newcastle United ...... 2 **Wolverhampton Wanderers** .... 0 *Division One*
Nattrass
Howard

22/9/73 **Arsenal** ...... 2 **Stoke City** ...... 1 *Division One*
Ball Greenhoff
Radford

Nottingham Forest ...... 1 **Preston North End** ...... 1 *Division Two*
O'Neill Burns

29/9/73 **West Bromwich Albion** ...... 1 **Sunderland** ...... 1 *Division Two*
A. Brown Halom

Manchester United ...... 0 **Liverpool** ...... 0 *Division One*

6/10/73 **Leeds United** ...... 1 **Stoke City** ...... 1 *Division One*
Jones Smith

West Ham United ...... 0 **Burnley** ...... 1 *Division One*
Waldron

13/10/73	**Southampton** ....**1** Channon (pen.)	**Liverpool** **0**	*Division One*
	Hereford United **0**	**Cambridge United** **0**	*Division Three*
20/10/73	**Derby County**.....................**2** Hector McGovern	**Leicester City** ....**1** Worthington	*Division One*
	Fulham **0**	**Sunderland** ....**2** Horswill Mullery (o.g.)	*Division Two*
27/10/73	**Manchester City**..................**0**	**Leeds United** ....**1** Bates	*Division One*
	Queens Park Rangers ....**2** Bowles Givens	**Arsenal** **0**	*Division One*
3/11/73	**Arsenal** **0**	**Liverpool** ....**2** Hughes Toshack	*Division One*
	Norwich City.......................**1** Rofe (o.g.)	**Leicester City** **0**	*Division One*
10/11/73	**Tottenham Hotspur**...............**2** Chivers Knowles	**Manchester United** ....**1** Best	*Division One*
	Bristol City **0**	**Crystal Palace** ....**1** Whittle	*Division Two*
17/11/73	**Manchester City**..................**1** Lee (pen.)	**Queens Park Rangers** **0**	*Division One*
	Wolverhampton Wanderers **0**	**West Ham United** **0**	*Division One*
24/11/73	**Everton** ....**1** Lyons	**Newcastle United** ....**1** Gibb	*Division One*
	Derby County **0**	**Leeds United** **0**	*Division One*
1/12/73	**Arsenal** ....**2** Hornsby Nelson	**Coventry City** ....**2** Cross Alderson	*Division One*
	Blackpool **0**	**Sunderland** ....**2** Halom Belfitt	*Division Two*
8/12/73	**Ipswich Town** **0**	**Leeds United** ....**3** Jones Yorath Clarke	*Division One*
	Queens Park Rangers **0**	**Sheffield United** **0**	*Division One*

15/12/73	**Luton Town** ....1 Anderson	**Aston Villa** 0	*Division Two*
	Newcastle United 0	**Derby County** ....2 Davies Hinton	*Division One*
22/12/73	**Liverpool** ....2 Keegan (pen.) Heighway	**Manchester United** 0	*Division One*
	Arsenal ....1 Ball	**Everton** 0	*Division One*
29/12/73	**Birmingham City** ....1 Latchford	**Leeds United** ....1 Jordan	*Division One*
	Leyton Orient......................1 Roffey	**Fulham** 0	*Division Two*
5/1/74	**Wolverhampton Wanderers** ....1 Richards	**Leeds United** ....1 Lorimer (pen.)	*FA Cup 3rd round*
	West Ham United ....1 Holland	**Hereford United** ....1 Redrobe	*FA Cup 3rd round*
	Manchester United ....1 Macari	**Plymouth Argyle** 0	*FA Cup 3rd round*
12/1/74	**Aston Villa** ....1 B. Rioch	**Middlesbrough** ....1 Craggs	*Division Two*
	Ipswich Town ....1 Johnson	**Stoke City**...........................1 Hurst	*Division One*
19/1/74	**Bristol Rovers**......................3 Warboys Rudge Bannister (pen.)	**AFC Bournemouth** 0	*Division Three*
	Everton 0	**Leeds United** 0	*Division One*
26/1/74	**Queens Park Rangers** ....2 Leach Givens	**Birmingham City** 0	*FA Cup 4th round*
	Fulham ....1 Mullery	**Leicester City** ....1 Glover	*FA Cup 4th round*
	Manchester United 0	**Ipswich Town** ....1 Beattie	*FA Cup 4th round*
2/2/74	**Carlisle United**....................3 Clarke (2) Laidlaw	**Leyton Orient**.......................0	*Division Two*
	Liverpool ....1 Cormack	**Norwich City**........................0	*Division One*
9/2/74	**Chelsea** ....1 Webb	**Manchester City**...................0	*Division One*

16/2/74	**Bristol City** ....1 Fear	**Leeds United** ....1 Bremner				*FA Cup 5th round*
	West Bromwich Albion 0	**Newcastle United** ....3 Tudor Macdonald Barrowclough				*FA Cup 5th round*
	Liverpool ....2 Hall Keegan	**Ipswich Town** 0				*FA Cup 5th round*
23/2/74	**Tottenham Hotspur**..............1 Pratt	**Ipswich Town** ....1 Whymark				*Division One*
	Leicester City ....1 Worthington	**Sheffield United** ....1 Salmons				*Division One*
2/3/74	**Queens Park Rangers** ....3 Givens Bowles Francis	**Tottenham Hotspur**..............1 Chivers (pen.)				*Division One*
	Sheffield United 0	**Manchester United** ....1 Macari				*Division One*
9/3/74	**Queens Park Rangers** 0	**Leicester City** ....2 Waters (2)				*FA Cup 6th round*
	Derby County....................1 Rioch (pen.)	**West Ham United** ....1 Bonds				*Division One*
16/3/74	**Liverpool** ....1 Heighway	**Leeds United** 0				*Division One*
	Leicester City 0	**Derby County**.....................1 McFarland				*Division One*
23/3/74	**Southampton** 0	**Birmingham City** ....2 Burns Francis				*Division One*
	Manchester United 0	**Tottenham Hotspur**..............1 Coates				*Division One*
30/3/74	**Leicester City** 0	**Liverpool** 0				*FA Cup semi-final*
6/4/74	**Hereford United** 0	**York City**...........................0				*Division Three*
	Leeds United ....2 Lorimer Bremner	**Derby County**.....................0				*Division One*
13/4/74	**Ipswich Town** ....1 Whymark	**Liverpool** ....1 Hughes				*Division One*
	Bristol Rovers....................1 Bannister	**Oldham Athletic** ....2 McVitie Garwood				*Division Three*

20/4/74	**Leyton Orient**......................1 Fairbrother	**Notts County**......................1 Masson	*Division Two*
	Liverpool...........................0	**Everton**..............................0	*Division One*
27/4/74	**West Ham United**................2 Lampard Brooking	**Liverpool**...........................2 Toshack Keegan	*Division One*
	Everton............................0	**Southampton**......................3 Osgood Channon O'Neil	*Division One*
4/5/74	**Liverpool**..........................3 Keegan (2) Heighway	**Newcastle United**...............0	*FA Cup final*
11/5/74	**Wales**...............................0	**England**...........................2 Bowles Keegan	*Home International Championship*
	Northern Ireland..................1 Cassidy	**Scotland**...........................0	*Home International Championship*
18/5/74	**Scotland**...........................2 Jordan Todd (o.g.)	**England**...........................0	*Home International Championship*
	Wales...............................1 Smallman	**Northern Ireland**..................0	*Home International Championship*
1/6/74	**Bulgaria**...........................0	**England**...........................1 Worthington	*Friendly*

MATCH OF THE SEASON
Tottenham Hotspur 2
Manchester United 1
at White Hart Lane,
Saturday 10 November 1973

Not necessarily a collectors' item in the great Spurs v. United series, perhaps, but a significant match for a number of reasons. They revolved around four individuals – Martin Chivers, George Best,

A powerhouse called Chivers. The Spurs centre forward puts them ahead, but can you name the Manchester United man making the desperate challenge? In fact, it's George Graham in an unusual role in his brief spell with United

the late Cyril Knowles who scored the goals, and Bill Nicholson, in the last of his 16 seasons as manager of Spurs.

Chivers was one of his best signings – yet finished up frustrating the perfectionist in Nicholson. The big centre-forward with the fierce shot in either foot came up with 174 goals for Spurs in 367 appearances. One in this match put Tottenham ahead.

United's equaliser was scored by George Best. He had come back from the first of his 'retirements', but his second spell with United was to last only 12 matches. Bearded now and heavier, he was discarded by Tommy Docherty well before United were relegated at the end of the season.

Spurs's winner came from a beautifully disguised free-kick, eventually wrapped around the United wall by the velvet left foot of left-back Cyril Knowles.

'Nice one, Cyril' was an appropriate response that day, and was quoted as an epitaph when, sadly, Knowles died from a brain disorder in the autumn of 1991.

Bill Nicholson attended his funeral and also the testimonial match Spurs held for Knowles's family. They had shared some fine moments together in the early 70s, when Spurs won the League Cup twice and the UEFA Cup to add to Nicholson's rich haul of trophies with his 'double' team of the early 60s.

Tottenham Hotspur: Jennings, Evans, Knowles, Pratt, England, Beal, Neighbour, Perryman, Chivers (sub. Gilzean), Peters, McGrath. Scorers: Chivers, Knowles

Manchester United: Stepney, Buchan, Young, Greenhoff, Holton, James, Morgan, Macari, Kidd, Graham, Best. Scorer: Best.

PLAYER OF THE SEASON
Billy Bremner
(Leeds United and Scotland)

When Doncaster Rovers, bottom of the Fourth Division, parted company with their manager on the first day of November 1991, his old club were top of the First Division for the first time since his playing days 17 years earlier. How times had changed for Billy Bremner.

He started the 1973/4 season in fine fettle, scoring twice against Spurs at White Hart Lane. He finished it as captain of Scotland in the World Cup finals in West Germany, brushing a post against Brazil with a shot that might have sent the unbeaten Scots close to the Final.

In between, Bremner and Leeds set about a promise he

made to Don Revie before their opening match – that they would go closer than ever before to completing a League season unbeaten. In fact, the run lasted 29 games, before Leeds lost 3–2 at Stoke after leading 2–0. They stumbled slightly, then recovered their balance by beating Derby, with Bremner scoring the clinching goal in front of the *Match of the Day* cameras.

Leeds were crowned League Champions, with Bremner's 10 goals from midfield just part of his contribution. His leadership qualities, technique and spirit shone through the early *Match of the Day* years.

AS MATCH OF THE DAY entered its second decade, the first close-up camera shot picked out Bill Shankly and Brian Clough standing side by side in the tunnel at Wembley. Shankly had just retired, and was leading Liverpool out for the last time; Clough had just arrived at Leeds to succeed Don Revie, but was to last just 44 days in the job.

The occasion was the first FA Charity Shield match to be played at Wembley, but it was not an auspicious start. Kevin Keegan of Liverpool and Leeds captain Billy Bremner were sent off for fighting, and subsequently suspended for 11 games for bringing the game into disrepute. It was an altogether contradictory opening to the season. The cameras covered Carlisle United's first match in the First Division. They beat Chelsea at Stamford Bridge and briefly led the table.

Also in August, Bill Nicholson resigned after 16 years as Tottenham manager. *Match of the Day* was at his last game, in which Spurs beat Derby 2–0 at White Hart Lane. But Derby, now managed by Nicholson's old warrior Dave Mackay, went on to win the Championship. Galvanised by the signings of Bruce Rioch and Francis Lee, they had emerged from their post-Clough gloom. Cloughie himself moved down the road to Nottingham Forest in January, too late to improve their poor position in the Second Division, where Manchester United romped to the Championship. A crowd of 60,000 saw United beat Sunderland at Old Trafford, and Bob Stokoe's team were also on the receiving end of the 'Goal of the Season' when Mickey Walsh hit a stupendous shot for Blackpool at Bloomfield Road.

The cameras were again at Blackpool when Aston Villa virtually made sure of promotion under Ron Saunders. They also won the League Cup, and when *Match of the Day* covered their derby with West Brom in March, the crowd at Villa Park numbered 47,574.

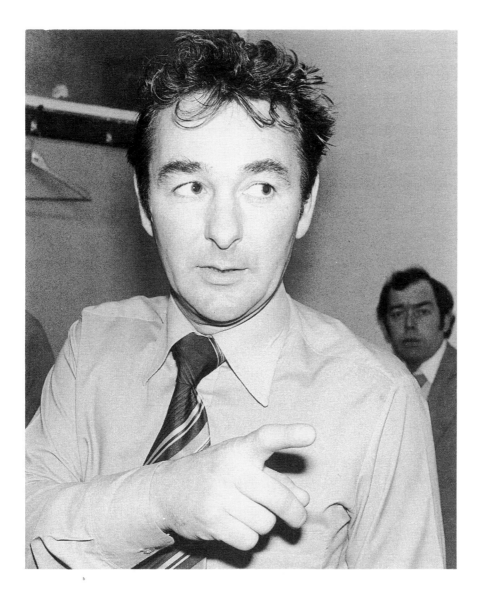

'Now look here, young man'. Brian
Clough back in business at
Nottingham Forest after short spells
at Brighton and Leeds. He would do
for Forest what he did for Derby – and
more

10/8/74	**Leeds United** ...... 1 Cherry (Liverpool won 6–5 on penalties)	**Liverpool** ...... 1 Boersma		*FA Charity Shield*
17/8/74	**Chelsea** 0	**Carlisle United** ...... 2 Green O'Neill		*Division One*
	Luton Town ...... 1 Butlin	**Liverpool** ...... 2 Smith Heighway		*Division One*
24/8/74	**Ipswich Town** ...... 2 Talbot (pen.) Whymark	**Burnley** 0		*Division One*
	Leeds United ...... 1 Clarke	**Birmingham City** 0		*Division One*
31/8/74	**Tottenham Hotspur** ...... 2 Neighbour (2)	**Derby County** 0		*Division One*
	Stoke City ...... 1 Ritchie (pen.)	**Middlesbrough** ...... 1 Souness		*Division One*
7/9/74	**Wolverhampton Wanderers** ...... 1 Richards	**Leicester City** ...... 1 Glover		*Division One*
	Arsenal 0	**Burnley** ...... 1 Noble		*Division One*
14/9/74	**West Bromwich Albion** ...... 1 Merrick	**Manchester United** ...... 1 Pearson		*Division Two*
	Manchester City ...... 2 Marsh Tueart	**Liverpool** 0		*Division One*
21/9/74	**Queens Park Rangers** ...... 1 Keeley (o.g.)	**Newcastle** ...... 2 Burns Tudor		*Division One*
	Peterborough United 0	**Preston North End** 0		*Division Three*
28/9/74	**Everton** ...... 3 Seargeant Lyons Clements	**Leeds United** ...... 2 Clarke Yorath		*Division One*
	Southampton 0	**Aston Villa** 0		*Division Two*
5/10/74	**Queens Park Rangers** ...... 1 Francis	**Ipswich Town** 0		*Division One*
	Carlisle United 0	**Liverpool** ...... 1 Kennedy		*Division One*
12/10/74	**Newcastle United** ...... 2 Keeley Tudor	**Stoke City** ...... 2 Salmons Mahoney		*Division One*
	Manchester United ...... 1 McIlroy	**Notts County** 0		*Division Two*

19/10/74	**Sunderland** 0		**Aston Villa** 0		*Division Two*
	Leeds United ....2 Clarke McKenzie		**Wolverhampton Wanderers** 0		*Division One*
26/10/74	**Burnley** ....1 Hankin		**Everton** ....1 Jones		*Division One*
	Ipswich Town ....1 Hamilton		**Manchester City**...................1 Bell		*Division One*
2/11/74	**Crystal Palace** ....1 Taylor		**Peterborough United**.............1 Galley		*Division Three*
	Ipswich Town ....1 Talbot		**Liverpool** 0		*Division One*
9/11/74	**Norwich City**........................0		**Bristol Rovers** ....1 Bannister		*Division Two*
	Middlesbrough 0		**Newcastle United** 0		*Division One*
16/11/74	**Everton** 0		**Liverpool** 0		*Division One*
	Fulham ....1 Mullery		**Sunderland** ....3 Moore (o.g.) Robson (2)		*Division Two*
23/11/74	**Manchester City**..................4 Tueart Daniels (2) Bell		**Leicester City** ....1 Birchenall		*Division One*
	Derby County ....2 Hector Rioch		**Ipswich Town** 0		*Division One*
30/11/74	**Manchester United** ....3 Pearson Morgan McIlroy		**Sunderland** ....2 Hughes (2)		*Division Two*
	Leeds United ....2 Cherry Clarke		**Chelsea** 0		*Division One*
7/12/74	**West Ham United** ....2 Gould Jennings		**Leeds United** ....1 McKenzie		*Division One*
	Norwich City........................1 Miller		**Cardiff City**.........................1 Reece		*Division Two*
14/12/74	**Coventry City** ....2 Cross Lloyd		**Newcastle United** 0		*Division One*
	Queens Park Rangers ....1 Rogers		**Sheffield United** 0		*Division One*

21/12/74	**Birmingham City** ....3 Taylor Kendall (pen.) Hatton	**Liverpool** ....1 Toshack	*Division One*
	Tottenham Hotspur..............1 Duncan	**Queens Park Rangers** ....2 Bowles (2) (1 pen.)	*Division One*
28/12/74	**Manchester City**..................1 Bell	**Derby County**.......................2 Newton Lee	*Division One*
	Leicester City 0	**Leeds United** ....2 F. Gray McKenzie	*Division One*
4/1/75	**Leyton Orient**......................2 Possee Queen	**Derby County**.......................2 Todd (2)	*FA Cup 3rd round*
	Liverpool ....2 Heighway Keegan	**Stoke City**...........................0	*FA Cup 3rd round*
	Southampton ....1 Channon (pen.)	**West Ham United** ....2 Lampard Gould	*FA Cup 3rd round*
11/1/75	**Leeds United** ....2 Clarke McKenzie	**West Ham United** ....1 Robson	*Division One*
	Stoke City 0	**Birmingham City** 0	*Division One*
18/1/75	**Sunderland** 0	**Manchester United** 0	*Division Two*
	Tottenham Hotspur..............1 Duncan	**Sheffield United** ....3 Currie Eddy Woodward	*Division One*
25/1/75	**Leatherhead** ....2 McGillicuddy Kelly	**Leicester City** ....3 Sammels Earle Weller	*FA Cup 4th round* *match played at Filbert Street*
	Plymouth Argyle..................1 Vassallo	**Everton** ....3 Pearson Lyons (2)	*FA Cup 4th round*
	Middlesbrough ....3 Murdoch Hickton (2 pens)	**Sunderland** ....1 Robson	*FA Cup 4th round*
1/2/75	**Blackpool** ....3 Alcock Davies Walsh	**Sunderland** ....2 Halom Kerr	*Division Two*
	West Ham United ....2 Jennings Holland	**Carlisle United**.....................0	*Division One*

8/2/75	**Liverpool** ....5 Hall Toshack (2) Lindsay Cormack	**Ipswich Town** ....2 Beattie Whymark	*Division One*
	Oxford United ....1 D. Clarke	**Manchester United** 0	*Division Two*
15/2/75	**Peterborough United**.............1 Nixon	**Middlesbrough** ....1 Mills	*FA Cup 5th round*
	Arsenal 0	**Leicester City** 0	*FA Cup 5th round*
	Mansfield Town 0	**Carlisle United**.....................1 Owen	*FA Cup 5th round*
22/2/75	**Liverpool** 0	**Everton** 0	*Division One*
	Middlesbrough 0	**Leeds United** ....1 Clarke	*Division One*
1/3/75	**Coventry City** 0	**Burnley** ....3 James Noble Fletcher	*Division One*
	Sunderland ....3 Halom Robson (2)	**West Bromwich Albion** 0	*Division Two*
8/3/75	**Arsenal** 0	**West Ham United** ....2 A. Taylor (2)	*FA Cup 6th round*
	Birmingham City ....1 Hatton	**Middlesbrough** 0	*FA Cup 6th round*
15/3/75	**Leeds United** 0	**Everton** 0	*Division One*
	Plymouth Argyle..................0	**Wrexham**..............................3 Griffiths Davies Whittle	*Division Three*
22/3/75	**Brighton & Hove Albion**..........0	**Blackburn Rovers** ....1 Kenyon	*Division Three*
	Sheffield United ....3 Currie (2) Woodward	**West Ham United** ....2 Gould Jennings	*Division One*
29/3/75	**Aston Villa** ....3 Leonard (2) Hamilton	**West Bromwich Albion** ....1 T. Brown	*Division Two*
	Liverpool ....1 Keegan (pen.)	**Birmingham City** 0	*Division One*
5/4/75	**West Ham United** 0	**Ipswich Town** 0	*FA Cup semi-final*

12/4/75	**Burnley** ....3 Noble (2) James (pen.)	**Tottenham Hotspur**..............2 Duncan Perryman	*Division One*
	Newcastle United 0	**Everton** ....1 Dobson	*Division One*
19/4/75	**Leicester City** 0	**Derby County**.......................0	*Division One*
	Blackpool 0	**Aston Villa** ....3 Phillips Hatton (o.g.) Little	*Division Two*
26/4/75	**Ipswich Town** ....4 Talbot Whymark Beattie Hunter	**West Ham United** ....1 Holland	*Division One*
	Chelsea ....1 Wilkins	**Everton** ....1 Latchford	*Division One*
3/5/75	**Fulham** 0	**West Ham United** ....2 A. Taylor (2)	*FA Cup final*
17/5/75	**Wales**................................2 Toshack Flynn	**Scotland** ....2 Rioch Jackson	*Home International Championship*
	Northern Ireland..................0	**England** 0	*Home International Championship*
23/5/75	**Northern Ireland**..................1 Finney	**Wales** 0	*Home International Championship*
24/5/75	**England** ....5 G. Francis (2) Beattie Bell Johnson	**Scotland** ....1 Rioch (pen.)	*Home International Championship*

MATCH OF THE SEASON

Leicester City 3
Leatherhead 2
(FA Cup 4th round)
at Filbert Street,
Saturday 25 January 1975

Five non-League clubs figured in the draw for the fourth round of the FA Cup, and Isthmian League Leatherhead came out of the bag at home to First Division Leicester. But the limitations of their ground at Fetcham Grove persuaded the Surrey side to switch the tie to Filbert Street.

After 27 minutes, ground advantage didn't seem to matter. Peter McGillicuddy had given the amateurs the lead, then striker Chris Kelly, nicknamed the 'Leatherhead Lip', headed in a free-kick to put Leatherhead two up.

Early in the second half, Kelly went round goalkeeper Mark Wallington and one of the shocks of the century seemed certain. But Leicester centre-half Malcolm Munro cleared off the line and his save turned the game.

Jon Sammels, Steve Earle and Keith Weller rescued the reputation of the First Division team, with centre-forward Frank Worthington the brains behind their recovery.

Chris Kelly later had a brief spell in the league limelight with Millwall.

Leicester: Wallington, Whitworth, Rofe, Earle, Munro, Cross, Weller, Sammels, Worthington, Birchenall, Glover.
Scorers: Sammels, Earle, Weller

Leatherhead: Swannell, Sargeant, Webb, Cooper, Reid, McGillicuddy, Woffinden, Lavers, Kelly, Smith, Doyle.
Scorers: McGillicuddy, Kelly

A fading dream. Leatherhead's two-goal lead disappears as Steve Earle equalises for Leicester. England amateur international goalkeeper John Swannell is grounded – later he was beaten again

PLAYER OF THE SEASON
Tony Currie (Sheffield United)

Sheffield United's achievement in finishing sixth in the First Division – their best position in modern times and close to a place in Europe – was due in no small part to one of the most extravagantly gifted players of the *Match of the Day* years.

Tony Currie looked languid, ran in loping strides, wore his blond hair untidily, and belonged to that category of 70s' non-conformists that included Stan Bowles, Alan Hudson, Charlie George and Frank Worthington.

But there was no better passer of the ball until the arrival of Glenn Hoddle, and Currie possessed the strength and ability to get into the thick of the action and score goals. He was also an exhibitionist. They still talk at Brammall

Lane of the time he sat on the ball against Arsenal, and when he ran down the wing against Stoke with the ball at his feet, applauding with his hands above his head.

His best televised goal was against West Ham. He beat the same bewildered opponent no fewer than four times before stroking the ball past Mervyn Day. The commentator called it 'a quality goal by a quality player'.

I T WAS ONE OF THE best-constructed goals ever scored in front of the *Match of the Day* cameras. It was a swift, incisive four-man move that took the ball from just outside one penalty area into the net at the other end.

It was scored by Queens Park Rangers against Liverpool on the opening day of the 1975/6 season, and said a lot about the months to come. Gerry Francis, who tucked the ball away after that continental build-up by Don Masson, Stan Bowles and Don Givens, was by now the captain of Don Revie's England.

His club manager, Dave Sexton, briefly made Rangers the cult team in London, much as he had done with Chelsea. Two of his former players, John Hollins and Dave Webb, together with Arsenal's double-winning captain Frank McLintock, were part of an all-star cast at the Shepherd's Bush football theatre.

Rangers ran Liverpool mighty close for the First Division Championship. Bob Paisley's team won their last match at Wolverhampton to take the title by just one point. They also won the UEFA Cup for the second time.

Behind Liverpool and Rangers in the First Division came Tommy Docherty's Manchester United. Their sparkling young team included two fresh, orthodox wingers, graduate Steve Coppell on the right, and on the left the unpredictable Gordon Hill, whose two goals against Derby at Hillsborough won the FA Cup semi-final covered by the BBC.

The season's FA Cup coverage also featured Malcolm Allison's fedora, as his Third Division Crystal Palace won impressively at Chelsea in front of the *Match of the Day* cameras, before losing in the semi-final to the eventual winners, Southampton. Lawrie McMenemy's team included several old favourites, and two of them produced a goal at Bradford in the sixth round which earned a special place in the BBC Library. Peter Osgood flicked the ball up from a free-kick, and Jim McCalliog volleyed in.

Eyes firmly on the ball, Gerry Francis led Queens Park Rangers to second place in the First Division, and also captained England. He later successfully managed Bristol Rovers, before taking over at Rangers in 1991

But viewers who voted the Gerry Francis effort the 'Goal of the Season', also had to consider an amazing effort by Malcolm Macdonald, with his 'wrong' foot, for Newcastle in the FA Cup at Bolton. 'Supermac' had Newcastle on course in two Cup competitions, but they lost in the League Cup final and the FA Cup quarter-final. In the summer, he left to join Arsenal.

9/8/75	**Derby County** ....2 Hector McFarland	**West Ham United** 0	*FA Charity Shield*
16/8/75	**Ipswich Town** 0	**Newcastle United** ....3 Macdonald (2) T. Craig (pen.)	*Division One*
	Queens Park Rangers ....2 Francis Leach	**Liverpool** 0	*Division One*
23/8/75	**Manchester United** ....5 Pearson (2) McIlroy Daly Badger (o.g.)	**Sheffield United** ....1 Guthrie	*Division One*
	Arsenal 0	**Stoke City** ....1 Hudson	*Division One*
30/8/75	**Fulham** ....4 Mitchell Howe (2) Busby	**West Bromwich Albion** 0	*Division Two*
	Everton ....2 Lyons Latchford	**Derby County** 0	*Division One*
6/9/75	**West Ham United** ....1 Lampard	**Manchester City** 0	*Division One*
	Newcastle United ....3 Macdonald (2) T. Craig	**Aston Villa** 0	*Division One*
13/9/75	**Stoke City** ....3 Conroy Pejic Greenhoff	**Leeds United** ....2 Lorimer (2) (1 pen.)	*Division One*
	Charlton Athletic ....1 Hales	**Blackpool** ....1 Walsh	*Division Two*
20/9/75	**Birmingham City** ....4 Campbell Withe Kendall Francis	**Burnley** 0	*Division One*
	Manchester United ....1 Houston	**Ipswich Town** 0	*Division One*
27/9/75	**Crystal Palace** ....1 Kemp	**Sheffield Wednesday** ....1 Potts	*Division Three*
	Everton 0	**Liverpool** 0	*Division One*

4/10/75	**Leeds United** ....2 Clarke Lorimer	**Queens Park Rangers** ....1 Bowles (pen.)	*Division One*
	Arsenal ....2 Ball Cropley	**Manchester City**..................3 Hartford Royle Marsh	*Division One*
11/10/75	**West Ham United** ....2 Curbishley A. Taylor	**Newcastle United** ....1 Howard	*Division One*
	Southampton ....4 Channon (2) (1 pen.) Stokes Holmes	**Chelsea** ....1 Wilkins	*Division Two*
18/10/75	**Sheffield United** 0	**Stoke City**...........................2 Greenhoff (2)	*Division One*
	Coventry City 0	**Liverpool** 0	*Division One*
25/10/75	**Manchester City**..................1 Bell	**Ipswich Town** ....1 Hamilton	*Division One*
	Sunderland ....2 Kerr Robson	**Luton Town** 0	*Division Two*
1/11/75	**Derby County**......................3 Gemmill George (pen.) Davies	**Leeds United** ....2 Cherry McKenzie	*Division One*
	Ipswich Town ....3 Peddelty Whymark Hamilton	**Aston Villa** 0	*Division One*
8/11/75	**Liverpool** ....3 Heighway Toshack Keegan	**Manchester United** ....1 Coppell	*Division One*
	Fulham ....1 Lloyd	**Charlton Athletic** ....1 Giles	*Division Two*
15/11/75	**Burnley** ....1 Hankin	**Wolverhampton Wanderers** ....5 Richards (2) Daley (2) Hibbitt	*Division One*
	Chelsea ....2 Garner R. Wilkins (pen.)	**Notts County** 0	*Division Two*

22/11/75	**Bristol City** .... 4 Ritchie (3) Merrick	**York City** .... 1 Seal	*Division Two*
	Norwich City .... 1 Sullivan	**Newcastle United** .... 2 Nulty (2)	*Division One*
29/11/75	**Queens Park Rangers** .... 3 Masson Clement Webb	**Stoke City** .... 2 Moores Bloor	*Division One*
	Bolton Wanderers .... 1 Greaves	**West Bromwich Albion** .... 2 Mayo Robson	*Division Two*
6/12/75	**Southampton** .... 4 Osgood (2) Holmes Blyth	**Sunderland** 0	*Division Two*
	Middlesbrough 0	**Manchester United** 0	*Division One*
13/12/75	**Ipswich Town** .... 2 Lambert Peddelty	**Leeds United** .... 1 McKenzie	*Division One*
	Leicester City .... 1 Weller	**Newcastle United** 0	*Division One*
20/12/75	**Liverpool** .... 2 Neal (pen.) Toshack	**Queens Park Rangers** 0	*Division One*
	Chelsea .... 1 Britton	**Sunderland** 0	*Division Two*
27/12/75	**Manchester United** .... 2 McIlroy Macari	**Burnley** .... 1 Hankin	*Division One*
	West Ham United .... 1 T. Taylor (pen.)	**Ipswich Town** .... 2 Lambert Peddelty	*Division One*
3/1/76	**West Ham United** 0	**Liverpool** .... 2 Keegan Toshack	*FA Cup 3rd round*
	Scarborough .... 1 Abbey	**Crystal Palace** .... 2 Taylor Evans	*FA Cup 3rd round*
	Queens Park Rangers 0	**Newcastle United** 0	*FA Cup 3rd round*
10/1/76	**Manchester United** .... 2 Hill McIlroy	**Queens Park Rangers** .... 1 Givens	*Division One*
	Cardiff City 0	**Brighton & Hove Albion** .... 1 Mellor	*Division Three*

17/1/76	**Wolverhampton Wanderers** ....**1** Gould	**Leeds United** ....**1** McAlle (o.g.)	Division One
	Manchester City..................**3** Royle (2) (1 pen.) Oakes	**West Ham United** **0**	Division One
24/1/76	**Stoke City**...........................**2** Salmons (pen.) Moores	**Tottenham Hotspur**...............**1** Perryman	FA Cup 3rd round replay
	Coventry City ....**1** Murphy	**Newcastle United** ....**1** Gowling	FA Cup 4th round
	Manchester United ....**3** Forsyth Hill McIlroy	**Peterborough United**.............**1** Cozens	FA Cup 4th round
31/1/76	**West Ham United** **0**	**Liverpool** ....**4** Toshack (3) Keegan	Division One
	Derby County......................**2** George (2) (1 pen.)	**Coventry City** **0**	Division One
7/2/76	**Bristol City** ....**1** Ritchie	**Southampton** ....**1** Holmes	Division Two
	Manchester City..................**2** Booth Hartford	**Aston Villa** ....**1** Gray	Division One
14/2/76	**Chelsea** ....**2** R. Wilkins Wicks	**Crystal Palace** ....**3** Taylor (2) Chatterton	FA Cup 5th round
	Bolton Wanderers ....**3** Allardyce G. Jones P. Jones	**Newcastle United** ....**3** Gowling Macdonald (2)	FA Cup 5th round
	Wolverhampton Wanderers ....**3** Richards (3)	**Charlton Athletic**..................**0**	FA Cup 5th round
21/2/76	**Sunderland** ....**4** Holden Moncur Robson Towers	**Charlton Athletic**..................**1** Bowman	Division Two
	Aston Villa ....**2** Gray McDonald	**Manchester United** ....**1** Macari	Division One
28/2/76	**Derby County**......................**1** George (pen.)	**Liverpool** ....**1** Kennedy	Division One
	Tottenham Hotspur..............**1** Chivers	**Leicester City** ....**1** Kember	Division One

6/3/76	**Derby County** .... 4 Rioch (2) Newton George	**Newcastle United** .... 2 Gowling (2)	*FA Cup 6th round*
	Bradford City 0	**Southampton** .... 1 McCalliog	*FA Cup 6th round*
13/3/76	**Manchester United** .... 3 Houston Daly Pearson	**Leeds United** .... 2 Cherry Bremner	*Division One*
	Peterborough United 0	**Mansfield Town** .... 3 Clarke (2) McCaffrey	*Division Three*
20/3/76	**West Bromwich Albion** .... 2 Mayo Wile	**Bolton Wanderers** 0	*Division Two*
	Middlesbrough 0	**Derby County** .... 2 Hector George	*Division One*
27/3/76	**Hereford United** .... 1 McNeil	**Brighton & Hove Albion** .... 1 Ward	*Division Three*
	Liverpool .... 2 Fairclough (2)	**Burnley** 0	*Division One*
3/4/76	**Derby County** 0	**Manchester United** .... 2 Hill (2)	*FA Cup semi-final*
10/4/76	**Bristol City** .... 2 Ritchie (2)	**Chelsea** .... 2 Swain Stanley	*Division Two*
	Wolverhampton Wanderers .... 5 Richards (3) Hibbitt Carr	**Newcastle United** 0	*Division One*
17/4/76	**Liverpool** .... 5 Neal (pen.) Toshack Kennedy Hughes Fairclough	**Stoke City** .... 3 Conroy Moores Bloor	*Division One*
	Norwich City .... 3 MacDougall Morris Boyer	**Queens Park Rangers** .... 2 Thomas Powell (o.g.)	*Division One*
24/4/76	**Leicester City** .... 2 Lee Garland	**Manchester United** .... 1 Coyne	*Division One*
	Oldham Athletic 0	**West Bromwich Albion** .... 1 T. Brown	*Division Two*

1/5/76	**Manchester United** 0	**Southampton** ....1 Stokes	*FA Cup final*
8/5/76	**Wales** 0	**England** ....1 Taylor	*Home International Championship*
	Northern Ireland..................0	**Scotland** ....3 Gemmill Masson Dalglish	*Home International Championship*
14/5/76	**Wales** ....1 James	**Northern Ireland**..................0	*Home International Championship*
15/5/76	**Scotland** ....2 Masson Dalglish	**England** ....1 Channon	*Home International Championship*
22/5/76	**Wales** ....1 Evans	**Yugoslavia** ....1 Katalinski (pen.)	*European Championship quarter-final second leg*

Match of the Season:

Liverpool 5
Stoke City 3
at Anfield,
Saturday 17 April 1976

The first of Bob Paisley's 20 trophies won in his 9 seasons as manager of Liverpool came the hard way. The League Championship race went to the very last match, but

Liverpool's reputation for staying the course was emphasised by the way they won 9 of their last 10 games. Their last home match against

Phil Neal, scorer of 60 goals from full back in 635 games for Liverpool, beats Peter Shilton from the penalty spot. Neal played in four European Cup finals for Liverpool – scoring in two – and managed Bolton Wanderers from 1985 to 1992

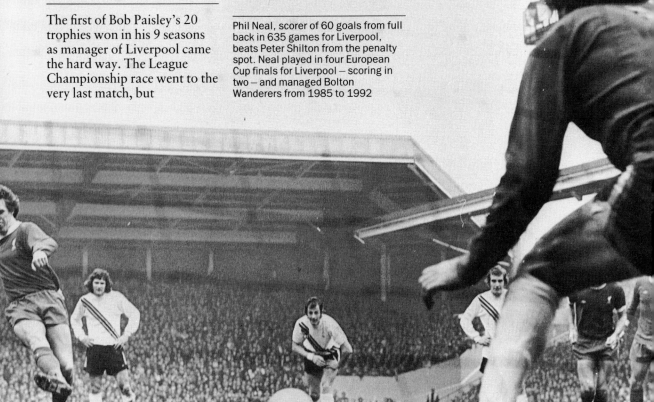

Stoke City, themselves championship contenders the season before, produced an eight-goal bonanza to delight any television audience. If Liverpool's football was not quite as perfect as in their 4–0 demolition of West Ham in front of the cameras in January, the Stoke game saw both teams going for the throat.

Tony Waddington's collection of veterans had charm and character. They took the lead at Anfield through Terry Conroy, from a cross by Jimmy Greenhoff.

A penalty by Phil Neal and a deflected shot from John Toshack gave Liverpool the lead at half-time. Ray Kennedy made it 3–1 from a delightful pass by Kevin Keegan, only for Ian Moores to pull one back for Stoke.

The irrepressible Keegan had a hand in the fourth and fifth Liverpool goals – scored by Emlyn Hughes and David Fairclough – before Alan Bloor completed the scoring at the Kop end.

Liverpool: Clemence, Smith, Neal, Thompson, Kennedy, Hughes, Keegan, Case (sub. Fairclough), Heighway, Toshack, Callaghan.
Scorers: Neal (pen.), Toshack, Kennedy, Hughes, Fairclough.

Stoke City: Shilton, Marsh, Pejic, Mahoney, Dodd, Bloor, Robertson, Greenhoff, Conroy, Moores, Salmons.
Scorers: Conroy, Moores, Bloor.

PLAYER OF THE SEASON
Mike Channon (Southampton)

Not many second division sides win the FA Cup, and certainly not with England's most prolific current goalscorer in their side. But it happened in 1975–6, a fairy tale season for Southampton and their locally born striker, Mike Channon.

He will never get the credit for the winning goal against Manchester United at Wembley – that belongs to Bobby Stokes – but quite apart from Channon's contribution to Saints' startling FA Cup run, it is often overlooked that he averaged a goal a game in nine internationals for England that same season.

Channon's infectious approach to the game made him a great favourite at the Dell, where his 185 goals were a Southampton career record. His 21 goals for England in 46 internationals put him in the all-time top ten goalscorers for his country.

Blessed with speed, flair and courage, Channon never lost his broad Hampshire accent or his love for the game. He played a full season for his old Southampton colleague Alan Ball at Portsmouth when he was 37, before finally giving up football to concentrate on his other big love – training racehorses.

Mike Channon's individual style said a lot about the entertainment value of football in the 70s. He would celebrate a goal by whirling his arm windmill-like, his cheeky, cheerful smile a reminder that the game could still be fun.

IT WAS PROBABLY the most bizarre moment ever seen on an English football ground, and certainly the strangest captured by the *Match of the Day* cameras. A First Division match came to a standstill while the groundsman walked on to the pitch with a pot of paint.

It happened at the muddy Baseball Ground on 30 April 1977, where Derby County, having sacked their manager Dave Mackay, were struggling against relegation. When they were awarded a penalty against Manchester City, the referee discovered that the penalty spot had been obscured by the mud. It had to be paced out and repainted by groundsman Bob Smith before Gerry Daly took the kick and scored Derby's fourth goal in a 4–0 win that helped preserve their First Division status.

Daly, signed from Manchester United, was one of several well-known faces in different shirts to pop up in new surroundings during this season. George Best and Rodney Marsh were playing for Fulham, Martin Peters for Norwich, Johnny Giles was the player-manager at West Bromwich Albion, Malcolm Macdonald was now scoring goals for Arsenal, Brian Kidd was getting them for his new club Manchester City, where he linked up with the old Everton favourite, Joe Royle.

One of Royle's former colleagues, Jimmy Husband, scored twice for Luton in a Second Division encounter screened from Brammall Lane, and Bryan 'Pop' Robson, a *Match of the Day* goalscorer at Newcastle and Sunderland, came back to London for a second spell with West Ham. While the Hammers avoided relegation thanks to a 0–0 draw at Anfield (the game was covered by the BBC because it confirmed Liverpool as champions), their neighbours Tottenham were not so fortunate. They *were* relegated – but viewers did get a glimpse of a young man who would become a household name over the next 10 years. Glenn Hoddle scored against Aston Villa at the end of April.

Brian Kidd joined the elite band of
players to score four goals in a
televised match when Manchester
City beat Leicester City 5–0 at Maine
Road in January 1977

14/8/76	**Liverpool** ....**1** Toshack	**Southampton** **0**	*FA Charity Shield*
21/8/76	**Queens Park Rangers** **0**	**Everton** ....**4** Parkes (o.g.) Latchford (2) Bernard (pen.)	*Division One*
	Leeds United ....**2** Harris Clarke	**West Bromwich Albion** ....**2** A. Brown T. Brown	*Division One*
28/8/76	**Sunderland** ....**2** Holden Robson	**Arsenal** ....**2** Ross Macdonald	*Division One*
	Bolton Wanderers ....**3** Taylor (2) Smith	**Millwall**................................**1** Lee	*Division Two*
4/9/76	**Manchester United** ....**2** Coppell Pearson	**Tottenham Hotspur**...............**3** Coates Moores Pratt	*Division One*
	Southampton ....**1** Channon	**Sheffield United** ....**1** Ludlam	*Division Two*
11/9/76	**Derby County**.......................**2** George Neal (o.g.)	**Liverpool** ....**3** Kennedy Toshack Keegan	*Division One*
	Fulham **0**	**Wolverhampton Wanderers** **0**	*Division Two*
18/9/76	**Brighton & Hove Albion**..........**7** Ward (2) Piper O'Sullivan Mellor (2) Fell	**York City**..............................**2** Hinch Pollard	*Division Three*
	Stoke City..........................**2** Tudor (2)	**Ipswich Town** ....**1** Whymark	*Division One*
25/9/76	**Manchester City**...................**1** Tueart	**Manchester United** ....**3** Coppell Daly McCreery	*Division One*
	West Ham United ....**1** Jennings	**Sunderland** ....**1** Bolton	*Division One*
2/10/76	**Norwich City**.......................**3** Peters (2) (1 pen.) Busby	**Newcastle United** ....**2** T. Craig (pen.) Gowling	*Division One*
	Chelsea ....**2** Swain Lewington	**Cardiff City**..........................**1** Charles (pen.)	*Division Two*

9/10/76	**Blackpool** 0	**Plymouth Argyle** ....2 Collins Horswill	*Division Two*
	Swindon Town ....1 Prophett	**Shrewsbury Town** 0	*Division Three*
16/10/76	**West Bromwich Albion** ....4 Giles A. Brown Cantello Treacy	**Manchester United** 0	*Division One*
	Hull City ....2 Hawley (2)	**Wolverhampton Wanderers** 0	*Division Two*
23/10/76	**Ipswich Town** ....1 Whymark	**Manchester City**...................0	*Division One*
	Crystal Palace ....2 Swindlehurst Evans	**Rotherham United** ....1 Gwyther	*Division Three*
30/10/76	**Liverpool** ....3 Callaghan Keegan McDermott	**Aston Villa** 0	*Division One*
	Birmingham City ....2 Burns Francis	**Queens Park Rangers** ....1 Eastoe	*Division One*
6/11/76	**Aston Villa** ....3 Mortimer Gray (2)	**Manchester United** ....2 Pearson Hill	*Division One*
	Everton 0	**Leeds United** ....2 Jordan McQueen	*Division One*
13/11/76	**Oldham Athletic** ....4 Halom (3) Shaw	**Carlisle United** ....1 Hoolickin	*Division Two*
	Tottenham Hotspur...............0	**Bristol City** ....1 Fear	*Division One*
20/11/76	**Nottingham Forest**................1 O'Neill	**Chelsea** ....1 Britton	*Division Two*
	Arsenal ....1 Armstrong	**Liverpool** ....1 Kennedy	*Division One*
27/11/76	**Blackpool** ....3 Hart Hatton Walsh	**Fulham** ....2 Mitchell (2)	*Division Two*
	Middlesbrough 0	**Ipswich Town** ....2 Mariner Talbot	*Division One*

4/12/76	**Arsenal** ....5 Ross Macdonald (3) Stapleton	**Newcastle United** ....3 Burns (2) Gowling	*Division One*

	Leicester City ....2 Kember Worthington (pen.)	**Birmingham City** ....6 Emmanuel Francis Burns (3) Rofe (o.g.)	*Division One*

11/12/76	**Coventry City** ....4 Beck Coop (pen.) Wallace Murphy	**Everton** ....2 King Kenyon	*Division One*

	Tottenham Hotspur..............2 Taylor (2)	**Manchester City**...................2 Kidd Power	*Division One*

18/12/76	**Bristol City** ....1 Merrick	**Middlesbrough** ....2 Armstrong (pen.) Brine	*Division One*

	Ipswich Town 0	**Derby County**.......................0	*Division One*

1/1/77	**Manchester United** ....2 Pearson (2)	**Aston Villa** 0	*Division One*

	Chelsea ....5 Swain Stanley R. Wilkins Finnieston Galley (o.g.)	**Hereford United** ....1 Paine	*Division Two*

8/1/77	**Southampton** ....1 Channon	**Chelsea** ....1 Locke	*FA Cup 3rd round*

	Cardiff City..........................1 Sayer	**Tottenham Hotspur**..............0	*FA Cup 3rd round*

	Blackpool 0	**Derby County**.......................0	*FA Cup 3rd round*

15/1/77	**Liverpool** ....1 Fairclough	**West Bromwich Albion** ....1 Cross	*Division One*

	Arsenal ....1 Rice	**Norwich City**........................0	*Division One*

22/1/77	**Manchester City**...................5 Kidd (4) Doyle	**Leicester City** 0	*Division One*

	Sheffield United 0	**Luton Town** ....3 R. Futcher Husband (2)	*Division Two*

29/1/77	**Colchester United**............1 Garwood	**Derby County**........................1 Hales	*FA Cup 4th round*
	Cardiff City.........................3 Giles Sayer Buchanan	**Wrexham**............................2 Whittle Ashcroft	*FA Cup 4th round*
	Manchester United..............1 Macari	**Queens Park Rangers** 0	*FA Cup 4th round*
5/2/77	**Leeds United**......................1 Jordan	**Coventry City** ....2 Green Murphy	*Division One*
	Arsenal 0	**Sunderland** 0	*Division One*
12/2/77	**Rotherham United** 0	**Brighton & Hove Albion**..........0	*Division Three*
	Manchester City..................1 Royle	**Arsenal** 0	*Division One*
19/2/77	**Liverpool** ....3 Toshack Jones Keegan	**Derby County**......................1 Hector	*Division One*
	Bristol City ....1 Garland	**Manchester City**..................0	*Division One*
26/2/77	**Leeds United** ....1 Cherry	**Manchester City**..................0	*FA Cup 5th round*
5/3/77	**Arsenal** ....1 Macdonald (pen.)	**Ipswich Town** ....4 Talbot Bertschin Wark (pen.) Mariner	*Division One*
	Liverpool ....1 Heighway	**Newcastle United** 0	*Division One*
12/3/77	**West Ham United** ....1 B. Robson	**Manchester City**..................0	*Division One*
	Manchester United..............1 Cherry (o.g.)	**Leeds United** 0	*Division One*
19/3/77	**Manchester United**..............2 Houston Macari	**Aston Villa** ....1 Little	*FA Cup 6th round*
	Everton ....2 Latchford Pearson	**Derby County**......................0	*FA Cup 6th round*
26/3/77	**Wolverhampton Wanderers** ....2 Richards Hibbitt	**Hull City** ....1 Hemmerman	*Division Two*
	Leicester City 0	**Bristol City** 0	*Division One*

2/4/77	**Chelsea** ....3 Wicks Finnieston (2)	**Blackburn Rovers** ....1 Waddington	*Division Two*
	Liverpool ....3 Neal (pen.) Fairclough Heighway	**Leeds United** ....1 McQueen	*Division One*
9/4/77	**Norwich City** 0	**Ipswich Town** ....1 Whymark	*Division One*
	Newcastle United 0	**Leicester City** 0	*Division One*
16/4/77	**Chelsea** ....2 Britton Finnieston	**Nottingham Forest** ....1 O'Neill	*Division Two*
	Liverpool ....2 Neal Keegan	**Arsenal** 0	*Division One*
23/4/77	**Everton** ....2 McKenzie Rioch	**Liverpool** ....2 McDermott Case	*FA Cup semi-final*
30/4/77	**Derby County** ....4 Gemmill Daniel Hector Daly (pen.)	**Manchester City** 0	*Division One*
	Tottenham Hotspur ....3 Hoddle Jones Taylor	**Aston Villa** ....1 Deehan	*Division One*
7/5/77	**Queens Park Rangers** ....1 Givens	**Liverpool** ....1 Case	*Division One*
	Luton Town ....1 Geddis	**Bolton Wanderers** ....1 Reid	*Division Two*
14/5/77	**Liverpool** 0	**West Ham United** 0	*Division One*
	Norwich City ....2 Reeves Busby	**Sunderland** ....2 Rowell Kerr	*Division One*
21/5/77	**Liverpool** ....1 Case	**Manchester United** ....2 Pearson J. Greenhoff	*FA Cup final*
28/5/77	**Northern Ireland** ....1 McGrath	**England** ....2 Channon Tueart	*Home International Championship*
	Wales 0	**Scotland** 0	*Home International Championship*
3/6/77	**Northern Ireland** ....1 Nelson	**Wales** ....1 Deacy	*Home International Championship*
4/6/77	**England** ....1 Channon (pen.)	**Scotland** ....2 McQueen Dalglish	*Home International Championship*

MATCH OF THE SEASON

Arsenal 5
Newcastle United 3
at Highbury,
Saturday 4 December 1976

Malcolm Macdonald was standing in the Highbury foyer when his old pals from Newcastle arrived. Goalkeeper Mike Mahoney stopped for a handshake, although 90 minutes later he must have wondered why.

The £333,333 transfer of 'Supermac' from the north-east back to his native London had caused a lot of unrest. Newcastle manager Gordon Lee, suspicious of the star syndrome, had shed no tears at Macdonald's departure and

without him had taken the Tynesiders to third place in the First Division.

They might have gone top had they won at Highbury that December afternoon. But Macdonald, the nearest thing to 'Roy of the Rovers', had other ideas. He scored a hat-trick, with Arsenal's other goals coming from a young Frank Stapleton and from Trevor Ross.

Mickey Burns scored twice for Newcastle who led 1–0, trailed 4–1, but in the end ran Arsenal close.

On the same day, the other *Match of the Day* feature was Leicester City's match against Birmingham at a frozen Filbert Street. Birmingham won 6–2,

giving the BBC a Saturday night spectacular with 16 goals.

Arsenal: Rimmer, Rice (sub. Matthews), Nelson, Ross, O'Leary, Howard, Ball, Brady, Macdonald, Stapleton, Armstrong.
Scorers: Macdonald (3), Ross, Stapleton.

Newcastle United: Mahoney, Nattrass, Kennedy, Cassidy, McCaffery, Nulty, Barrowclough, Cannell, Burns, Gowling, T. Craig.
Scorers: Gowling, Burns(2).

Roy of the Rovers. Macdonald turns away after completing a hat-trick in his first match against his old club

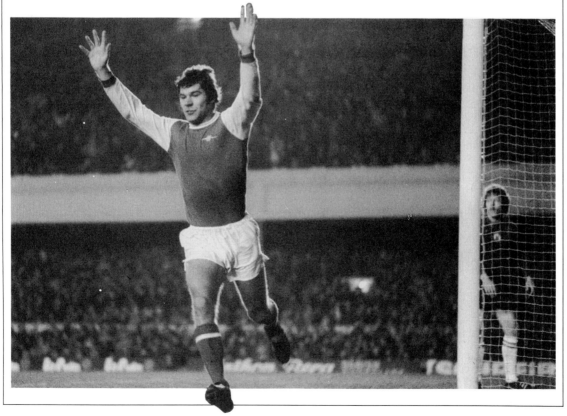

PLAYER OF THE SEASON
Kevin Keegan (Liverpool)

Nobody did more to earn Liverpool their second European trophy in consecutive seasons – and their first Champions Cup – than a self-made superstar who came out of the Doncaster Sunday League to elevate himself into the game's European parliament.

Everybody remembers how Kevin Keegan outwitted the prodigous German defender, Bertie Vogts, to help Liverpool win the 1977 European Cup final against Borussia Mönchengladbach. A year earlier, he had played a leading role in their UEFA Cup triumph against Bruges. But Keegan became more than a mere match winner.

Since the demise of George Best, the English game had looked for a suitable replacement around whom it could wrap its dreams. Keegan never pretended to be in Best's class as a footballer, but his capacity for getting the best out of what he had enabled him to win more medals, and to achieve lasting fame in more places.

These included Hamburg, where he was twice voted European Footballer of the Year; Southampton, where he was top scorer in the first division; and Newcastle, where he led the Geordies back to the first division in 1984 and eight years later returned as manager.

But it was Liverpool who developed Keegan, signed for £35,000 from Scunthorpe by Bill Shankly. And to an extent it was Keegan who made the modern Liverpool, helping them retain their Championship in 1977 and setting them on course for the richest harvest of trophies ever gathered so quickly by one club.

The 1976–77 season was the climax to his six-year stint at Anfield, where his partnership with John Toshack holds a special place in the memory bank.

The Hamilton Heartache

It was traditional in this period for the BBC to cover one of the FA Cup semi-finals and ITV the other. Recorded highlights were shown first on Saturday night, then on Sunday afternoon. The BBC's choice this season was the Merseyside derby between Liverpool and Everton, played at Maine Road, Manchester.

Paisley's team were going for the 'treble' of League, Cup and European Cup, while Gordon Lee had arrived as manager to take Everton to the last stages of two Cup competitions.

Liverpool had won their two previous semi-finals against Everton in 1950 and 1971, and Terry McDermott's opening goal, brilliantly chipped over goalkeeper David Lawson and voted the BBC's 'Goal of the Season', set them on their way on this occasion.

But Everton levelled through Duncan McKenzie and when Jimmy Case restored Liverpool's lead, Bruce Rioch pulled the Blues back to 2–2.

That was how things stood with three minutes to go. Then Everton's Ronnie Goodlass crossed from the left. McKenzie helped it on, and

substitute Bryan Hamilton nudged the ball past Ray Clemence from the 6-yard line.

Liverpool's faces fell as Everton celebrated what everybody in the ground believed was the winning goal. Everybody, that is, apart from referee Clive Thomas of Wales.

To the consternation of Everton, the relief of Liverpool, and the amazement of the crowd, he stood steadfast in the Liverpool penalty area and awarded a free-kick against Hamilton.

Even Jimmy Hill's analysis was inconclusive. Most people felt that Thomas had disallowed the effort for handball, although the pictures clearly showed the ball going in off Hamilton's hip. There was the faintest suspicion of offside, although when McKenzie played the ball on, Hamilton was fractionally behind Joey Jones, the last defender.

Thomas would only say that there had been 'an infringement'. But Everton's chance had gone. They lost the replay 3–0.

Two years earlier, playing in a semi-final replay for Ipswich against West Ham at Stamford Bridge, Hamilton had had *two* goals disallowed. Again the doors of Wembley were slammed in his face.

Again the referee was Clive Thomas.

No goal. Bryan Hamilton is incredulous as referee Clive Thomas refuses to stamp Everton's passport to Wembley. The disallowed goal remains one of the biggest mysteries in *Match of the Day*'s history

SEEN IN HINDSIGHT, this was the year democracy made its last stand in the English game – the last season when the three major domestic trophies were all won by clubs outside what became known as the élitist 'big five'.

It was Nottingham Forest, under Brian Clough now rejoined by Peter Taylor, and Ipswich Town, smoothly managed on a tight budget by Bobby Robson, who delayed a little longer the growing power base of Liverpool, Manchester United, Arsenal, Everton and Tottenham.

Forest, fresh out of the Second Division, were the surprise package. They won the League Championship by seven points from Liverpool, losing just three matches and remaining unbeaten from mid November until the end of the season.

Clough's team, who also beat Liverpool in a replayed League Cup final, carried that unbeaten sequence through a further 16 matches at the start of the following season, setting a fabulous record of 42 First Division matches without defeat over a calendar year.

Match of the Day cameras caught up with them early in their First Division renaissance. They won 3–2 at Wolverhampton, but Clough clearly wasn't satisfied and quickly signed Peter Shilton and Archie Gemmill. By the time the cameras picked up their 4–0 win at Old Trafford in December, followed by a January victory over Arsenal, Forest were unstoppable.

The only exception was in the FA Cup, where they lost at West Bromwich in the sixth round on the day the *Match of the Day* programme first had to deal with a frightening outbreak of crowd misbehaviour. The football hooligan had arrived, and the referee had to take the Millwall and Ipswich teams off the field while order was restored at The Den. Ipswich went on to win 6–1 and delighted the whole of Suffolk, and much of the nation, by beating Arsenal at Wembley.

BBC Viewers will also remember the part played by Northern League Blyth Spartans, who took Wrexham to a fifth round replay. It was a thoroughly good year for the underdog.

Match of the Day also picked up Liverpool's first home defeat for 20 months – inflicted by Andy Gray and Aston Villa – and some of Bob Latchford's goals, as the Everton striker earned a £10,000 prize from a national newspaper for scoring 30 times in League matches.

Firepower from the Forest. Tony Woodcock scores against Arsenal – part of an unbeaten sequence of 42 First Division games, and the platform for two European Cup achievements

13/8/77	**Liverpool** 0	**Manchester United** 0	*FA Charity Shield*
20/8/77	**Ipswich Town** ....1 Geddis	**Arsenal** 0	*Division One*
	Manchester City 0	**Leicester City** 0	*Division One*
27/8/77	**West Ham United** 0	**Manchester City** ....1 Royle	*Division One*
	Leeds United ....1 Hankin	**Birmingham City** 0	*Division One*
3/9/77	**Queens Park Rangers** ....3 Givens Francis Needham	**Leicester City** 0	*Division One*
	Derby County 0	**Manchester United** ....1 Macari	*Division One*
10/9/77	**Wolverhampton Wanderers** ....2 Bell Daley (pen.)	**Nottingham Forest**...............3 Withe Bowyer Woodcock	*Division One*
	Crystal Palace ....2 Bourne Swindlehurst	**Sunderland** ....2 Rowell Rostron	*Division Two*
17/9/77	**Blackpool** 0	**Tottenham Hotspur**...............2 Duncan Hoddle	*Division Two*
	Ipswich Town ....1 Whymark	**Liverpool** ....1 Dalglish	*Division One*
24/9/77	**West Bromwich Albion** ....3 Regis T. Brown (2) (1 pen.)	**Birmingham City** ....1 Connolly	*Division One*
	Brighton & Hove Albion........2 Ward (2)	**Sheffield United** ....1 Cattlin (o.g.)	*Division Two*
1/10/77	**Arsenal** ....3 Stapleton Rice Brady (pen.)	**West Ham United** 0	*Division One*
	Manchester United ....2 Macari McIlroy	**Liverpool** 0	*Division One*
8/10/77	**Southampton** ....4 Nicholl Boyer Williams Holmes	**Sunderland** ....2 Rowell Lee	*Division Two*
	Newcastle United ....1 Burns	**Derby County**.......................2 Hughes McFarland	*Division One*

15/10/77	**Nottingham Forest**...............2	**Manchester City**..................1	*Division One*
	Woodcock	Kidd	
	Withe		
	Chelsea 0	**Middlesbrough** 0	*Division One*
22/10/77	**Tottenham Hotspur**...............9	**Bristol Rovers**......................0	*Division Two*
	Lee (4)		
	Moores (3)		
	Hoddle		
	Taylor		
	Liverpool 0	**Everton** 0	*Division One*
29/10/77	**Derby County**......................2	**Norwich City**.....................2	*Division One*
	Daly	Reeves (2)	
	Hughes		
	Bolton Wanderers 2	**Luton Town** 1	*Division Two*
	Morgan	R. Futcher	
	Worthington		
5/11/77	**Liverpool** 1	**Aston Villa** 2	*Division One*
	Carrodus (o.g.)	Gray (2)	
	Coventry City......................1	**West Ham United** 0	*Division One*
	Wallace		
12/11/77	**Everton** 2	**Birmingham City** 1	*Division One*
	Latchford (2)	Bertschin	
	Southampton 2	**Blackpool** 0	*Division Two*
	Baker		
	Peach (pen.)		
19/11/77	**Wrexham**...........................2	**Colchester United**................1	*Division Three*
	Shinton	Wignall	
	Cook (o.g.)		
26/11/77	**Bolton Wanderers** 1	**Tottenham Hotspur**..............0	*Division Two*
	Greaves		
	Leicester City 0	**Liverpool** 4	*Division One*
		Fairclough	
		Heighway	
		Dalglish	
		McDermott	
3/12/77	**Leeds United** 3	**Queens Park Rangers** 0	*Division One*
	Needham (o.g.)		
	Flynn		
	Currie		
	Oxford United 1	**Shrewsbury Town** 1	*Division Three*
	Foley	Bates	

10/12/77	**Sunderland** ....1 Rowell (pen.)	**Tottenham Hotspur** ....2 Duncan (2)	*Division Two*
	Aston Villa ....3 Gray Gidman Cowans	**West Bromwich Albion** 0	*Division One*
17/12/77	**Manchester United** 0	**Nottingham Forest** ....4 Woodcock (2) Robertson B. Greenhoff (o.g.)	*Division One*
	Birmingham City 0	**Everton** 0	*Division One*
31/12/77	**Manchester City**...................2 Barnes Kidd	**Aston Villa** 0	*Division One*
	Luton Town ....1 Boersma	**Brighton & Hove Albion**..........0	*Division Two*
7/1/78	**Carlisle United** ....1 MacDonald	**Manchester United** ....1 Macari	*FA Cup 3rd round*
14/1/78	**Everton** ....1 King	**Aston Villa** 0	*Division One*
	Bristol City 0	**Leicester City** 0	*Division One*
21/1/78	**Nottingham Forest**...............2 Needham Gemmill	**Arsenal** 0	*Division One*
	Norwich City.......................1 Gibbins	**Manchester City**...................3 Kidd (2) Owen	*Division One*
28/1/78	**Manchester United** ....1 Coppell	**West Bromwich Albion** ....1 Johnston	*FA Cup 4th round*
	Newcastle United ....2 Bird Blackhall	**Wrexham**...........................2 McNeil (2)	*FA Cup 4th round*
	Arsenal ....2 Sunderland Macdonald	**Wolverhampton Wanderers** ....1 Hibbitt	*FA Cup 4th round*
4/2/78	**Burnley** ....3 Kindon (2) Cochrane	**Southampton** ....3 MacDougall Boyer Peach	*Division Two*
	Coventry City ....1 Ferguson	**Liverpool** 0	*Division One*

RESULTS
1977-8

11/2/78	**Leicester City** ....1 Williams	**Arsenal** ....1 Brady (pen.)	*Division One*
	Blackburn Rovers ....2 Round Brotherston	**Luton Town** 0	*Division Two*
18/2/78	**Wrexham** ....1 McNeil	**Blyth Spartans** ....1 Johnson	*FA Cup 5th round*
	Queens Park Rangers ....1 Busby	**Nottingham Forest**...............1 O'Neill	*FA Cup 5th round*
	Arsenal ....4 Stapleton (2) Macdonald Sunderland	**Walsall** ....1 Buckley	*FA Cup 5th round*
25/2/78	**Liverpool** ....3 Souness Case Kennedy	**Manchester United** ....1 McIlroy	*Division One*
	Leeds United ....2 F. Gray Currie	**Chelsea** 0	*Division One*
4/3/78	**Arsenal** ....3 Sunderland Price Young	**Manchester City**...................0	*Division One*
	Bolton Wanderers ....1 Reid	**Brighton & Hove Albion**..........1 Horton (pen.)	*Division Two*
11/3/78	**West Bromwich Albion** ....2 Martin Regis	**Nottingham Forest**...............0	*FA Cup 6th round*
	Millwall...............................1 Mehmet	**Ipswich Town** ....6 Burley Mariner (3) Wark Talbot	*FA Cup 6th round*
18/3/78	**Bristol Rovers**......................2 Randall Daines (o.g.)	**Tottenham Hotspur**...............3 Jones McNab Pratt	*Division Two*
	Derby County......................1 Curran	**Birmingham City** ....3 Connolly Francis Bertschin	*Division One*

25/3/78	**West Ham United** ....3 Brooking Green Holland	**Chelsea** ....1 Garner	*Division One*
	Nottingham Forest................2 Robertson (pen.) Anderson	**Newcastle United** 0	*Division One*
1/4/78	**Preston North End** 0	**Peterborough United**..............1 Robson	*Division Three*
	Arsenal ....3 Brady Macdonald (2)	**Manchester United** ....1 Jordan	*Division One*
8/4/78	**Ipswich Town** ....3 Talbot Mills Wark	**West Bromwich Albion** ....1 T. Brown (pen.)	*FA Cup semi-final*
15/4/78	**Watford**..............................1 Jenkins	**Southend United** ....1 Moody (pen.)	*Division Four*
	Everton ....1 Latchford (pen.)	**Ipswich Town** 0	*Division One*
22/4/78	**Coventry City** 0	**Nottingham Forest**................0	*Division One*
	Middlesbrough 0	**Everton** 0	*Division One*
29/4/78	**Wolverhampton Wanderers** ....2 Patching Eves	**Manchester United** ....1 B. Greenhoff	*Division One*
	Southampton 0	**Tottenham Hotspur**...............0	*Division Two*
6/5/78	**Arsenal** 0	**Ipswich Town** ....1 Osborne	*FA Cup final*
13/5/78	**Scotland** ....1 Johnstone	**Northern Ireland**...................1 O'Neill	*Home International Championship*
	Wales...............................1 Dwyer	**England** ....3 Latchford Currie Barnes	*Home International Championship*
19/5/78	**Wales**...............................1 Deacy (pen.)	**Northern Ireland**...................0	*Home International Championship*
20/5/78	**Scotland** 0	**England** ....1 Coppell	*Home International Championship*

MATCH OF THE SEASON

Tottenham Hotspur 9
Bristol Rovers 0
at White Hart Lane, Saturday
22 October 1977

Colin Lee did not even know his way to the dressing room when he arrived in the Tottenham car park for his debut after his £60,000 transfer from Torquay United.

The man who signed him, Spurs manager Keith Burkinshaw, wasn't even there to welcome him. He was away on a scouting mission, and never witnessed what proved to be an historic occasion.

It was Spurs's record league victory, and the lanky Lee scored four times. His attacking partner Ian Moores weighed in with three, and a new record was set for *Match of the Day*.

Previously, Leeds United and Brighton & Hove Albion had recorded the highest score on the programme. Both had managed seven, but Spurs showed that their sojourn in the Second Division would be a brief one by overwhelming a Bristol Rovers side that included one Bobby Gould at centre-forward.

Gould could only admire the ice-cool finishing of the shy west country lad. Colin Lee wasn't even known to his team-mates until just before the game. By 11 o'clock that Saturday night he was known to millions.

Tottenham: Daines, Naylor, Holmes, Hoddle, McAllister, Perryman, Pratt, McNab, Moores, Lee, Taylor.
Scorers: Lee (4), Moores (3), Taylor, Hoddle.

Bristol Rovers: Jones, Bater, T. Taylor, Day, S. Taylor, Prince, Williams, Aitken, Gould, Staniforth, Evans.

Leaping Lee. The Spurs debutant gave the BBC cameras on the 'old' East Stand at White Hart Lane a day to remember. Tottenham's 9–0 victory remains a *Match of the Day* record.

PLAYER OF THE SEASON
Peter Shilton
(Nottingham Forest)

Brian Clough and Peter Taylor hankered after Peter Shilton throughout their highly successful partnership at Derby County. They never got him then. But when the pair were reunited in management at Nottingham Forest, he became a prime target.

So much so, that when Forest opened their First Division campaign with four wins in their first five games, Clough and Taylor were still not satisfied. Shilton was signed from Stoke for £250,000 to replace the England U21 goalkeeper John Middleton.

In the next 37 games, Shilton conceded just 18 goals, his massive presence enabling Forest to win the championship at their first attempt.

One save sums up his towering contribution. On the day Forest clinched the title in front of the *Match of the Day* cameras at Coventry, a tight 0–0 draw giving them the point they required, the best chance fell to Coventry forward Mick Ferguson. His point-blank header from inside the 6-yard box would probably only have been saved by one goalkeeper in the world. But Shilton happened to be between the posts that day – and saves like that explain why he was still playing at the top level in his 43rd year.

ALTHOUGH ENGLAND were not present, the World Cup in Argentina precipitated a revolution in the Football League. In a wave of ticker-tape, Ossie Ardiles and Ricky Villa arrived at Tottenham, Alberto Tarrantini joined Birmingham and Alex Sabella linked up with Sheffield United. Suddenly, overseas players were all the rage. Arnold Muhren brought his subtle skills from Holland to Ipswich, Ivan Golac became a popular full-back at Southampton and, within 18 months, nearly every First and Second Division club had at least flirted with imports.

Jimmy Hill, discussing the affair with Everton manager Gordon Lee in the first *Match of the Day* of the new season, thought that it was a positive step. 'We've always been too insular in our thinking,' was the verdict of the BBC's soccer pundit.

Come November, Hill's own island was invaded. ITV announced they had pulled off an exclusive deal with the Football League for future coverage of their matches. It was headlined: 'Snatch of the Day'. The referee from the Office of Fair Trading blew his whistle on the deal. But the BBC lost their inherent right to Saturday night football. For the next four seasons, the two channels would alternate, with *Match of the Day* switching to Sunday afternoons for seasons 1980/1 and 1982/3.

On the field, the First Division Championship was dominated by Liverpool. They regained their title with a record 68 points, scoring 85 goals and conceding just 16 – only 4 of them at Anfield. And it was all achieved by just 15 players. On the second Saturday of the season, Liverpool showed why they had been European Champions for the two previous seasons. They thrashed Manchester City 4–1 at Maine Road in front of the *Match of the Day* cameras. In December, they inflicted on Nottingham Forest their first league defeat for over 12 months, and New Year victories at Anfield over West Brom, Arsenal and Manchester United were all covered by the BBC cameras.

It takes two to tango, Argentina style.
Ricky Villa (left) watches admiringly
as his compatriot Ossie Ardiles turns
away from the Nottingham Forest
defence in the South American pair's
debut match for Spurs

When *Match of the Day* dipped into the Third Division,* it was to spotlight two aspiring managers who guided their clubs, ultimately, from the Fourth to the First. Graham Taylor was busy building up Watford for Elton John, and John Toshack – groomed by Liverpool – was still scoring goals as player-manager of Swansea.

---

* During the 70s and early 80s the BBC's contract with the Football League stipulated that the programme would show 14 matches from the Second Division every season, and 4 from the Third and Fourth. Of these, half had to be screened as the main match. The BBC also undertook to visit every First Division ground at least once a season.

| 19/8/78 | **Bolton Wanderers** 1
Gowling | **Bristol City** 2
Mann
Ritchie | *Division One* |

| | **Chelsea** ....0 | **Everton** 1
King | *Division One* |

| 26/8/78 | **Manchester City**...................1
Kidd | **Liverpool** 4
Souness (2)
R. Kennedy
Dalglish | *Division One* |

| | **Brighton** 2
Ward (2) | **Sunderland** ....0 | *Division Two* |

| 2/9/78 | **Gillingham**..........................2
Overton
Westwood | **Watford**..............................3
Joslyn (2)
Blissett | *Division Three* |

| | **Manchester United** 1
Buchan | **Everton** 1
King | *Division One* |

| 9/9/78 | **Burnley** 3
Brennan
Fletcher
Thomson | **West Ham United** 2
Cross (2) | *Division Two* |

| | **Tottenham Hotspur**...............1
Rodgers (o.g.) | **Bristol City** ....0 | *Division One* |

| 16/9/78 | **Arsenal** 1
Stapleton | **Bolton Wanderers** ....0 | *Division One* |

| | **Middlesbrough** ....0 | **Queens Park Rangers** 2
Eastoe
Harkouk | *Division One* |

| 23/9/78 | **Crystal Palace** 1
Swindlehurst | **Oldham Athletic** ....0 | *Division Two* |

| | **Coventry City** ....0 | **Leeds United** ....0 | *Division One* |

| 30/9/78 | **Norwich City**.........................3
Ryan
Reeves
Robb | **Derby County**.........................0 | *Division One* |

| | **Wrexham**............................1
Lyons | **Cardiff City**...........................2
Buchanan (2) (1 pen.) | *Division Two* |

| 7/10/78 | **Sheffield United** 3
Anderson (2)
Finnieston | **Sunderland** 2
Rowell
Lee | *Division Two* |

| | **West Bromwich Albion** ....0 | **Tottenham Hotspur**...............1
Taylor | *Division One* |

14/10/78	**Aston Villa** ....2 Gregory (2)	**Manchester United** ....2 Macari McIlroy	*Division One*
	Southampton ....1 MacDougall	**Queens Park Rangers** ....1 Goddard	*Division One*
21/10/78	**West Ham United** ....1 Brooking	**Stoke City** ....1 Richardson	*Division Two*
	Nottingham Forest...............1 O'Neill	**Ipswich Town** 0	*Division One*
28/10/78	**Everton** ....1 King	**Liverpool** 0	*Division One*
	Wolverhampton Wanderers ....2 Hibbitt Daley	**Manchester United** ....4 J. Greenhoff (2) B. Greenhoff Jordan	*Division One*
4/11/78	**Arsenal** ....4 Stapleton (3) Nelson	**Ipswich Town** ....1 Mariner	*Division One*
	West Bromwich Albion ....1 Trewick	**Birmingham City** 0	*Division One*
11/11/78	**Queens Park Rangers** ....1 Eastoe	**Liverpool** ....3 Heighway R. Kennedy Johnson	*Division One*
	Bristol City ....4 Ritchie Royle (2) Rodgers	**Bolton Wanderers** ....1 Walsh	*Division One*
18/11/78	**West Ham United** ....1 Bonds	**Crystal Palace** ....1 Elwiss	*Division Two*
	Wolverhampton Wanderers ....1 Daniel	**Leeds United** ....1 Currie	*Division One*
25/11/78	**Manchester City**...................1 Hartford	**Ipswich Town** ....2 Gates Talbot	*Division One*
	Chelsea 0	**Manchester United** ....1 J. Greenhoff	*Division One*
2/12/78	**Stoke City**............................0	**Leicester City** 0	*Division Two*
9/12/78	**Liverpool** ....2 McDermott (2) (1 pen.)	**Nottingham Forest**...............0	*Division One*
	Coventry City ....1 Thompson	**Queens Park Rangers** 0	*Division One*

16/12/78	**Manchester United** **2**	**Tottenham Hotspur**...............**0**	*Division One*
	Ritchie		
	McIlroy		
	Fulham **1**	**Newcastle United** **3**	*Division Two*
	Guthrie	Shoulder	
		Connolly	
		Withe	
23/12/78	**Tottenham Hotspur**.............**0**	**Arsenal** **5**	*Division One*
		Sunderland (3)	
		Brady	
		Stapleton	
	Manchester City...................**0**	**Nottingham Forest**...............**0**	*Division One*
30/12/78	**Ipswich Town** **5**	**Chelsea** **1**	*Division One*
	Osman	Langley	
	Muhren (2)		
	Mariner		
	Wark		
	Bristol City **1**	**Manchester City**...................**1**	*Division One*
	Ritchie	R. Futcher	
6/1/79	**Leicester City** **3**	**Norwich City**.........................**0**	*FA Cup 3rd round*
	May		
	Weller		
	Henderson		
	Shrewsbury Town **3**	**Cambridge United** **1**	*FA Cup 3rd round*
	Maguire	Biley	
	Turner		
	Chapman		
13/1/79	**Norwich City**......................**1**	**West Bromwich Albion** **1**	*Division One*
	Peters	Regis	
	Bristol City **0**	**Tottenham Hotspur**...............**0**	*Division One*
20/1/79	**Brighton & Hove Albion**..........**1**	**Stoke City**...........................**1**	*Division Two*
	Jones (o.g.)	O'Callaghan	
	Tottenham Hotspur.............**1**	**Leeds United** **2**	*Division One*
	Hoddle	Hankin	
		Hart	
27/1/79	**Shrewsbury Town** **2**	**Manchester City**...................**0**	*FA Cup 4th round*
	Maguire		
	Chapman		
	Arsenal **2**	**Notts County** **0**	*FA Cup 4th round*
	Talbot		
	Young		
3/2/79	**Liverpool** **2**	**West Bromwich Albion** **1**	*Division One*
	Dalglish	A. Brown	
	Fairclough		
	Watford.............................**2**	**Rotherham United** **2**	*Division Three*
	Jenkins (2)	Phillips	
		Gwyther	

10/2/79	**Manchester City**...................0	**Manchester United**...............3 Coppell (2) Ritchie	*Division One*
	Arsenal 0	**Middlesbrough** 0	*Division One*
17/2/79	**Southampton** ....3 Peach (pen.) Baker Boyer	**Everton** 0	*Division One*
	Brighton & Hove Albion..........0	**Crystal Palace** 0	*Division Two*
24/2/79	**Derby County**......................0	**Liverpool** ....2 Dalglish R. Kennedy	*Division One*
	Portsmouth........................1 Hemmerman	**Grimsby Town**......................3 Ford (2) Brolly	*Division Four*
3/3/79	**Stoke City**...........................2 Doyle Randall	**West Ham United** 0	*Division Two*
	Ipswich Town ....1 Brazil	**Nottingham Forest**................1 Birtles	*Division One*
10/3/79	**No programme due to industrial action**		
17/3/79	**Chelsea** ....1 Shanks (o.g.)	**Queens Park Rangers** ....3 Goddard Roeder Busby	*Division One*
	Bristol City.........................1 Gow	**Middlesbrough** ....1 Armstrong	*Division One*
24/3/79	**Arsenal** ....1 Sunderland	**Manchester City**...................1 Channon	*Division One*
	Sunderland ....1 Rowell	**Leyton Orient**.......................0	*Division Two*
31/3/79	**Arsenal** ....2 Stapleton Sunderland	**Wolverhampton Wanderers** 0	*FA Cup semi-final*
7/4/79	**West Bromwich Albion** ....1 A. Brown	**Everton** 0	*Division One*
	Leeds United ....1 Cherry	**Ipswich Town** ....1 Gates	*Division One*
14/4/79	**Liverpool** ....2 Neal Dalglish	**Manchester United** 0	*Division One*
	Birmingham City ....1 Ainscow	**Wolverhampton Wanderers** ....1 Richards	*Division One*

Date	Home		Away		Competition
21/4/79	**Swindon Town** Jenkins (o.g.) Rowland	2	Watford	0	*Division Three*
	Derby County Daly Buckley	2	Arsenal	0	*Division One*
28/4/79	**Nottingham Forest**	0	Liverpool	0	*Division One*
	West Ham United Bonds	1	Wrexham Shinton	1	*Division Two*
5/5/79	**Liverpool** Neal (2)	2	Southampton	0	*Division One*
	Plymouth Argyle Binney Bason	2	Swansea City Curtis Toshack	2	*Division Three*
12/5/79	**Arsenal** Talbot Stapleton Sunderland	3	Manchester United McQueen McIlroy	2	*FA Cup final*
19/5/79	**Wales** Toshack (3)	3	Scotland	0	*Home International Championship*
	Northern Ireland	0	England Watson Coppell	2	*Home International Championship*
25/5/79	**Northern Ireland** Spence	1	Wales James	1	*Home International Championship*
26/5/79	**England** Barnes Coppell Keegan	3	Scotland Wark	1	*Home International Championship*

MATCH OF THE SEASON
Everton 1 Liverpool 0
at Goodison Park,
Saturday 28 October 1978

There were tears on the
Everton bench when the referee
blew the final whistle, but
unlike the semi-final the

You little beauty. Everton manager
Gordon Lee hugs goalscorer Andy
King as they celebrate the end of a
seven-year wait. Moments later, a
BBC interviewer was pushed off the
pitch by a police inspector as he tried
to interview King for *Grandstand*

previous year, this time they were tears of joy. Everton had beaten Liverpool for the first time in seven years.

Their victory brought to an end not only one of the most one-sided spells in nearly a century of local rivalry, but also spiked Liverpool's magnificent start to the season. They had won 10 and drawn 1 of their 11 opening games.

But Everton, with six wins and five draws, were themselves unbeaten and second to Liverpool in the table. The only ingredient missing from the occasion was captain, Mike Lyons, who was out injured.

He joined the 53,000 crowd to celebrate a moment Evertonians will always savour. Andy King's second-half volley, a sweetly-struck shot from 20 yards after a cross by Mike Pejic and a header down by Martin Dobson, has a permanent place in Goodison's hall of memories.

Even though Everton finished fourth as Liverpool romped away with the Championship, King's goal has a cherished place in the *Match of the Day* library, as has the moment when a policeman pushed him and an interviewer off the pitch after the game.

Everton: Wood, Todd, Pejic, Kenyon, Wright, Nulty, King, Dobson, Latchford, Walsh, Thomas   Scorer: King

Liverpool: Clemence, Neal, A. Kennedy, Thompson, R. Kennedy, Hansen, Dalglish, Case, Heighway, Johnson, Souness

PLAYER OF THE SEASON
Liam Brady (Arsenal)

If this was the season of the overseas import, then Dublin-born Liam Brady could trade intrinsic skill with any of them. And when the traffic started in the other direction, he was one of the first Football League exports to Italy.

Brady's slight frame belied his enormous influence on the game. His was the best left foot in the business, described by Arsenal coach Bobby Campbell as 'the claw', because of the sharpness it had in reaching parts of the field beyond the vision of others.

His unfailing courtesy made him part of an Irish connection which, along with Frank Stapleton and David O'Leary, did Arsenal's image proud.

Against Spurs at Christmas Brady scored with a stunning shot in Arsenal's 5–0 victory at White Hart Lane, besides abetting Alan Sunderland's hat-trick in front of the cameras. And come the FA Cup final, Brady was the ace in Arsenal's pack against Manchester United. He had a hand in all three goals and was voted 'Player of the Year' by his peers in the PFA.

ENGLISH FOOTBALL stumbled into a new decade down a stairway of financial chaos. This was the season when Manchester City paid Wolves £1.4 million for Steve Daley, only for Wolves to break the transfer record almost at once with the Daley money financing the signing of Andy Gray. It was Malcolm Allison, back at Maine Road, who believed Daley and another expensive acquisition, centre forward Michael Robinson for £750,000, would make his second coming a successful one.

The *Match of the Day* cameras followed Allison's progress closely. A goalless draw with promoted Crystal Palace on the opening day of the season was followed by 4–0 thrashings by West Bromwich Albion in September and Liverpool in October.

In November, the gloom was lifted by victory over United in the Manchester derby. Robinson scored, and did so again when City beat Derby in front of the cameras just before Christmas.

By now Liverpool were pulling clear of the rest with some vintage performances. They won 3–1 at Derby on a day when the two BBC matches produced *four* penalties – two in the game at Meadow Lane where Notts County and Newcastle drew 2–2.

It was another Second Division match which produced the season's biggest score on *Match of the Day*. Queens Park Rangers beat Burnley 7–0 at Loftus Road. There were goals to enjoy in the FA Cup too. Nottingham Forest, now European Champions, scored four at Leeds in the third round; Second Division Watford beat non-League Harlow Town 4–3 in the fourth round; and in the fifth, Everton put five past Wrexham.

Sunderland also scored five for the cameras, when they ensured promotion against Watford at Roker Park. And a week later, on the last League Saturday, Liverpool made up for their marathon FA Cup semi-final defeat by Arsenal, by beating Aston Villa 4–1 to retain the Championship. In 14 appearances on *Match of the Day*, Bob Paisley's team scored 38 times.

Lionhearted centre forwards didn't come cheap. Wolves paid a British record £1.5 million for Andy Gray, who led them to the Football League Cup final only six months later and scored the winning goal at Wembley

11/8/79	**Arsenal** 1	**Liverpool** 3	*FA Charity Shield*
	Sunderland	McDermott (2)	
		Dalglish	
18/8/79	**Southampton** 1	**Manchester United** 1	*Division One*
	Peach (pen.)	McQueen	
	Manchester City 0	**Crystal Palace** 0	*Division One*
25/8/79	**Sunderland** 2	**Fulham** 1	*Division Two*
	Arnott	Gale	
	Robson (pen.)		
	Derby County 0	**Everton** 1	*Division One*
		King	
1/9/79	**Leicester City** 1	**Luton Town** 3	*Division Two*
	May	Moss (2) (1 pen.)	
		Hill	
	Bristol City 2	**Wolverhampton Wanderers** 0	*Division One*
	Gow		
	Royle		
	Leeds United 1	**Arsenal** 1	*Division One*
	Hart	Nelson	
8/9/79	**Liverpool** 4	**Coventry City** 0	*Division One*
	Johnson (2)		
	Case		
	Dalglish		
	Aston Villa 0	**Manchester United** 3	*Division One*
		Coppell	
		Thomas (pen.)	
		Grimes	
15/9/79	**West Bromwich Albion** 4	**Manchester City** 0	*Division One*
	A. Brown		
	Owen		
	Robson (2)		
	West Ham United 2	**Sunderland** 0	*Division Two*
	Cross		
	Pearson		
22/9/79	**Stoke City** 1	**Crystal Palace** 2	*Division One*
	Smith	Hilaire	
		Cannon	
	Newcastle United 1	**Wrexham** 0	*Division Two*
	Shoulder (pen.)		
29/9/79	**Nottingham Forest** 1	**Liverpool** 0	*Division One*
	Birtles		
	Sheffield United 3	**Oxford United** 1	*Division Three*
	Bourne (pen.)	Graydon (pen.)	
	Briggs (o.g.)		
	Matthews		

(*Left*) Arguably the most memorable of the five thousand goals shown on *Match of the Day*. Ronnie Radford's 40-yard screamer for Southern League Hereford against First Division Newcastle in the FA Cup third round replay on 5 February 1972

(*Below*) Justin Fashanu might contest the description of Radford's goal. The shot he delivered for Norwich against Liverpool at Carrow Road in February 1980 was pure television theatre. In more recent years, his younger brother John Fashanu was a *Match of the Day* goalscorer with Wimbledon

George Graham (*above*) set out to become the most successful Arsenal manager since Herbert Chapman. He broke the Liverpool monopoly of the First Division scene by winning two championships in the space of three seasons

Double delight (*left*). Kenny Dalglish's son Paul helps him celebrate Liverpool's league and FA Cup success in 1986 — Dalglish senior's first year as player-manager

Leading by example (*right*). Nottingham Forest captain Stuart Pearce, England's left back, salutes his opening goal from a free kick in the 1991 FA Cup final. Nearly 15 million BBC viewers saw Spurs fight back to win 2-1

Stretching to make history (*left*), Wimbledon captain Dave Beasant became the first goalkeeper to save a penalty in the FA Cup final

It enabled him to collect the most famous trophy in football (*above*) only eleven years after Wimbledon had left the Southern League

Television faces of the nineties. Gary Lineker and Paul Gascoigne (*right*) presented widely differing images, but both were among the most instantly recognisable figures in the country. At the end of the 1991-92 season, Lineker retired from international football and announced that he was leaving Spurs to join the Japanese team Grampus Eight. As for Gascoigne, after a year out of the game with injury he passed a rigorous fitness test so that his £5.5 million transfer to Lazio could go ahead

The name's the same. The Robsons (*below*) spanned the *Match of the Day* period on and off the field. Bryan was Bobby's captain in two World Cups, but injuries meant he missed the quarter final in 1986 and the semi-final in 1990

Commentators conference. Kenneth
Wolstenholme, the BBC's voice of
football for over 20 years, with the
author. Wolstenholme covered 21 FA
Cup finals and when Motson
commentated on Liverpool v
Sunderland in 1992 it was his 15th

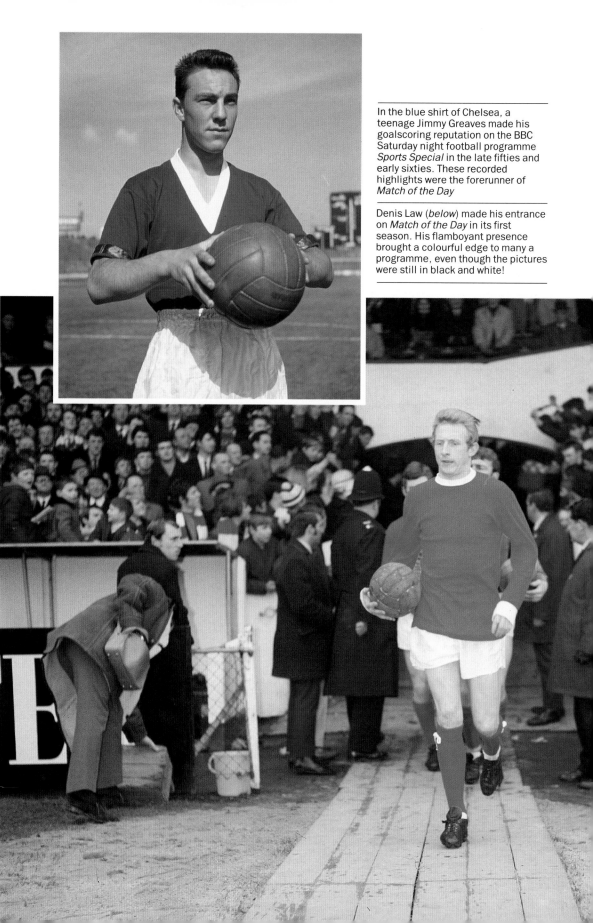

In the blue shirt of Chelsea, a teenage Jimmy Greaves made his goalscoring reputation on the BBC Saturday night football programme *Sports Special* in the late fifties and early sixties. These recorded highlights were the forerunner of *Match of the Day*

Denis Law (*below*) made his entrance on *Match of the Day* in its first season. His flamboyant presence brought a colourful edge to many a programme, even though the pictures were still in black and white!

Roger Hunt (*below*), Liverpool's record goalscorer, scored the first-ever goal on *Match of the Day* against Arsenal in August 1964. He figured with West Ham's Geoff Hurst (*right*) in England's World Cup winning team of 1966. Hurst, who scored a hat-trick in the final, became a household name when the BBC beamed the World Cup across the globe

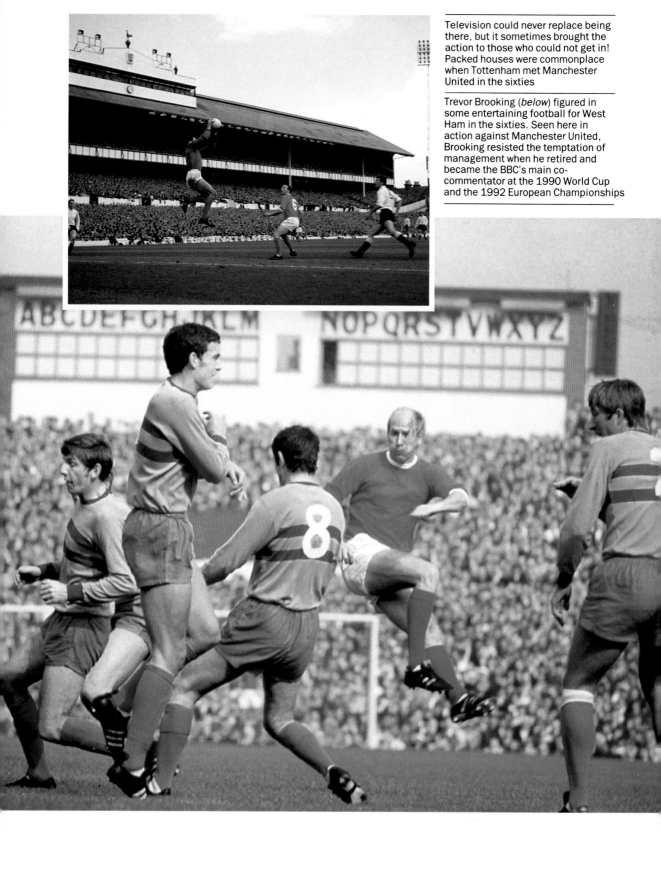

Television could never replace being there, but it sometimes brought the action to those who could not get in! Packed houses were commonplace when Tottenham met Manchester United in the sixties

Trevor Brooking (*below*) figured in some entertaining football for West Ham in the sixties. Seen here in action against Manchester United, Brooking resisted the temptation of management when he retired and became the BBC's main co-commentator at the 1990 World Cup and the 1992 European Championships

6/10/79	**Crystal Palace** ....**1** Walsh	**Tottenham Hotspur** ....**1** Villa	*Division One*

6/10/79	**Crystal Palace** **1**	**Tottenham Hotspur** **1**	*Division One*
	Walsh	Villa	
	Coventry City **2**	**Everton** **1**	*Division One*
	Wallace (2)	King	
	Leeds United **2**	**Ipswich Town** **1**	*Division One*
	Cherry Hird (pen.)	Mariner	
13/10/79	**Luton Town** **2**	**Sunderland** **0**	*Division Two*
	Moss (2)		
	Wolverhampton Wanderers **1**	**Norwich City** **0**	*Division One*
	Carr		
20/10/79	**Manchester United** **1**	**Ipswich Town** **0**	*Division One*
	Grimes		
	Arsenal **0**	**Stoke City** **0**	*Division One*
	West Bromwich Albion **4**	**Southampton** **0**	*Division One*
	Owen Robson Deehan A. Brown		
27/10/79	**Queens Park Rangers** **7**	**Burnley** **0**	*Division Two*
	Goddard (2) Shanks McCreery Roeder Allen (2) (1 pen.)		
	Southampton **1**	**Leeds United** **2**	*Division One*
	Boyer	Entwhistle Curtis	
	Manchester City **0**	**Liverpool** **4**	*Division One*
		Johnson R. Kennedy Dalglish (2)	
3/11/79	**Liverpool** **3**	**Wolverhampton Wanderers** **0**	*Division One*
	Dalglish (2) R. Kennedy		
	Middlesbrough **0**	**Tottenham Hotspur** **0**	*Division One*
10/11/79	**Manchester City** **2**	**Manchester United** **0**	*Division One*
	Henry Robinson		
	Birmingham City **1**	**Cambridge United** **0**	*Division Two*
	Lynex		
17/11/79	**Nottingham Forest** **0**	**Brighton & Hove Albion** **1**	*Division One*
		Ryan	
	Arsenal **2**	**Everton** **0**	*Division One*
	Stapleton (2)		

24/11/79	**Ipswich Town** ....3 Gates Wark Brazil	**Southampton** ....1 Williams	*Division One*
	Derby County......................4 Daly Duncan (2) Emery	**Nottingham Forest**...............1 Robertson (pen.)	*Division One*
1/12/79	**Nottingham Forest**...............1 Birtles	**Arsenal** ....1 Stapleton	*Division One*
	Liverpool ....4 McDermott Hansen Johnson R. Kennedy	**Middlesbrough** 0	*Division One*
8/12/79	**Manchester United** ....1 Thomas	**Leeds United** ....1 Connor	*Division One*
	Queens Park Rangers ....2 Goddard (2)	**Wrexham**...........................2 Edwards Vinter	*Division Two*
	Luton Town ....1 Moss	**Newcastle United** ....1 Rafferty	*Division Two*
15/12/79	**Tottenham Hotspur**...............1 Ardiles	**Aston Villa** ....2 Geddis Cowans (pen.)	*Division One*
	West Bromwich Albion ....2 Robson Trewick	**Arsenal** ....2 Nelson Stapleton	*Division One*
	Manchester City...................3 Robinson Henry Webb (o.g.)	**Derby County**......................0	*Division One*
22/12/79	**Notts County** ....2 O'Brien (2 pens)	**Newcastle United** ....2 Shoulder Connolly	*Division Two*
	Derby County......................1 Davies (pen.)	**Liverpool** ....3 Davies (o.g.) McDermott (pen.) Johnson	*Division One*
29/12/79	**Coventry City** 0	**Nottingham Forest**...............3 Robertson (2) (1 pen.) Bowles	*Division One*
	Wrexham...........................2 McNeil Vinter	**Chelsea** 0	*Division Two*

Date	Home		Away		Competition
5/1/80	**Leeds United**	1	**Nottingham Forest**	4	*FA Cup 3rd round*
	Lloyd (o.g.)		F. Gray		
			Birtles		
			Bowyer		
			Robertson		
	Cardiff City	0	**Arsenal**	0	*FA Cup 3rd round*
	Yeovil Town	0	**Norwich City**	3	*FA Cup 3rd round*
			Paddon		
			Robson		
			Fashanu		
12/1/80	**Chelsea**	4	**Newcastle United**	0	*Division Two*
	Fillery				
	Barton (o.g.)				
	Walker				
	Langley				
	Bolton Wanderers	0	**Brighton & Hove Albion**	2	*Division One*
			Ward (2)		
19/1/80	**Coventry City**	1	**Liverpool**	0	*Division One*
	Dyson				
	Southampton	4	**Manchester City**	1	*Division One*
	Channon		Power		
	Ball				
	Watson				
	Moran				
	West Ham United	2	**Preston North End**	0	*Division Two*
	Stewart (pen.)				
	Allen				
26/1/80	**Nottingham Forest**	0	**Liverpool**	2	*FA Cup 4th round*
			Dalglish		
			McDermott (pen.)		
	Wolverhampton Wanderers	1	**Norwich City**	1	*FA Cup 4th round*
	Gray		Bond		
	Watford	4	**Harlow Town**	3	*FA Cup 4th round*
	Poskett		Prosser		
	Bolton		McKenzie (2)		
	Patching (2)				
2/2/80	**Manchester City**	1	**West Bromwich Albion**	3	*Division One*
	Lee		Regis		
			Barnes (2)		
	Leicester City	1	**Newcastle United**	0	*Division Two*
	Smith (pen.)				
	Aston Villa	2	**Crystal Palace**	0	*Division One*
	Cowans				
	Mortimer				

9/2/80	**Norwich City** 3	**Liverpool** 5	*Division One*
	Peters	Fairclough (3)	
	Reeves	Dalglish	
	Fashanu	Case	
	Swindon Town 1	**Sheffield Wednesday** 2	*Division Three*
	McHale (pen.)	Johnson	
		Taylor	
	Arsenal 3	**Aston Villa** 1	*Division One*
	Sunderland (2)	Mortimer	
	Rix		
16/2/80	**Wolverhampton Wanderers** 0	**Watford**................................3	*FA Cup 5th round*
		Poskett (2)	
		Blissett	
	Blackburn Rovers 1	**Aston Villa** 1	*FA Cup 5th round*
	Evans (o.g.)	Geddis	
	Everton 5	**Wrexham** 2	*FA Cup 5th round*
	Megson	Vinter (2)	
	Eastoe (2)		
	Ross (pen.)		
	Latchford		
23/2/80	**Manchester United** 4	**Bristol City** 0	*Division One*
	Jordan (2)		
	McIlroy		
	Merrick (o.g.)		
	Sunderland 1	**Luton Town** 0	*Division Two*
	Cooke		
	West Bromwich Albion 1	**Aston Villa** 2	*Division One*
	Robson	Little	
		McNaught	
1/3/80	**Everton** 1	**Liverpool** 2	*Division One*
	Eastoe	Neal (pen.)	
		Johnson	
	Southampton 1	**West Bromwich Albion** 1	*Division One*
	Baker	Regis	
	Luton Town 1	**West Ham United** 1	*Division Two*
	Hill	Stewart	
8/3/80	**Tottenham Hotspur**................0	**Liverpool** 1	*FA Cup 6th round*
		McDermott	
	Watford..............................1	**Arsenal** 2	*FA Cup 6th round*
	Poskett	Stapleton (2)	
15/3/80	**Grimsby Town** 2	**Millwall**...............................0	*Division Three*
	Kilmore		
	Drinkell		
	Bristol City 1	**Liverpool** 3	*Division One*
	Mabbutt	R. Kennedy	
		Dalglish (2)	

22/3/80	**Queens Park Rangers** ....2 Goddard (2)	**Luton Town** ....2 Hill Stein		*Division Two*
	Manchester United ....1 Thomas	**Manchester City** 0		*Division One*
29/3/80	**Ipswich Town** ....1 Gates	**Derby County** ....1 Swindlehurst		*Division One*
	Brighton & Hove Albion ....1 Williams	**Nottingham Forest** 0		*Division One*
5/4/80	**Sheffield United** ....1 MacPhail	**Sheffield Wednesday** ....1 Curran		*Division Three*
	Wolverhampton Wanderers ....1 Richards	**Tottenham Hotspur** ....2 Jones Galvin		*Division One*
	Aston Villa ....3 Evans Bremner Lloyd (o.g.)	**Nottingham Forest** ....2 Birtles Bowyer		*Division One*
12/4/80	**West Ham United** ....1 Pearson	**Everton** ....1 Kidd (pen.)		*FA Cup semi-final*
	Manchester United ....4 Ritchie (3) Wilkins	**Tottenham Hotspur** ....1 Ardiles		*Division One*
19/4/80	**Birmingham City** ....1 Bertschin	**Luton Town** 0		*Division Two*
	Manchester City ....3 Robinson Deyna Tueart	**Bristol City** ....1 Rodgers		*Division One*
	Bristol Rovers ....2 Barrowclough Bates	**Sunderland** ....2 Robson Dunn		*Division Two*
26/4/80	**Sunderland** ....5 Robson (2) Buckley Elliott (2)	**Watford** 0		*Division Two*
	Derby County ....3 Swindlehurst Reid (o.g.) Biley (pen.)	**Manchester City** ....1 Tueart		*Division One*
3/5/80	**Liverpool** ....4 Johnson (2) Cohen Blake (o.g.)	**Aston Villa** ....1 Cohen (o.g.)		*Division One*
	Leeds United ....2 Parlane Hird (pen.)	**Manchester United** 0		*Division One*

10/5/80	**Arsenal** 0	**West Ham United** .... 1 Brooking	*FA Cup final*
17/5/80	**Wales** .... 4 Thomas Walsh James Thompson (o.g.)	**England** .... 1 Mariner	*Home International Championship*
23/5/80	**Wales** 0	**Northern Ireland** .... 1 Brotherston	*Home International Championship*
24/5/80	**Scotland** 0	**England** .... 2 Brooking Coppell	*Home International Championship*

MATCH OF THE SEASON

Norwich City 3 Liverpool 5
at Carrow Road,
Saturday 9 February 1980

This was the day when David Fairclough, the red-haired Liverpool forward, stuck with the label 'super-sub', could have reasonably expected to hog the headlines. In one of only 64 games he actually started in his seven seasons with the club, he scored a hat-trick at Carrow Road.

But even then, Fairclough was condemned to a secondary role. Not by Liverpool perhaps, because his splendidly-taken goals kept them top of the table, but by the *Match of the Day* viewers who remember the game more for a priceless piece of skill from Justin Fashanu.

Long after the rest of his chequered career is forgotten, or overtaken by that of his brother John, the elder Fashanu's goal will stay in the memory. A flick up with his right foot to take the ball away from Alan Kennedy, a thumping volley with his left from outside the penalty area which beat Ray Clemence's right hand and nestled in the top corner of the net.

It was voted the BBC's 'Goal of the Season'. But it couldn't save the game for Norwich. With two minutes to go and the score 3–3, Kenny Dalglish and Jimmy Case came up with two late goals for Liverpool.

Norwich City: Keelan, Bond, Downs, Ryan, Brown, Jones, Mendham (sub. McGuire), Reeves, Fashanu, Paddon, Peters.
Scorers: Peters, Reeves, Fashanu

Liverpool: Clemence, Neal, A. Kennedy, Thompson, R. Kennedy, Hansen, Dalglish, Case, Fairclough, Kennedy, Lee.
Scorers: Fairclough (3), Dalglish, Case

'Stop calling me super-sub'. David Fairclough (centre) arches a beautiful shot past Norwich goalkeeper Kevin Keelan. Despite his hat-trick, Fairclough still finished up in a supporting role at Liverpool

PLAYER OF THE SEASON
Kenny Dalglish (Liverpool)

As a young player with Celtic, Kenny Dalglish worshipped Denis Law, nursing one of Law's Scotland shirts as a treasured souvenir. Later, Dalglish would wear the national shirt himself over 100 times, dominating the second decade of *Match of the Day* very much the way Law had marched imperiously across the programme's first 10 years.

In the 1979/80 season, when Dalglish scored 16 goals to help Liverpool retain the Championship, he kindly arranged to score more than half of them in front of the BBC cameras. Coventry, Manchester City, Wolves, Nottingham Forest, Norwich and Bristol City all found themselves watching television

again in the evening to find out how they had been outfoxed by one of the most skilful and strategic players to grace the post-war era.

Later, at Ipswich in 1983, *Match of the Day* viewers would see Dalglish's 100th league goal in England, to match the century he scored for Celtic in Scotland.

AFTER 16 SEASONS in an unchallenged Saturday night slot, *Match of the Day* now moved to Sunday afternoon. Jimmy Hill and co-presenter Bob Wilson swapped suits and ties for shirtsleeves and pullovers, as the four-year plan to alternate with ITV entered its second year. And the first Sunday programme proved a prescient one. It showed Spurs beating Nottingham Forest with a new strike force of Archibald and Crooks, and Ipswich winning at Leicester with a goal by John Wark.

In the months that followed, Wark amassed 36 goals from midfield as Bobby Robson's home-bred side came within a whisker of a 'treble'. They won the UEFA Cup (in which Wark scored 14 goals alone), came second in the League, and were narrowly beaten in the FA Cup semi-final by Manchester City.

It was in the FA Cup that Spurs prospered. Their first trophy since the retirement of Bill Nicholson owed much to the Argentine connection of Ardiles and Villa, but Crooks and Archibald scored 47 goals between them.

The team that Spurs beat in the Cup final, Manchester City, were rescued in the autumn by John Bond, who arrived from Norwich to see them lose to Birmingham in front of the *Match of the Day* cameras, but then proceeded to haul them away from relegation and through to Wembley.

Talking of Wembley, the BBC were able to cover the Football League Cup final there for the first time since 1967. It produced one of the season's great controversies, when referee Clive Thomas allowed Alan Kennedy's shot to count even though Liverpool's Sammy Lee was lying on the ground in front of West Ham goalkeeper Phil Parkes.

Match of the Day was also present on the day the First Division Championship was decided. Although Aston Villa lost 2–0 at Highbury, their nearest challengers, Ipswich, were beaten at Middlesbrough on the same afternoon.

Manager Ron Saunders won the title with only 14 players, of which 7 were ever-present. The midfield thrust of Denis Mortimer was as potent a weapon as the wing play of Tony Morley, and the deadly duo of Peter Withe and Gary Shaw.

When the final whistle went at Arsenal, it signalled a jubilant invasion by Villa fans. Television still couldn't replace the transistor radio when it came to following two matches at once!

Never change a winning team. Aston Villa manager Ron Saunders was able to keep ten of the eleven positions virtually unchanged as Villa won their first League Championship since 1910

16/8/80	**Tottenham Hotspur**..............2 Hoddle (pen.) Crooks	**Nottingham Forest**...............0		Division One
	Leicester City....................0	**Ipswich Town**.....................1 Wark		Division One
	Sheffield Wednesday...........2 McCulloch Taylor	**Newcastle United**................0		Division Two
23/8/80	**Sunderland**........................1 Allardyce	**Southampton**.....................2 Nicholl George		Division One
	Birmingham City................0	**Manchester United**..............0		Division One
	Queens Park Rangers...........0	**Swansea City**.....................0		Division Two
30/8/80	**Liverpool**..........................4 Hansen McDermott A. Kennedy Johnson	**Norwich City**.......................1 Bennett		Division One
	Brighton & Hove Albion..........1 Robinson	**West Bromwich Albion**..........2 Regis Owen		Division One
	Arsenal..............................2 Price Stapleton	**Tottenham Hotspur**..............0		Division One
6/9/80	**Coventry City**.....................3 Daly (2) Blair	**Crystal Palace**.....................1 Allen		Division One
	Everton.............................2 Eastoe Wright	**Wolverhampton Wanderers**....0		Division One
	Sheffield United.................3 Kenworthy (pen.) Peters Trusson	**Swindon Town**.....................0		Division Three
13/9/80	**Nottingham Forest**...............3 Birtles Bowyer Wallace	**Manchester City**..................2 Bennett Henry		Division One
	Queens Park Rangers...........1 Hazell	**Newcastle United**.................2 Boam Hibbitt		Division Two
	Manchester United..............5 Coppell Grimes Macari Jovanovic (2)	**Leicester City**.....................0		Division One

Date	Home	Score	Away	Score	Division
20/9/80	**Southampton** Nicholl Boyer	2	**Liverpool** Souness Fairclough	2	*Division One*
	Bristol City	0	**Notts County** Masson	1	*Division Two*
	Derby County	0	**Wrexham** Edwards	1	*Division Two*
27/9/80	**Manchester United** Coppell Albiston	2	**Manchester City** Reeves Palmer	2	*Division One*
	Portsmouth Gregory	1	**Fulham**	0	*Division Three*
	Wolverhampton Wanderers	0	**Ipswich Town** Brazil Mariner	2	*Division One*
4/10/80	**Middlesbrough** McAndrew Jankovic (2) Woods (o.g.) Johnston Armstrong	6	**Norwich City** Fashanu	1	*Division One*
	AFC Bournemouth Massey Heffernan	2	**Scunthorpe United** Lambert O'Berg	2	*Division Four*
	Aston Villa Evans (2) Morley Shaw	4	**Sunderland**	0	*Division One*
11/10/80	**Liverpool** McDermott (pen.)	1	**Ipswich Town** Thijssen	1	*Division One*
	Leicester City Lineker	1	**Coventry City** Dyson Gooding English	3	*Division One*
	West Ham United Cross (2)	2	**Blackburn Rovers**	0	*Division Two*
18/10/80	**Nottingham Forest** Bowyer Mills	2	**West Bromwich Albion** Moses	1	*Division One*
	Manchester City	0	**Birmingham City** Gemmill (pen.)	1	*Division One*
	Crystal Palace Hilaire Allen (pen.)	2	**Leicester City** Young	1	*Division One*

25/10/80	**Chelsea** 6	**Newcastle United** 0	*Division Two*
	Lee (3)		
	Fillery		
	Walker		
	Chivers		
	Burnley 2	**Brentford** 0	*Division Three*
	Dobson (pen.)		
	Cavener		
	Leeds United 1	**Crystal Palace** 0	*Division One*
	Connor		
1/11/80	**Everton** 2	**Tottenham Hotspur** 2	*Division One*
	Eastoe	Archibald (2)	
	McMahon		
	Fulham 1	**Chesterfield** 1	*Division Three*
	Wilson	Birch	
	Luton Town 3	**Sheffield Wednesday** 0	*Division Three*
	Moss (2) (1 pen.)		
	White		
8/11/80	**Liverpool** 0	**Nottingham Forest** 0	*Division One*
	West Bromwich Albion 0	**Aston Villa** 0	*Division One*
	West Ham United 2	**Grimsby Town** 1	*Division Two*
	Cross (2)	Stone	
15/11/80	**Ipswich Town** 3	**Leicester City** 1	*Division One*
	Gates	Williams	
	D'Avray		
	Williams (o.g.)		
	Plymouth Argyle 1	**Colchester United** 1	*Division Three*
	Kemp	Bremner	
	Arsenal 2	**West Bromwich Albion** 2	*Division One*
	Batson (o.g.)	Barnes	
	Sunderland	Owen (pen.)	
22/11/80	**Brighton & Hove Albion**..........1	**Manchester United** 4	*Division One*
	Ritchie	Jordan (2)	
		McIlroy	
		Duxbury	
	Stoke City...........................1	**Crystal Palace** 0	*Division One*
	O'Callaghan		
	Harlow Town 0	**Charlton Athletic** 2	*FA Cup 1st round*
		Hales	
		Robinson	

29/11/80	**Sunderland** ....2 Brown Cummins	**Liverpool** ....4 Johnson McDermott Lee (2)	Division One
	Notts County ....1 Harkouk	**Chelsea** ....1 Bumstead	Division Two
	Tottenham Hotspur ....2 Lacy Perryman	**West Bromwich Albion** ....3 A. Brown Robson Barnes	Division One
6/12/80	**Norwich City** ....2 Jovanovic (o.g.) Fashanu	**Manchester United** ....2 Bond (o.g.) Coppell	Division One
	Manchester City ....1 Gow	**Ipswich Town** ....1 Muhren	Division One
	Southampton ....1 Holmes	**Coventry City** 0	Division One
13/12/80	**Swansea City** ....4 L. James R. James (2) Charles	**Newcastle United** 0	Division One
	Aston Villa ....3 Geddis (2) Shaw	**Birmingham City** 0	Division One
	Colchester United ....1 Wignall	**Yeovil Town** ....1 Green	FA Cup 2nd round
20/12/80	**Chelsea** 0	**Leyton Orient** ....1 Mayo	Division Two
	Brighton & Hove Albion ....1 Robinson	**Aston Villa** 0	Division One
	Nottingham Forest ....3 Ponte Walsh Francis	**Sunderland** ....1 Rowell	Division One
27/12/80	**West Bromwich Albion** ....3 Owen (pen.) Regis Barnes	**Manchester United** ....1 Jovanovic	Division One
	Arsenal ....1 Sunderland	**Ipswich Town** ....1 Wark (pen.)	Division One
	Lincoln City ....1 Carr	**Mansfield Town** ....1 Thompson (o.g.)	Division Four

3/1/81	**Ipswich Town** ....1 Mariner	**Aston Villa** 0		*FA Cup 3rd round*
	Everton ....2 Lyons Sansom (o.g.)	**Arsenal** 0		*FA Cup 3rd round*
	Swansea City 0	**Middlesbrough** ....5 Angus Ashcroft Hodgson (2) Cochrane		*FA Cup 3rd round*
10/1/81	**Sheffield Wednesday** 0	**Chelsea** 0		*Division Two*
	Crystal Palace ....1 Boyle	**Stoke City** 0		*Division One*
	Aston Villa ....2 Withe Mortimer	**Liverpool** 0		*Division One*
17/1/81	**Everton** 0	**Ipswich Town** 0		*Division One*
	Birmingham City 0	**Southampton** ....3 Moran Channon Keegan		*Division One*
	Tottenham Hotspur...............2 Archibald (2)	**Arsenal** 0		*Division One*
24/1/81	**Nottingham Forest**...............1 Francis	**Manchester United** 0		*FA Cup 4th round*
	Manchester City...................6 Reeves Gow MacKenzie Bennett Power McDonald	**Norwich City**........................0		*FA Cup 4th round*
	Watford...............................1 Armstrong	**Wolverhampton Wanderers** ....1 Rice (o.g.)		*FA Cup 4th round*
31/1/81	**Derby County** ....2 Wilson Hector	**Luton Town** ....2 Moss Ingram		*Division Two*
	Southampton ....2 Keegan (2)	**Sunderland** ....1 Chisholm		*Division One*
	Arsenal ....2 Talbot Stapleton	**Coventry City** ....2 Bodak Daly		*Division One*

7/2/81	**Shrewsbury Town** 0	**West Ham United** 2	*Division Two*
		Cross	
		Devonshire	
	Everton 1	**Aston Villa** 3	*Division One*
	Ross (pen.)	Morley	
		Mortimer	
		Cowans (pen.)	
	Tottenham Hotspur...............1	**Leeds United** 1	*Division One*
	Archibald	Harris	
14/2/81	**Tottenham Hotspur**.............3	**Coventry City** 1	*FA Cup 5th round*
	Ardiles	English	
	Hughton		
	Archibald		
	Peterborough United 0	**Manchester City**..................1	*FA Cup 5th round*
		Booth	
	Wolverhampton Wanderers 3	**Wrexham** 1	*FA Cup 5th round*
	Bell (2)	Fox	
	Richards		
21/2/81	**Charlton Athletic** 1	**Exeter City** 0	*Division Three*
	Walker		
	Ipswich Town 3	**Wolverhampton Wanderers** 1	*Division One*
	Wark	Gray	
	Gates		
	Beattie		
	Southampton 2	**West Bromwich Albion** 2	*Division One*
	Golac	Robson	
	Moran	Regis	
28/2/81	**Crystal Palace** 2	**Everton** 3	*Division One*
	Hilaire	Eastoe	
	Allen (pen.)	McMahon	
		Varadi	
	Grimsby Town.....................0	**Blackburn Rovers** 0	*Division Two*
	Coventry City 0	**Ipswich Town** 4	*Division One*
		Brazil	
		Gates	
		McCall	
		Osman	
8/3/81	**Everton** 2	**Manchester City**..................2	*FA Cup 6th round*
	Eastoe	Gow	
	Ross (pen.)	Power	
	Middlesbrough 1	**Wolverhampton Wanderers** 1	*FA Cup 6th round*
	Cochrane	Gray	
15/3/81	**Liverpool** 1	**West Ham United** ....1 **(a.e.t.)**	*League Cup final*
	A. Kennedy	Stewart (pen.)	
	(Liverpool won the replay 2—1)		

| 22/3/81 | **Chelsea** ....0 | **Blackburn Rovers** ....0 | *Division Two* |

| | **Brighton & Hove Albion**..........1
Robinson | **Stoke City**............................1
Ursem | *Division One* |

| | **Liverpool** 1
Bailey (o.g.) | **Everton** ....0 | *Division One* |

| 29/3/81 | **Huddersfield Town**................0 | **Chester City** ....0 | *Division Three* |

| | **Leyton Orient**......................2
Jennings
P. Taylor | **Sheffield Wednesday** ....0 | *Division Two* |

| | **Aston Villa** 2
Morley
Geddis | **Southampton** 1
Evans (o.g.) | *Division One* |

| 5/4/81 | **West Bromwich Albion** 3
A. Brown
Batson
Barnes | **Ipswich Town** 1
Brazil | *Division One* |

| | **Tottenham Hotspur**...............2
Galvin
Crooks | **Everton** 2
Hartford
Varadi | *Division One* |

| | **Sheffield Wednesday** 3
Mirocevic
Curran (2) | **Luton Town** 1
Ingram | *Division Two* |

| 12/4/81 | **Manchester City**...................1
Power | **Ipswich Town** ....0 | *FA Cup semi-final* |

| 19/4/81 | **Ipswich Town** ....0 | **Arsenal** 2
Sansom
Nicholas | *Division One* |

| | **Notts County** ....0 | **Preston North End** ....0 | *Division Two* |

| | **Manchester United** 2
Jordan
Macari | **West Bromwich Albion** 1
Regis | *Division One* |

| 26/4/81 | **Aston Villa** 3
Shaw
Withe
Evans | **Middlesbrough** ....0 | *Division One* |

| | **Manchester United** 1
Jordan | **Norwich City**.........................0 | *Division One* |

| | **Swansea City** 3
Robinson
Hadziabdic
R. James | **Chelsea** ....0 | *Division Two* |

3/5/81	**Arsenal** ....2 Young McDermott	**Aston Villa** 0	*Division One*
	Brighton & Hove Albion ....2 Foster Ritchie	**Leeds United** 0	*Division One*
9/5/81	**Manchester City** ....1 Hutchison (Tottenham Hotspur won the replay 3–2)	**Tottenham Hotspur** .....1 (a.e.t.) Hutchison (o.g.)	*FA Cup final*
16/5/81	**Wales** ....2 Walsh (2)	**Scotland** 0	*Home International Championship*

MATCH OF THE SEASON

Chelsea 6
Newcastle United 0
at Stamford Bridge,
Saturday 25 October 1980

It was anniversary time at Chelsea. Geoff Hurst was celebrating one year as manager with his team riding high in the Second Division, and centre forward Colin Lee was also glad to see the *Match of the Day* cameras – it was exactly three years since he had scored four goals on his Tottenham debut (*see* Match of the Season, 1977/8).

The opposition was ready made for them. Newcastle's new manager, Arthur Cox, brought to London a team which included three players new to League football – including a lanky 19-year-old forward called Chris Waddle.

Chelsea simply took them apart. Lee, thriving on the service of orthodox wingers Phil Driver and Peter Rhoades-Brown, helped himself to a hat-trick. Other goals came from Mike Fillery, Clive Walker and full-back Gary Chivers.

Sadly for Hurst, it was one of his last enjoyable afternoons in football. He was sacked when Chelsea slumped in the second half of the season, winning only 3 of their last 23 matches and failing to score in 19 of them.

Chelsea: Borota, Chivers, Rofe, Bumstead, Droy, Nutton, Driver, Fillery, Lee, Walker (sub. Britton), Rhoades-Brown.
Scorers: Lee (3), Fillery, Walker, Chivers

Newcastle: Carr, Carney, Withe, Martin, Boam, Halliday, Shinton, Cartwright, Waddle (sub. Koenan), Rafferty, Wharton

Gary Chivers climaxes a sweeping Chelsea move by running over 60 yards to meet a cross. But the hero of the afternoon (left) was that man Colin Lee again

PLAYER OF THE SEASON
Glenn Hoddle (Tottenham)

The 'Noes' in the great Hoddle debate used to go to their lobby saying he couldn't tackle. As if he needed to, said the 'Ayes', with *his* range of skills. Yet strangely, the Spurs supremo wins the vote for this season largely because he was at his most competitive.

A rerun of the FA Cup final against Manchester City – especially the first match when City's midfield bristled with aggression – shows Hoddle getting stuck in with the best of them. It was his free-kick that flew off the head of Tommy Hutchison to earn Spurs a replay. And it was his stunning pass, an instant chip right out of the Hoddle repertoire, which slowed up just enough for Garth Crooks to steer Spurs level in the second game.

The early 80s were governed by the Hoddle factor at White Hart Lane, and to an extent on television. His mastery of the long pass, his peripheral vision and his supply of goals – 51 in 3 seasons for Spurs from midfield – made him the role model for many a schoolboy and junior footballer.

Later he played in France, for Monaco, and in 1991 he took over as manager of Swindon Town.

The Clive Allen 'Goal'

It was an altogether strange few months for Clive Allen. In June 1980, just a month after his 19th birthday, the Queens Park Rangers goalscorer was transferred to Arsenal for £1.25 million. It looked a dream move for the latest model from the Allen family production line. But two months later, with pre-season training still in progress and without playing a competitive game for Arsenal, Allen was moved on to Crystal Palace in a deal that took Kenny Sansom to Highbury.

He must have been in a state of some shock when Palace played at Coventry in early September. Without being unkind to Clive, it might be said that the BBC cameras tumbled across a 'one in a million' happening.

Palace were awarded a free-kick just outside the Coventry penalty area – ideal territory for Allen to exercise his powerful right foot. His shot sped past the Coventry wall and goalkeeper Jim Blyth. Those who had blinked and missed it then saw the ball bounce back on to the field.

What the referee and linesman had failed to spot, however, was that the ball had hit the stanchion at the rear of the goal net and rebounded out. From where the officials were standing, they could be forgiven for thinking it had hit the underside of the bar.

Despite the legitimate protests of Allen and his team, a goal was not given. Palace lost the match 3–1, and a month later lost their manager, Terry Venables, who left his so-called 'Team of the 80s' to rejoin his old club Queens Park Rangers.

One 'net' result of the Coventry incident was that most clubs redesigned their goals afterwards, pulling the netting away from the stanchion so that the ball would stay in the goal and not fly out as it did at Highfield Road. One of the chief instigators of this was the then chairman of Coventry City . . . who just happened to be the presenter of *Match of the Day*!

Clive Allen was to be much travelled in the future. He rejoined Venables at QPR for a couple of years, before joining Spurs and scoring 49 goals in season 1986–7. After a short spell in France with Bordeaux, he joined Manchester City and then Chelsea in 1991.

Three months later he went to West Ham for £300,000.

The camera didn't lie. Irrefutable evidence that Allen's shot *did* go into the net. The ball then rebounded off the stanchion and out of Jim Blyth's goal area. The referee waved play on

MATCH OF THE DAY
SEASON
1981-2

THE INTRODUCTION of three points for a win was designed to produce brighter football, and the return of *Match of the Day* to Saturday nights immediately featured a 5–1 win for promoted Swansea City over Leeds United.

It would prove a significant season for both clubs. Swansea, under John Toshack, had made their way from the Fourth Division to the First in a little more than three years, and with 12 games to go in their first season in the First Division they actually led the Championship race. *Match of the Day* cameras captured victories over both Manchester clubs at the Vetch Field, and also an emotional occasion at Anfield, where Toshack's men drew 2–2 just a few days after the death of Bill Shankly. In the end, Swansea finished sixth, which was a creditable performance and a whole lot better than that of their opponents on the first day of the season, Leeds, who were relegated.

For a while it looked as though the mighty might be in for a heavier fall, because Liverpool found themselves in the bottom half of the table when the BBC covered their Boxing Day defeat by Manchester City at Anfield. But with a super-charge which was to become their trade mark in the 80s, Liverpool carried all before them in the second half of the season, losing just two more games and claiming their fifth Championship in seven seasons with a televised victory over Spurs on the last day of the season.

Watford won promotion from the Second Division to earn a place among the 'Establishment'. Their brand of football caused endless arguments, but it was exciting and effective. Interviewed on *Match of the Day* after his team had beaten Leicester, manager Graham Taylor vociferously challenged a suggestion that Watford might be found out by more 'sophisticated' opponents. Taylor obviously knew a bit more about it than his questioner. A year later, Watford were runners-up in the First Division, and eight years later, he was manager of England!

When Bob Latchford scored against Manchester City in April, First Division newcomers Swansea City were championship contenders. But they lost five of their last six games, finished sixth, and four years later found themselves back in the Fourth Division which they had left in 1978

22/8/81	**Aston Villa** ....2 Withe (2)	**Tottenham Hotspur** ....2 Falco (2)	*FA Charity Shield*
29/8/81	**Nottingham Forest**...............2 Francis (2)	**Southampton** ....1 Keegan	*Division One*
	Manchester City...................2 Tueart Hutchison	**West Bromwich Albion** ....1 Mills (pen.)	*Division One*
	Swansea City ....5 Charles Curtis Latchford (3)	**Leeds United** ....1 Parlane	*Division One*
5/9/81	**Manchester United** ....1 Stapleton	**Ipswich Town** ....2 Wark Brazil	*Division One*
	West Bromwich Albion ....4 Regis (3) MacKenzie	**Swansea City** ....1 Robinson	*Division One*
12/9/81	**Luton Town** 0	**Sheffield Wednesday** ....3 Megson Bannister McCulloch	*Division Two*
	Aston Villa ....1 Cowans	**Manchester United** ....1 Stapleton	*Division One*
19/9/81	**Liverpool** 0	**Aston Villa** 0	*Division One*
	Norwich City........................2 Watson Jack	**Newcastle United** ....1 Waddle	*Division Two*
26/9/81	**West Ham United** ....1 Pike	**Liverpool** ....1 Johnson	*Division One*
	Manchester City...................0	**Tottenham Hotspur**...............1 Falco	*Division One*
3/10/81	**Queens Park Rangers** ....2 Gregory Allen	**Blackburn Rovers** 0	*Division Two*
	Liverpool ....2 McDermott (2) (2 pens)	**Swansea City** ....2 L. James (pen.) Latchford	*Division One*
	Notts County ....2 Hunt Kilcline	**Arsenal** ....1 Hawley	*Division One*
10/10/81	**Ipswich Town** ....1 O'Callaghan	**Wolverhampton Wanderers** 0	*Division One*
	Bristol City 0	**Preston North End** 0	*Division Three*

Date	Home		Away		Division
17/10/81	**Leeds United** ....3 Graham Cherry Connor		**West Bromwich Albion** ....1 Mills		*Division One*
	Arsenal ....1 Meade		**Manchester City**..................0		*Division One*
24/10/81	**Wolverhampton Wanderers** 0		**Aston Villa** ....3 Shaw (2) Palmer (o.g.)		*Division One*
	Crystal Palace 0		**Derby County**.......................1 Swindlehurst		*Division Two*
31/10/81	**Everton** 0		**Manchester City**..................1 Tueart		*Division One*
	Leicester City 0		**Sheffield Wednesday** 0		*Division Two*
7/11/81	**Liverpool** ....3 Dalglish (2) Rush		**Everton** ....1 Ferguson		*Division One*
	Stoke City..........................0		**Southampton** ....2 Keegan Armstrong		*Division One*
14/11/81	**Watford**............................0		**Cardiff City**..........................0		*Division Two*
	Middlesbrough 0		**Sunderland** 0		*Division One*
21/11/81	**Tottenham Hotspur**...............3 Hazard Roberts Archibald		**Manchester United** ....1 Birtles		*Division One*
	Birmingham City 0		**Wolverhampton Wanderers** ....3 Richards Gray Brazier		*Division One*
28/11/81	**Aston Villa** ....3 Bremner (2) Withe		**Nottingham Forest**...............1 Walsh		*Division One*
	Fulham 0		**Millwall**..............................0		*Division Three*
5/12/81	**West Ham United** ....1 Pearson		**Arsenal** ....2 Whyte Hollins (pen.)		*Division One*
	Everton ....3 Sharp O'Keefe (2)		**Swansea City** ....1 Latchford		*Division One*
12/12/81	**Swansea City** ....1 R. James		**Nottingham Forest**...............2 Young Robertson (pen.)		*Division One*
	Queens Park Rangers ....1 Flanagan		**Barnsley**.............................0		*Division Two*

19/12/81	**Everton** ....2 Lyons Eastoe	**Aston Villa** 0	*Division One*
	Chelsea ....1 Lee	**Blackburn Rovers** ....1 Miller	*Division Two*
26/12/81	**Liverpool** ....1 Whelan	**Manchester City**..................3 Hartford Bond (pen.) Reeves	*Division One*
	Portsmouth 0	**Bristol Rovers** 0	*Division Three*
2/1/82	**Leicester City** ....3 Young (2) Lineker	**Southampton** ....1 Keegan	*FA Cup 3rd round*
	Barnet 0	**Brighton & Hove Albion**..........0	*FA Cup 3rd round*
	Swansea City 0	**Liverpool** ....4 Hansen Rush (2) Lawrenson	*FA Cup 3rd round*
9/1/82	**Manchester City**..................1 Francis	**Stoke City**..........................1 O'Callaghan	*Division One*
	Huddersfield Town..............2 Cowling Brown	**Oxford United** 0	*Division Three*
16/1/82	**Coventry City** ....2 Hunt Daly	**Ipswich Town** ....4 Wark Muhren Mariner Brazil	*Division One*
	Liverpool ....2 Whelan Dalglish	**Wolverhampton Wanderers** ....1 Atkinson	*Division One*
23/1/82	**Watford**............................2 Armstrong Callaghan	**West Ham United** 0	*FA Cup 4th round*
	Tottenham Hotspur..............1 Crooks	**Leeds United** 0	*FA Cup 4th round*
	Manchester City..................1 Bond (pen.)	**Coventry City** ....3 Hunt Hateley Bodak	*FA Cup 4th round*
30/1/82	**Luton Town** ....2 White Donaghy	**Leicester City** ....1 Lineker	*Division Two*
	Swansea City ....2 Curtis R. James	**Manchester United** 0	*Division One*

6/2/82	**Colchester United**................5 Houston (o.g.) McDonough Allinson (2) Bremner	**Sheffield United**..................2 Kenworthy (pen.) Edwards	*Division Four*
	Southampton ....2 G. Baker Armstrong	**Manchester City**..................1 McDonald	*Division One*
	Tottenham Hotspur..............6 Hoddle (pen.) Villa (3) Crooks Falco	**Wolverhampton Wanderers** ....1 Hibbitt	*Division One*
13/2/82	**Tottenham Hotspur**..............1 Falco	**Aston Villa** 0	*FA Cup 5th round*
	Leicester City ....2 O'Neill Terry (o.g.)	**Watford**...............................0	*FA Cup 5th round*
	West Bromwich Albion ....1 Regis	**Norwich City**.......................0	*FA Cup 5th round*
20/2/82	**Watford**...............................1 Rostron	**Luton Town** ....1 Stein	*Division Two*
	Manchester United 0	**Arsenal** 0	*Division One*
27/2/82	**Brighton & Hove Albion**..........2 Ritchie Robinson	**West Bromwich Albion** ....2 Cross Bennett	*Division One*
	Everton 0	**West Ham United** 0	*Division One*
6/3/82	**Chelsea** ....2 Fillery Mayes	**Tottenham Hotspur**..............3 Archibald Hoddle Hazard	*FA Cup 6th round*
	Leicester City ....5 May Griffin (o.g.) Melrose (2) Lineker	**Shrewsbury Town** ....2 Bates Keay	*FA Cup 6th round*
13/3/82	**Oldham Athletic** 0	**Sheffield Wednesday** ....3 Pearson Megson Bannister	*Division Two*
	Arsenal ....1 Robson	**Ipswich Town** 0	*Division One*

20/3/82	**Tottenham Hotspur**..............3 Roberts (3)	**Southampton** ....2 G. Baker Armstrong	*Division One*
	Notts County ....1 Harkouk	**Manchester United** ....3 Coppell (2) Stapleton	*Division One*
27/3/82	**Sheffield Wednesday** ....2 Taylor Megson	**Leyton Orient**......................0	*Division Two*
	Manchester United 0	**Sunderland** 0	*Division One*
3/4/82	**Queens Park Rangers** ....1 Allen	**West Bromwich Albion** 0	*FA Cup semi-final*
	Sunderland 0	**Middlesbrough** ....2 Ashcroft Baxter	*Division One*
10/4/82	**Gillingham**.......................2 Bruce Powell	**Fulham** 0	*Division Three*
	Manchester City...................0	**Liverpool** ....5 Lee Neal (pen.) Rush A. Kennedy Johnston	*Division One*
17/4/82	**Swansea City** ....2 Stanley Latchford	**Manchester City**...................0	*Division One*
	Blackburn Rovers ....1 Stonehouse (pen.)	**Watford**.............................2 Callaghan Blissett (pen.)	*Division Two*
24/4/82	**Rotherham United** ....2 Moore Seasman	**Luton Town** ....2 Fuccillo Money	*Division Two*
	Brighton & Hove Albion..........0	**Manchester United** ....1 Wilkins	*Division One*
1/5/82	**Ipswich Town** ....3 Wark Brazil Muhren	**Middlesbrough** ....1 Thomas	*Division One*
	Liverpool ....2 Johnston (2)	**Nottingham Forest**...............0	*Division One*
8/5/82	**Birmingham City** 0	**Liverpool** ....1 Rush	*Division One*
	Watford...........................3 Barnes (2) Blissett	**Leicester City** ....1 Melrose	*Division Two*

15/5/82	**Liverpool** 3	**Tottenham Hotspur** 1		*Division One*
	Lawrenson	Hoddle		
	Dalglish			
	Whelan			
	Ipswich Town 1	**Nottingham Forest** 3		*Division One*
	Brazil	Davenport (3)		
22/5/82	**Queens Park Rangers** 1	**Tottenham Hotspur** .....1 (a.e.t.)		*FA Cup final*
	Fenwick	Hoddle		
	(Tottenham Hotspur won the replay 1–0)			
29/5/82	**Scotland** 0	**England** 1		*Home International Championship*
		Mariner		

MATCH OF THE SEASON

Leicester City 5
Shrewsbury Town 2
(*FA Cup 6th round*)
at Filbert Street,
Saturday 6 March 1982

Leicester's 21-year-old forward Gary Lineker had the world at his feet, but in all the global adventures that lay ahead, he never again played in a team that changed their goalkeeper three times during a game.

When Jack Keay put Shrewsbury 2–1 ahead in the first half of this all-Second Division quarter-final, it was clear that Leicester's goalkeeper, Mark Wallington, could not continue. He was hobbling badly after bruising a thigh in a collision with Chic Bates.

Lineker's striking partner

Stand-in goalkeeper Alan Young receives attention for concussion after replacing Mark Wallington. Manager Jock Wallace (right) had to use a third keeper, Steve Lynex, before Young recovered and went back in goal

Alan Young took over in goal, and substitute Jim Melrose came on up front. Before half-time, an own goal by Shrewsbury defender Colin Griffin made the score 2–2.

In the second half, Young himself was stunned in a collision, and handed over the goalkeeper's jersey to right-winger Steve Lynex for 10 minutes – but Shrewsbury couldn't beat him either. Instead, they swopped over again when Young's head cleared, and almost at once Lynex made Leicester's third goal for Melrose.

Lineker and Melrose added further goals to stamp Leicester's passport to the semi-finals, and when he was England captain years later, it became Lineker's favourite quiz question: 'Which was the game when seven goals were scored and two goalkeepers kept clean sheets?'

Leicester: Wallington (sub. Melrose), Williams, Friar, Peake, May, O'Neill, Lynex, Lineker, Young, Wilson, Kelly. Scorers: Melrose (2), May, Lineker, Griffin (o.g.)

Shrewsbury: Wardle, King (sub.Dungworth), Johnson, Cross, Griffin, Keay, Tong, McNally, Atkins, Biggins, Bates. Scorers: Bates, Keay

PLAYER OF THE SEASON
Ray Clemence
(Tottenham Hotspur)

If the match at Leicester found a place in football's version of trivial pursuits, the last day of the season threw up another poser with a neat twist: 'Which goalkeeper got a standing ovation from his own fans when he was playing for the opposition?'

The scene was Anfield. Liverpool, needing to beat Spurs to win the championship, were trailing at half-time to a wonder goal from Glenn Hoddle. But the fans on the Kop were typically generous.

As Spurs goalkeeper Ray Clemence ran towards them, cap and gloves in hand, they gave him a reception which said everything about Clemence's 11 seasons in Liverpool's first team, in which he missed just 6 games.

He won five Championship medals, three European Cup winners' medals, two UEFA Cup and a winners' medal in both the League Cup and the FA Cup. Then there were 61 England caps, which would have been doubled, but for the concurrent career of Peter Shilton.

In this, his first season at Spurs, Clemence won another FA Cup winners' medal. But he couldn't prevent his old Liverpool chums from putting three past him in the second half that day at Anfield as they secured the championship again.

His manager at Spurs, Keith Burkinshaw, said simply: 'He was one of the best professionals I ever worked with.'

FRUSTRATED BY A back injury which limited his World Cup contribution to just 27 minutes' play, England's Kevin Keegan made the first headlines of the new season when he left Southampton to join Newcastle.

Match of the Day viewers had an early glimpse of the impact Keegan would make on Tyneside. On the first Saturday of October, Newcastle won 5–1 at Rotherham in front of the cameras, and Keegan scored four times.

Not to be outdone, Liverpool's Ian Rush repeated the feat a month later. His four goals came in the Merseyside derby at Goodison Park and marked the first hat-trick in the fixture since 1935. Everton's on-loan defender Glen Keeley was sent off on this his debut appearance!

There was no holding Liverpool. In Bob Paisley's last season, they won their sixth Championship in eight seasons, as well as lifting the Milk Cup for the third year running.

The Wembley final against Manchester United was played before a capacity crowd on a Saturday afternoon, with highlights on *Match of the Day* 24 hours later. The programme was back on Sundays for a year as BBC and ITV continued their 'turn and turn about' arrangement.

Liverpool's retirement tributes to Paisley included sending him up the steps of the Royal Box to receive the Milk Cup ahead of his players, and bringing him on to the pitch at Anfield to lift the championship trophy before the last home game of the season against Aston Villa. Paisley's team led the League from the end of October, eventually finishing 11 points ahead of Watford. Liverpool eased up towards the end, taking only two points from their last seven matches.

Watford's achievement in finishing runners-up in their first season silenced many of their critics. Graham Taylor had proved that he could operate in the big boys' playground.

'Why don't you retire and give somebody else a chance?' Bob Paisley with the League Championship trophy after winning it for the sixth time in eight seasons

28/8/82	**Wolverhampton Wanderers** ....2 Eves (2)	**Blackburn Rovers** ....1 Garner	*Division Two*
	Norwich City ....1 Deehan	**Manchester City**...................2 Cross Power	*Division One*
4/9/82	**Arsenal** 0	**Liverpool** ....2 Neal Hodgson	*Division One*
	Ipswich Town ....1 Mariner	**Coventry City** ....1 Thomas	*Division One*
11/9/82	**Sheffield Wednesday** ....2 Bannister Megson	**Leeds United** ....3 Worthington (2) Butterworth	*Division Two*
	Manchester United ....3 Whiteside (2) Coppell	**Ipswich Town** ....1 Mariner	*Division One*
18/9/82	**Southampton** 0	**Manchester United** ....1 Macari	*Division One*
	Swansea City 0	**Liverpool** ....3 Rush (2) Johnston	*Division One*
25/9/82	**Tottenham Hotspur**...............4 Mabbutt (2) Crooks (2)	**Nottingham Forest**...............1 Birtles	*Division One*
	Leicester City 0	**Queens Park Rangers** ....1 O'Neill (o.g.)	*Division Two*
2/10/82	**Rotherham United** ....1 McBride	**Newcastle United** ....5 Keegan (4) (1 pen.) Todd	*Division Two*
	Ipswich Town ....1 D'Avray	**Liverpool** 0	*Division One*
9/10/82	**Everton** ....2 King McMahon	**Manchester City**...................1 Cross	*Division One*
	Chelsea 0	**Leeds United** 0	*Division Two*
16/10/82	**Newcastle United** ....1 Keegan (pen.)	**Fulham** ....4 Davies (2) Coney Houghton	*Division Two*
	Stoke City...........................3 Thomas McIlroy M. Chamberlain	**Brighton & Hove Albion**..........0	*Division One*

23/10/82	**Nottingham Forest**............3 Proctor Birtles Wallace	**Arsenal** 0	*Division One*
	Watford..........................0	**Coventry City** 0	*Division One*
30/10/82	**Aston Villa** ....4 Cowans (2) (1 pen.) Morley Shaw	**Tottenham Hotspur**............0	*Division One*
	Manchester City...............2 Tueart Hartford	**Swansea City** ....1 Latchford	*Division One*
6/11/82	**Everton** 0	**Liverpool** ....5 Rush (4) Lawrenson	*Division One*
	Coventry City 0	**Aston Villa** 0	*Division One*
13/11/82	**Manchester United**............1 Muhren	**Tottenham Hotspur**............0	*Division One*
	West Ham United ....1 Clark	**Norwich City**....................0	*Division One*
20/11/82	**Watford**..........................4 Blissett (2 pens) Barnes Taylor	**Brighton & Hove Albion**.........1 Ryan	*Division One*
	Sunderland 0	**Nottingham Forest**............1 Wallace	*Division One*
	Blackpool ....3 Pashley Bamber Deary (pen.)	**Horwich RMI** 0	*FA Cup 1st round*
27/11/82	**Crystal Palace** ....3 Cannon Jones Hinshelwood	**Wolverhampton Wanderers** ....4 Matthews (2) Clarke Gray	*Division Two*
	Luton Town ....3 Hill Stein Goodyear	**Southampton** ....3 Wallace Cassells Armstrong	*Division One*
4/12/82	**Lincoln City** ....3 Neale Bell Cockerill	**Millwall**...........................1 Massey	*Division Three*
	Notts County ....3 McCulloch Hooks Christie	**Nottingham Forest**............2 Wallace Young	*Division One*

11/12/82	**Liverpool** ....3 Rush Neal (2 pens)	**Watford**................................1 Rostron	*Division One*
	Brighton & Hove Albion..........3 Case Ritchie Robinson	**Norwich City**.........................0	*Division One*
	Boston United......................1 Lumby	**Sheffield United** ....1 Edwards	*FA Cup 2nd round*
18/12/82	**Wolverhampton Wanderers** ....4 Humphrey Clarke Palmer (pen.) Dodd	**Queens Park Rangers** 0	*Division Two*
	Tottenham Hotspur...............2 Mabbutt (2)	**Birmingham City** ....1 Langan	*Division One*
1/1/83	**Manchester United** ....3 Stapleton (2) Coppell	**Aston Villa** ....1 Cowans (pen.)	*Division One*
	Fulham ....1 Lewington	**Wolverhampton Wanderers** ....3 Pender Eves Clarke	*Division Two*
8/1/83	**Manchester United** ....2 Coppell Stapleton	**West Ham United** 0	*FA Cup 3rd round*
	Northampton Town 0	**Aston Villa** ....1 Walters	*FA Cup 3rd round*
	Tottenham Hotspur...............1 Hazard	**Southampton** 0	*FA Cup 3rd round*
15/1/83	**West Bromwich Albion** 0	**Liverpool** ....1 Rush	*Division One*
	Middlesbrough ....1 Bell	**Sheffield Wednesday** ....1 Pearson	*Division Two*
22/1/83	**Watford**...............................2 Nicholl (o.g.) Blissett	**Southampton** 0	*Division One*
	Stoke City............................1 Painter	**Ipswich Town** 0	*Division One*
29/1/83	**Aston Villa** ....1 Withe	**Wolverhampton Wanderers** 0	*FA Cup 4th round*
	Watford...............................1 Lohman	**Fulham** ....1 Coney	*FA Cup 4th round*
	Brighton & Hove Albion..........4 Case Smillie Robinson (2)	**Manchester City**...................0	*FA Cup 4th round*

5/2/83	**Luton Town** ....1 Stein	**Liverpool** ....3 Rush A. Kennedy Souness	*Division One*
	Queens Park Rangers ....1 Sealy	**Oldham Athletic** 0	*Division Two*
	Charlton Athletic ....2 Hales Simonsen (pen.)	**Cambridge United** ....1 Cartwright	*Division Two*
12/2/83	**Huddersfield Town**...............5 Lillis Russell (2) Hanvey Wilson	**Millwall**...............................1 Madden	*Division Three*
	Tottenham Hotspur...............1 Crooks	**Swansea City** 0	*Division One*
19/2/83	**Norwich City**.......................1 Bertschin	**Ipswich Town** 0	*FA Cup 5th round*
	Crystal Palace 0	**Burnley** 0	*FA Cup 5th round*
	Derby County......................0	**Manchester United** ....1 Whiteside	*FA Cup 5th round*
26/2/83	**Fulham** ....2 Davies Lock (pen.)	**Newcastle United** ....2 Varadi McDermott	*Division Two*
	Birmingham City ....1 Harford	**Nottingham Forest**...............1 Davenport	*Division One*
5/3/83	**Queens Park Rangers** ....6 Allen (3) Gregory Micklewhite Flanagan	**Middlesbrough** ....1 Kennedy (pen.)	*Division Two*
	Manchester City...................1 Reeves	**Manchester United** ....2 Stapleton (2)	*Division One*
12/3/83	**Arsenal** ....2 Woodcock Petrovic	**Aston Villa** 0	*FA Cup 6th round*
	Burnley ....1 Cassidy	**Sheffield Wednesday** ....1 Bannister	*FA Cup 6th round*
19/3/83	**Liverpool** 0	**Everton** 0	*Division One*
	Ipswich Town ....2 Mariner (2)	**Nottingham Forest**...............0	*Division One*
26/3/83	**Liverpool** ....2 A. Kennedy Whelan	**Manchester United** .....1 (a.e.t.) Whiteside	*Milk Cup final*

2/4/83	**Fulham** ....1 Lock	**Chelsea** ....1 Canoville	*Division Two*
	Luton Town 0	**Norwich City** ....1 Bennett	*Division One*
9/4/83	**Brighton & Hove Albion**..........1 Smith (pen.)	**Everton** ....2 Sheedy (2)	*Division One*
	Nottingham Forest................2 Davenport Bowyer	**Tottenham Hotspur**..............2 Brazil Mabbutt	*Division One*
	Queens Park Rangers ....2 Gregory Sealy	**Leicester City** ....2 Lineker (2)	*Division Two*
16/4/83	**Manchester United** ....2 Robson Whiteside	**Arsenal** ....1 Woodcock	*FA Cup semi-final*
	Southampton ....3 Moran (pen.) Holmes (2)	**Liverpool** ....2 Dalglish Johnston	*Division One*
23/4/83	**Manchester United** ....2 Cunningham Grimes (pen.)	**Watford**.............................0	*Division One*
	West Ham United ....2 Bonds Swindlehurst	**Aston Villa** 0	*Division One*
30/4/83	**Wolverhampton Wanderers** ....1 Gray	**Crystal Palace** 0	*Division Two*
	Swansea City ....1 Rajkovic	**Ipswich Town** ....1 Mariner	*Division One*
7/5/83	**Liverpool** ....1 Johnston	**Aston Villa** ....1 Shaw (pen.)	*Division One*
	Brighton & Hove Albion..........0	**Manchester City**...................1 Reeves	*Division One*
14/5/83	**Southampton** 0	**Birmingham City** ....1 Harford	*Division One*
	Manchester City..................0	**Luton Town** ....1 Antic	*Division One*
	Brighton & Hove Albion..........2 Smith Stevens	**Manchester United** .....2 (a.e.t.) Stapleton Wilkins	*FA Cup final*
	(Manchester United won the replay 4—0)		

Jig of joy. David Pleat off the starting blocks for his televised sprint across the pitch at Maine Road. Note the pained expression of Manchester City's acting manager John Benson (left) whose team had just been relegated

MATCH OF THE SEASON

Manchester City 0
Luton Town 1
at Maine Road,
Saturday 14 May 1983

The climax to the First Division season came not at the top, where Liverpool had the title tucked away weeks before, but at the bottom, where not even the most imaginative match-maker could have contrived a finish like the one at Maine Road.

Luton Town, in their first season after promotion, seemed doomed to make a quick return to the Second Division. Only a victory would keep them up, while their opponents in that last game, Manchester City, knew that just a draw would preserve *their* First Division status. Quite simply, one of the two teams would go down.

With less than five minutes to go, the odds were heavily on City surviving. There was no score, and David Pleat had pushed on his substitute, the Yugoslav Raddy Antic, in a desperate last throw of the dice.

Then Brian Stein found a yard of space on the right wing and hooked a long cross into the City penalty box. Goalkeeper Alex Williams came off his line to punch clear, only for Antic to drive the loose ball past five helpless City defenders, as well as the goalkeeper, from the edge of the area. Luton had survived.

When the final whistle went, a jubilant Pleat ran from the dug-out in a jig of joy to embrace his captain Brian Horton. His emotional response was understandable, as was City's despair at being relegated before their own fans when they were just four minutes from safety.

It was one of the biggest acts of escapology ever seen on *Match of the Day*.

Manchester City: Williams, Ranson, McDonald, Reid, Bond, Caton, Tueart, Reeves, Baker (sub. Kinsey), Hartford, Power

Luton Town: Godden, Stephens, Goodyear, Horton, Elliott, Donaghy, Hill, Aylott, Walsh, Turner (sub. Antic), Stein.
Scorer: Antic

PLAYER OF THE SEASON
Frank Stapleton
(Manchester United)

It was typical of Frank Stapleton that he finished the Milk Cup final against Liverpool as an emergency centre-half – and still got voted Man of the Match by most neutrals. His was a classy, uncomplaining brand of professionalism that sustained him through a long and successful career.

The young Stapleton had first caught the eye of *Match of the Day* viewers as a 20-year-old playing for Arsenal alongside Malcolm Macdonald (*see* 'Match of the Season', page 106). Together with his young Irish colleagues Liam Brady and David O'Leary, he played in three consecutive FA Cup finals. When Ron Atkinson bought him for £1 million soon after taking over at Old Trafford, Stapleton returned to the club who had taken him on their books as a schoolboy, but had then let him go.

His disappointment on losing to Liverpool at Wembley was soon forgotten when United returned in the FA Cup final, and Stapleton scored their first goal against Brighton. He was the first player to score in two FA Cup finals for different clubs.

His winners' medal was followed by another in 1985 (he shared the record of five FA Cup final appearances), and Frank still figured in *Match of the Day* FA Cup coverage in 1990, when he played and scored for Blackburn Rovers.

In the 1991/2 season, Stapleton followed a spell as player-coach to Huddersfield Town by taking the manager's job at Bradford City.

NOT ONLY WAS *Match of the Day* back on a Saturday night, but there was Friday night football on BBC too. Under a two-year agreement with the Football League, the two broadcasting companies were each allowed to screen seven live matches. ITV chose their favoured Sunday afternoon slot, while BBC experimented with Friday evening transmission.

The first game, not untypically, was between Manchester United and Spurs and, again not untypically, it produced six goals. United won 4–2 before a crowd of 33,616 – 10,000 below their average. Playing on a Friday night did not disturb Liverpool, who marked Joe Fagan's first season as manager with a treble – a third successive Championship, the Milk Cup for the fourth year running, and the European Cup for the fourth time.

Ian Rush scored 3 of his 48 goals in a Friday live match at Villa Park, and 2 more when Liverpool beat Newcastle 4–0 at Anfield in the first live FA Cup tie. Not a happy return for Kevin Keegan.

Not a happy time, either, for Howard Kendall. His Everton team were booed off the pitch after a goalless draw against Coventry at the end of 1983, and Kendall's job was said to be in jeopardy.

But in the Milk Cup quarter-final at Oxford in front of the BBC *Sportsnight* cameras, a back pass from Kevin Brock was intercepted by Adrian Heath, and in one moment Everton's season was tranformed. They reached two Wembley finals and beat Watford to lift the FA Cup.

It was revival time, too, at Chelsea, Sheffield Wednesday and Newcastle, as three famous clubs regained their First Division status (*see* 'Match of the Season', page 172).

Arsenal's attempt to recapture past glories with the signing of Charlie Nicholas from Celtic fell on stony ground. Manager Terry Neill was sacked in December.

Neither was it an auspicious autumn for *Match of the Day*. A

Taking on the big boys. Watford manager Graham Taylor was able to celebrate three promotions, runners-up spot in the first division, as well as trips to Wembley and into Europe. His ten years at Watford were followed by three at Aston Villa, where he again won promotion and finished second in Division One. Taylor took over as England manager in 1990

technical dispute at the BBC meant that outside broadcasts were disrupted, and for four Saturdays in a row there was no programme owing to industrial action.

It was a prelude to a turbulent time for the programme. After 20 years, *Match of the Day* would not remain sacrosanct for much longer.

20/8/83	**Liverpool** 0	**Manchester United** ....2 Robson (2)	*FA Charity Shield*
27/8/83	**Aston Villa** ....4 Evans Walters Shaw Ormsby	**West Bromwich Albion** ....3 Zondervan Regis Thompson	*Division One*
	Manchester United ....3 Muhren (2) (1 pen.) Stapleton	**Queens Park Rangers** ....1 Allen	*Division One*
3/9/83	**Liverpool** ....1 Rush	**Nottingham Forest**...............0	*Division One*
	Fulham 0	**Portsmouth**........................2 Hateley Biley	*Division Two*
10/9/83	**Arsenal** 0	**Liverpool** ....2 Dalglish Johnston	*Division One*
	Wolverhampton Wanderers ....1 Eves	**Birmingham City** ....1 Wright (pen.)	*Division One*
17/9/83	**Southampton** ....3 Williams (2) D. Armstrong	**Manchester United** 0	*Division One*
	Tottenham Hotspur...............1 Falco	**Everton** ....2 Reid Sheedy	*Division One*
24/9/83	**Manchester United** ....1 Stapleton	**Liverpool** 0	*Division One*
	Watford.............................2 Rostron Callaghan (pen.)	**Tottenham Hotspur**...............3 Hoddle Archibald Hughton	*Division One*
1/10/83	**Stoke City**...........................3 Painter M. Chamberlain Thomas	**West Ham United** ....1 Stewart (pen.)	*Division One*
	Luton Town ....1 Moss (pen.)	**Aston Villa** 0	*Division One*
8/10/83	**Newcastle United** ....2 Keegan (2)	**Charlton Athletic** ....1 Curtis	*Division Two*
	Manchester City...................2 Parlane Davidson	**Swansea City** ....1 Latchford	*Division Two*

15/10/83	**West Ham United** ....1 Devonshire	**Liverpool** ....3 Robinson (3)	*Division One*
	Leicester City 0	**Southampton** 0	*Division One*
	(Match abandoned — waterlogged pitch)		

22/10/83, 29/10/83, 5/11/83, 12/11/83 No programme due to strikes

19/11/83	**Luton Town** ....2 Stein Walsh	**Tottenham Hotspur**...............4 Cooke Dick Archibald (2)	*Division One*
	Aston Villa ....3 Withe Rideout McMahon	**Leicester City** ....1 Lynex (pen.)	*Division One*
26/11/83	**Ipswich Town** ....1 Wark	**Liverpool** ....1 Dalglish	*Division One*
	West Bromwich Albion ....1 Thompson	**Wolverhampton Wanderers** ....3 Crainie (2) Clarke	*Division One*
3/12/83	**Chelsea** 0	**Manchester City**...................1 Tolmie	*Division Two*
	Sunderland ....1 Rowell	**Ipswich Town** ....1 Gates	*Division One*
10/12/83	**Coventry City** ....4 Platnauer Gibson (3)	**Liverpool** 0	*Division One*
	West Ham United ....3 Brooking Whyte (o.g.) Pike	**Arsenal** ....1 Whyte	*Division One*
16/12/83	**Manchester United** ....4 Graham (2) Moran (2)	**Tottenham Hotspur**...............2 Brazil Falco	*Division One*
	(BBC's first ever live *Match of the Day*)		
31/12/83	**Aston Villa** ....2 McMahon Evans (pen).	**Queens Park Rangers** ....1 Charles	*Division One*
	Everton 0	**Coventry City** 0	*Division One*
6/1/84	**Liverpool** ....4 Robinson Rush (2) Johnston	**Newcastle United** 0	*FA Cup 3rd round*
7/1/84	**Fulham** 0	**Tottenham Hotspur**...............0	*FA Cup 3rd round*
13/1/84	**Queens Park Rangers** ....1 Fenwick	**Manchester United** ....1 Robson	*Division One*

RESULTS
1983-4

20/1/84	**Aston Villa** ....1 Mortimer	**Liverpool** ....3 Rush (3)	*Division One*

28/1/84	**Shrewsbury Town** ....2 Hackett Robinson	**Ipswich Town** 0	*FA Cup 4th round*
	Tottenham Hotspur 0	**Norwich City** 0	*FA Cup 4th round*
	Portsmouth 0	**Southampton** ....1 Moran	*FA Cup 4th round*

4/2/84	**Grimsby Town** ....1 Wilkinson	**Manchester City** ....1 Parlane	*Division Two*
	Blackpool ....3 Mercer Moore Britton	**York City** 0	*Division Four*

11/2/84	**Notts County** ....3 Harkouk Christie (2) (1 pen.)	**Watford** ....5 Hunt (o.g.) Callaghan (2) Reilly Johnston	*Division One*
	Sheffield Wednesday ....4 Bannister Shirtliff Cunningham Varadi	**Charlton Athletic** ....1 Moore	*Division Two*

17/2/84	**Blackburn Rovers** 0	**Southampton** ....1 Armstrong	*FA Cup 5th round*

25/2/84	**Nottingham Forest** 0	**Arsenal** ....1 Mariner	*Division One*
	Norwich City ....1 Deehan	**West Ham United** 0	*Division One*

3/3/84	**Leicester City** ....4 Peake (2) Lineker A. Smith	**Watford** ....1 Rostron	*Division One*
	Chelsea ....3 Speedie Dixon McAndrew (pen.)	**Oldham Athletic** 0	*Division Two*

10/3/84	**Birmingham City** ....1 Terry (o.g.)	**Watford** ....3 Barnes (2) Taylor	*FA Cup 6th round*
	Plymouth Argyle 0	**Derby County** 0	*FA Cup 6th round*
	Notts County ....1 Chiedozie	**Everton** ....2 Gray Richardson	*FA Cup 6th round*

16/3/84	**Southampton** ....2 Wallace (2)	**Liverpool** 0	*Division One*
24/3/84	**Queens Park Rangers** ....4 Wicks Micklewhite Allen Waddock	**Southampton** 0	*Division One*
	Wimbledon ....2 Cork Downes	**Walsall** 0	*Division Three*
31/3/84	**Leeds United** ....1 Ritchie	**Sheffield Wednesday** ....1 Bannister	*Division Two*
	Birmingham City ....2 Stevenson Gayle	**Aston Villa** ....1 Withe	*Division One*
7/4/84	**Queens Park Rangers** ....1 Allen	**Ipswich Town** 0	*Division One*
	Swansea City 0	**Manchester City**..................2 Parlane Kinsey	*Division Two*
14/4/84	**Plymouth Argyle**..................0	**Watford**............................1 Reilly	*FA Cup semi-final*
21/4/84	**Manchester United** ....4 Hughes (2) McGrath Wilkins	**Coventry City** ....1 Daly	*Division One*
	Sheffield Wednesday ....1 Sterland (pen.)	**Grimsby Town** 0	*Division Two*
28/4/84	**Liverpool** ....2 A. Kennedy Rush	**Ipswich Town** ....2 Gates (2)	*Division One*
	Nottingham Forest...............0	**Stoke City** 0	*Division One*
4/5/84	**Manchester City**..................0	**Chelsea** ....2 Nevin Dixon	*Division Two*
12/5/84	**Notts County** 0	**Liverpool** 0	*Division One*
	Newcastle United ....3 Keegan Waddle Beardsley	**Brighton & Hove Albion**..........1 Ryan	*Division Two*
19/5/84	**Everton** ....2 Sharp Gray	**Watford**............................0	*FA Cup final*
2/6/84	**England** 0	**USSR**................................2 Gotsmanov Protasov	*Friendly*

MATCH OF THE SEASON

Newcastle United 3
Brighton & Hove Albion 1
at St James' Park,
Saturday 12 May 1984

Promotion was already assured, but the pilgrimage the Geordie fans made on the last day of the season was to say goodbye to the man whose Messianic qualities had brought the good times back to Tyneside. It was Kevin Keegan's 500th league game – and his last.

Keegan's decision to retire at the age of 33 had been announced weeks earlier. His last challenge – leading Newcastle back to the First Division – had taken two years

to accomplish and had made him a hero all over again.

He stage-managed the occasion brilliantly, scoring the first goal himself, and bringing the best out of Chris Waddle and Peter Beardsley, who added further goals in a carnival atmosphere.

On the final whistle, the whole crowd rose to acclaim Keegan. He must have shaken hands with half the fans in the stadium, and the last word belonged to *Match of the Day* commentator Alan Parry: 'So ends the final chapter in one of the most remarkable and moving stories in English football history. Kevin Keegan, after 16 years and 500 league games, has rounded off his

career in the style that made him the great player he is.'

Newcastle United: Carr, Anderson, Wharton, McCreery, Carney, Roeder, Keegan, Beardsley, Waddle, McDermott, Trewick.
Scorers: Keegan, Beardsley, Waddle

Brighton: Corrigan, Jones, Hutchings, Case, E. Young, Gatting, Wilson, Ryan, A. Young, Connor (sub. Smillie), Pearce.
Scorer: Ryan

Fond farewells. The fans who said goodbye to Kevin Keegan at Newcastle in 1984 welcomed him back as manager eight years later

PLAYER OF THE SEASON
Ian Rush (Liverpool)

His third season as a Liverpool regular brought Ian Rush a golden haul of 48 goals, as well as winners' medals in the League Championship, the Milk Cup and the European Cup. Even the great goalscorers of the past, like Jimmy Greaves, never had a season like it.

Rush scored 32 goals in 41 league games, 8 in 12 league cup matches, 2 in the FA Cup and registered 6 goals in 9 European games.

He wasn't fussy about how he got them. Some were gentle tap-ins, others the manifestation of his acceleration and anticipation, which got him behind opponents. A few were spectacular – like the volley at Villa Park live on *Match of the Day*.

Rush did better than that against Luton – scoring five in one match. His understanding with Kenny Dalglish bordered on the telepathic and his capacity to punish defensive slackness was quite unforgiving.

For six years, he was a lucky mascot. In all that time, Liverpool never lost a match in which Rush scored.

SEASON
1984–5

ATCH OF THE DAY'S 21st birthday celebrations were rendered overwhelmingly irrelevant by two of the biggest disasters ever to hit football. The Bradford fire on the last Saturday of the league season claimed 56 lives, and less than three weeks later a further 39 people perished in the Heysel tragedy.

Before disaster struck, the season on the field was dominated by a rejuvenated Everton. Kendall's team built on their FA Cup success the previous season, giving due notice of their intent when they won at Anfield in October.

Graeme Sharp's goal that day was one of the finest seen on *Match of the Day*. He controlled the ball with one touch on his left foot, then with his right volleyed an unstoppable shot past Grobbelaar from outside the penalty area.

Everton never looked back. Their 4–1 victory over Sunderland in April included two classic diving headers from Andy Gray, and the nation saw the pedigree of the new champions. It was Everton's first title in 15 years.

In the FA Cup, they beat Luton after extra-time in an exciting semi-final, but lost to Manchester United in the final just three days after lifting the European Cup Winners' Cup in Rotterdam.

It was the first time for 10 years that Liverpool had ended a season empty-handed. The Milk Cup went to Norwich City, although both the winners and their Wembley opponents Sunderland were later relegated.

One of the clubs to replace them were Second Division champions Oxford United, whose two apperances on *Match of the Day* were a personal triumph for striker John Aldridge. He scored hat-tricks against Leeds and Oldham, helping Oxford win both matches 5–2.

The cameras also caught Manchester City's return to the top grade, thanks to a 5–1 win over Charlton. On the same afternoon,

A goal to remember. Everton's
Graeme Sharp captured in mid-air as
his ferocious volley flies past Mark
Lawrenson. That goal gave Everton
their first victory at Anfield for 14
years and helped them win their first
Championship since 1970

the Bradford disaster sent the football world into mourning. Then
Heysel sent the English game into exile for five years.

Nobody noticed that *Match of the Day* had come of age. It
would now be off the screen altogether for eight months.

25/8/84	**Manchester United** ....1 Strachan (pen.)	**Watford**.....................1 Callaghan	*Division One*
	Aston Villa ....1 Bremner	**Coventry City** 0	*Division One*
31/8/84	**Chelsea** 0	**Everton** ....1 Richardson	*Division One*
8/9/84	**Arsenal** ....3 Talbot (2) Woodcock	**Liverpool** ....1 A. Kennedy	*Division One*
	Sheffield Wednesday ....2 Marwood Varadi	**Tottenham Hotspur**...............1 Falco	*Division One*
15/9/84	**Southampton** ....2 Jordan Watson (o.g.)	**Norwich City**........................1 Donowa	*Division One*
	Hull City ....1 McEwan (pen.)	**Preston North End** ....2 Clark M. Jones	*Division Three*
22/9/84	**Manchester United** ....1 Strachan (pen.)	**Liverpool** ....1 Walsh	*Division One*
	Aston Villa 0	**Tottenham Hotspur**...............1 Chiedozie	*Division One*
29/9/84	**Manchester City**..................2 Kinsey Smith	**Crystal Palace** ....1 Irvine	*Division Two*
	Newcastle United ....1 Beardsley	**West Ham United** ....1 Allen	*Division One*
6/10/84	**Aston Villa** ....3 Evans Rideout Withe	**Manchester United** 0	*Division One*
	Nottingham Forest...............1 Davenport (pen.)	**Stoke City**...........................1 Berry	*Division One*
12/10/84	**Tottenham Hotspur**...............1 Crooks	**Liverpool** 0	*Division One*
20/10/84	**Liverpool** 0	**Everton** ....1 Sharp	*Division One*
	Ipswich Town ....2 Gates Sunderland	**West Bromwich Albion** 0	*Division One*
27/10/84	**West Ham United** ....3 Cottee Goddard Pike	**Arsenal** ....1 Allinson	*Division One*
	West Bromwich Albion 0	**Southampton** 0	*Division One*

2/11/84	**Manchester United** ....4 Robson Strachan (2) Hughes	**Arsenal** ....2 Allinson Woodcock	*Division One*
10/11/84	**Nottingham Forest**...............1 Davenport	**Tottenham Hotspur**...............2 Hazard Galvin	*Division One*
	Blackburn Rovers ....2 Garner Randell	**Brighton & Hove Albion**..........0	*Division Two*
17/11/84	**Watford**....................1 Barnes	**Sheffield Wednesday** 0	*Division One*
	Charlton Athletic ....2 Lee Aizlewood	**Birmingham City** ....1 Morley	*Division Two*
	Metropolitan Police 0	**Dartford** ....3 Borg Cowley Burman	*FA Cup 1st round*
24/11/84	**Sunderland** ....3 Walker (3) (2 pens)	**Manchester United** ....2 Hughes Robson	*Division One*
	Oxford United ....5 Aldridge (3) Briggs Hamilton	**Leeds United** ....2 Lorimer Wright	*Division Two*
1/12/84	**Arsenal** ....3 Allinson Woodcock Anderson	**Luton Town** ....1 B. Stein	*Division One*
	Watford.............................2 Reilly Sterling	**Nottingham Forest**...............0	*Division One*
	Oldham Athletic 0	**Manchester City**...................2 Melrose Smith	*Division Two*
8/12/84	**Nottingham Forest**...............3 Hodge Mills Metgod	**Manchester United** ....2 Strachan (2) (1 pen.)	*Division One*
	Tottenham Hotspur...............3 Falco (2) Roberts (pen.)	**Newcastle United** ....1 Waddle	*Division One*
	Dagenham..........................1 Dunwell	**Peterborough** 0	*FA Cup 2nd round*

15/12/84	**West Ham United** 0	**Sheffield Wednesday** 0	*Division One*
	Coventry City ....2 Peake Shilton (o.g.)	**Southampton** ....1 Jordan	*Division One*
21/12/84	**Queens Park Rangers** 0	**Liverpool** ....2 Rush Wark	*Division One*
29/12/84	**Newcastle United** ....1 Beardsley (pen.)	**Arsenal** ....3 Talbot Nicholas (2)	*Division One*
	Ipswich Town 0	**Everton** ....2 Sharp (2)	*Division One*
4/1/85	**Leeds United** 0	**Everton** ....2 Sharp (pen.) Sheedy	*FA Cup 3rd round*
12/1/85	**Queens Park Rangers** ....2 Bannister (2)	**Tottenham Hotspur**..............2 Falco Crooks	*Division One*
	Norwich City......................1 Deehan	**Southampton** 0	*Division One*
19/1/85	**Chelsea** ....1 Speedie	**Arsenal** ....1 Mariner	*Division One*
	Coventry City 0	**Aston Villa** ....3 Walters (2) Rideout	*Division One*
	Manchester City.................3 Smith Baker Phillips	**Wimbledon** 0	*Division Two*
26/1/85	**York City**...........................1 Houchen (pen.)	**Arsenal** 0	*FA Cup 4th round*
	Leyton Orient......................0	**Southampton** ....2 Jordan Moran	*FA Cup 4th round*
	Grimsby Town....................1 Foley	**Watford**...........................3 Blissett (2) Gilligan	*FA Cup 4th round*
2/2/85	**Luton Town** ....2 B. Stein Nwajiobi	**Tottenham Hotspur**..............2 Falco Roberts	*Division One*
	Sheffield Wednesday ....1 Marwood	**Liverpool** ....1 Lawrenson	*Division One*

Date	Home		Away		Competition
9/2/85	**Manchester City** ....**1** Phillips		**Carlisle United** ....**3** Poskett (2) Bishop		*Division Two*
	Barnsley ....**2** Campbell Wylde		**Portsmouth** ....**2** Blake Bamber		*Division Two*
	Brighton & Hove Albion ....**1** Hutchings		**Cardiff City** **0**		*Division Two*
15/2/85	**Blackburn Rovers** **0**		**Manchester United** ....**2** McGrath Strachan		*FA Cup 5th round*
23/2/85	**Leicester City** ....**1** Lynex		**Everton** ....**2** Gray (2)		*Division One*
	Blackburn Rovers ....**1** Quinn		**Oxford United** ....**1** Brock		*Division Two*
	Ipswich Town ....**1** D'Avray		**Norwich City** **0**		*Milk Cup semi-final first leg*
2/3/85	**Manchester United** ....**1** Olsen		**Everton** ....**1** Mountfield		*Division One*
	Bradford City ....**1** Campbell		**Gillingham** ....**1** Shearer		*Division Three*
9/3/85	**Manchester United** ....**4** Hughes Whiteside (3) (1 pen.)		**West Ham United** ....**2** Allen Hogg (o.g.)		*FA Cup 6th round*
	Everton ....**2** Sheedy Mountfield		**Ipswich Town** ....**2** Zondervan Wilson		*FA Cup 6th round*
	Luton Town ....**1** Turner		**Watford** **0**		*FA Cup 6th round*
15/3/85	**West Ham United** ....**2** Stewart (pen.) Duxbury (o.g.)		**Manchester United** ....**2** Stapleton Robson		*Division One*
24/3/85	**Norwich City** ....**1** Chisholm (o.g.)		**Sunderland** **0**		*Milk Cup final*
30/3/85	**Southampton** ....**1** Jordan		**Everton** ....**2** Richardson (2)		*Division One*
	Stoke City ....**2** Dyson Painter		**Arsenal** **0**		*Division One*
6/4/85	**Everton** ....**4** Gray (2) Steven Sharp		**Sunderland** ....**1** Wallace		*Division One*
	Portsmouth ....**1** Webb		**Brighton & Hove Albion** ....**1** Ferguson		*Division Two*

13/4/85	**Everton** 2	**Luton Town** ....1 (a.e.t.)	*FA Cup semi-final*
	Sheedy	Hill	
	Mountfield		
20/4/85	**Liverpool** 3	**Newcastle United** 1	*Division One*
	Wark	N. McDonald	
	Walsh		
	Gillespie		
	Oxford United 5	**Oldham Athletic** 2	*Division Two*
	Brock	Quinn	
	B. McDonald	McGuire	
	Aldridge (3)		
27/4/85	**Manchester United** 2	**Sunderland** 2	*Division One*
	Robson	Pickering	
	Moran	Walker	
	Chelsea 1	**Tottenham Hotspur** 1	*Division Two*
	Nevin	Galvin	
4/5/85	**Sheffield Wednesday** 0	**Everton** 1	*Division One*
		Gray	
	Blackburn Rovers 0	**Portsmouth** 1	*Division Two*
		Tait	
11/5/85	**Manchester City** 5	**Charlton Athletic** 1	*Division Two*
	Phillips (2)	Lee	
	May		
	Melrose		
	Simpson		
	Southampton 2	**Coventry City** 1	*Division One*
	Moran	Regis	
	Stephens (o.g.)		
18/5/85	**Everton** 0	**Manchester United** .....1 (a.e.t.)	*FA Cup final*
		Whiteside	

The moment that sent shivers down the spine of Arsenal supporters, as Houchen's penalty skips across the frosty surface into the net. Note the BBC camera on a hoisted crane which became a feature of *Match of the Day* coverage at smaller grounds

MATCH OF THE SEASON

York City 1 Arsenal 0
(*FA Cup 4th round*)
at Bootham Crescent,
Saturday 26 January 1985

The day started with York's manager Denis Smith and his assistant, Viv Busby, helping a team of volunteers to sweep snow off the pitch at Bootham Crescent. Only after that was the match certain to go ahead.

Busby had a score to settle with the FA Cup. Thirteen years earlier, while on loan to Newcastle, he had been on the wrong end of that shock defeat at Hereford. The BBC cameras owed him a favour.

It came in the 89th minute, courtesy of Arsenal's England midfielder Steve Williams. As York's Keith Houchen set off on the last attack of the game, Williams pushed him over and gave away a penalty.

Houchen rolled the ball into the corner of the net to give York a famous victory and bring another Cup upset into millions of living rooms.

Two years later, Houchen scored an even more memorable goal, in the final itself this time, for Coventry against Spurs.

York City: Astbury, Senior, Hay, Sbragia, MacPhail, Haslegrave, Ford, Butler, Walwyn, Houchen, Pearce. Scorer: Houchen (pen.)

Arsenal: Lukic, Anderson, Sansom, Talbot, O'Leary, Caton, Robson, Williams, Mariner, Woodcock, Nicholas (sub. Allinson)

PLAYER OF THE SEASON

Derek Mountfield (Everton)

Fourteen goals from centre-half, and not one of them a penalty. That was Derek Mountfield's contribution to Everton's best-ever season, quite apart from his main job in shackling most of the strikers he played against.

Mountfield, an Everton fan as a boy, was signed from Tranmere Rovers for a modest £30 000. In this, only his second season as an Everton regular, he outclassed his opponents in his own penalty area and generally outjumped them in theirs.

Most of his goals came from free-kicks and corners, and how timely some of them were. Like the last-minute equaliser against Ipswich in the sixth round of the FA Cup, and the winner in extra-time in the semi-final against Luton.

In a period when set plays settled more and more matches, Mountfield's prolific total – including 10 goals in League games alone – made his a season to remember.

THE RELATIONSHIP between the television companies and the football authorities had always been a tender one. Now, it broke down altogether as negotiations for a new contract ended in deadlock. The argument was mainly about money. Football had felt for some years that it was being short-changed by BBC and ITV acting together in a cartel. But, after Heysel, the image of the game was tarnished. Was the product still of compulsive value?

The first half of the season suggested otherwise. Crowds were noticeably down, a heavy police presence suggested that hooliganism was now the game's biggest enemy and the television audience was starved of football – other than the Charity Shield and the occasional international match – until after Christmas.

Then an interim deal was done until the end of the season. When the FA Cup third round weekend arrived *Match of the Day* was back in business with new faces on show.

One of these was Frank McAvennie. His partnership with Tony Cottee produced the winning goal against Charlton the day the programme returned, and the pair scored 53 goals between them as West Ham finished third in the table. Gary Lineker managed 40 by himself in his one and only season at Everton – including a goal in the FA Cup final – but the defending champions, like the Hammers, had to accede to the might of Liverpool.

In Kenny Dalglish's first season as player-manager, the Anfield aristocrats became the third club this century to win the League and Cup double. Dalglish himself scored the goal at Chelsea which tied up Liverpool's 16th championship.

But what the season really proved on the television front was a disaffection by both channels with recorded highlights. Live football was what the television controllers wanted. The Saturday night *Match of the Day* concept was shelved indefinitely. It would be seven years before it returned.

A study in concentration. With the
outside of his right foot Kenny
Dalglish glides in the goal at Chelsea
which clinched Liverpool's sixteenth
Championship in front of millions of
Match of the Day viewers. A week
later, Liverpool beat Everton at
Wembley to complete the League and
Cup double in Dalglish's first season
as player-manager

10/8/85	**Everton** ....2 Steven Heath	**Manchester United** 0		*FA Charity Shield*

There was no *Match of the Day* between August and 5/1/86 due to a protracted dispute between the television companies and the Football League

5/1/86	**Charlton Athletic** 0	**West Ham United** ....1 Cottee		*FA Cup 3rd round*
12/1/86	**Watford**..............................2 Jackett Lohman	**Liverpool** ....3 Walsh (2) Rush		*Division One*
18/1/86	**Manchester United** ....2 Olsen (2) (1 pen.)	**Nottingham Forest**...............3 Walsh (2) Clough		*Division One*
	Birmingham City 0	**Everton** ....2 Lineker (2)		*Division One*
	West Bromwich Albion 0	**Chelsea** ....3 Speedie Murphy Nevin		*Division One*
25/1/86	**Sunderland** 0	**Manchester United** 0		*FA Cup 4th round*
	Manchester City..................1 Davies	**Watford**.............................1 Jackett (pen.)		*FA Cup 4th round*
	Notts County ....1 McParland	**Tottenham Hotspur**...............1 C. Allen		*FA Cup 4th round*
9/2/86	**Liverpool** ....1 Wark	**Manchester United** ....1 C. Gibson		*Division One*
2/3/86	**Tottenham Hotspur**...............1 Waddle	**Liverpool** ....2 Rush Molby		*Division One*
8/3/86	**Bury** 0	**Watford**.............................3 Callaghan West Sterling		*FA Cup 5th round*
	Luton Town ....2 Harford Stein	**Everton** ....2 Sharp Heath		*FA Cup 6th round*
	Brighton & Hove Albion..........0	**Southampton** ....2 Moran Cockerill		*FA Cup 6th round*

22/3/86	**Manchester United** ....2 C. Gibson Strachan (pen.)	**Manchester City**..................2 Wilson Albiston (o.g.)	*Division One*

22/3/86 **Manchester United** 2   **Manchester City**..................2   *Division One*
C. Gibson   Wilson
Strachan (pen.)   Albiston (o.g.)

Southampton 0   **Chelsea** 1   *Division One*
   Pates

Sheffield United 2   **Norwich City**.......................5   *Division Two*
Edwards (2)   Smith (o.g.)
   Drinkell
   Mendham
   Barham
   Biggins

31/3/86 **Manchester United** 0   **Everton** 0   *Division One*

Liverpool 2   **Manchester City**..................0   *Division One*
McMahon (2)

Brighton & Hove Albion..........2   **Portsmouth**.......................3   *Division Two*
Saunders   Quinn (2) (1 pen.)
O'Regan   Hilaire

5/4/86 **Everton** 2   **Sheffield Wednesday**...1 (a.e.t.)   *FA Cup semi-final*
Harper   Shutt
Sharp

19/4/86 **Everton** 1   **Ipswich Town** 0   *Division One*
Sharp

Watford...............................0   **West Ham United** 2   *Division One*
   Cottee
   McAvennie

3/5/86 **Everton** 6   **Southampton** 1   *Division One*
Mountfield   Puckett
Steven
Lineker (3)
Sharp

West Bromwich Albion 2   **West Ham United** 3   *Division One*
Madden   Cottee
Reilly (pen.)   McAvennie
   Stewart (pen.)

Chelsea 0   **Liverpool** 1   *Division One*
   Dalglish

10/5/86 **Everton** 1   **Liverpool** 3   *FA Cup final*
Lineker   Rush (2)
   Johnston

MATCH OF THE DAY
SEASON
1985-6

MATCH OF THE SEASON

Manchester United 2
Nottingham Forest 3
at Old Trafford,
Saturday 18 January 1986

Brian Clough was so delighted with his team's performance at Old Trafford that he rang the BBC and asked for copies of the full-match video for every member of his team.

Maybe there was a touch of the proud father about it. Clough's son, Nigel, still only 19, headed the winner from a corner in the last minute of a match watched by 46 000 at Old Trafford and several million on the first Saturday night *Match of the Day* since the previous May.

Earlier, Jesper Olsen had scored twice for Manchester United, once from a penalty, and Colin Walsh twice for Forest. It was the sort of

A choirboy admonished. But Nigel Clough got up to score the winning goal at Old Trafford

football that the television audience had been missing.

Manchester United: Bailey, Gidman, Albiston, Whiteside, Moran, Garton, Olsen, Strachan, Hughes, Stapleton, C. Gibson.
Scorer: Olsen (2) (1 pen.)

Nottingham Forest: Sutton, Fleming, Williams, Walker, Metgod, Bowyer, Carr, Webb, Clough, Davenport, Walsh.
Scorers: Walsh (2), Clough

186

PLAYER OF THE SEASON
Frank McAvennie (West Ham)

The fact that Frank McAvennie burst on to the scene when there was no televised football made his impact all the more impressive. By the time the cameras picked up the flaxen-haired forward in January he had already scored 19 goals.

Signed from St Mirren for £340 000 in close competition with Luton, McAvennie started off in midfield but was immediately switched to partner Tony Cottee when Paul Goddard was injured in West Ham's opening game.

The move worked a treat. McAvennie scored 26 League goals in 41 matches as the Hammers remained in contention for the Championship until the last day of the season. In the end they finished third – the best position in the club's history.

McAvennie never had another season like it. Although he remained a firm favourite at Upton Park, he moved back to Scotland after one more season in the south.

His return from Celtic for a second spell with West Ham was less successful, although he scored 10 goals in their promotion season of 1990/1 before he was injured and missed the FA Cup semi-final against Nottingham Forest.

THE NEW TWO-YEAR deal between television and football that started after the Mexico World Cup was heavily loaded towards live matches. Recorded highlights were left to the discretion of the television companies, who only took up the option on Cup weekends.

The BBC's live fixtures had now found a settled spot, like those of their competitors, on Sunday afternoons. The schedulers maintained that their audiences of six and seven million comfortably exceeded the disappointing figures for recorded football.

Inevitably, the selection process for live games centred on the glamour clubs with the widest appeal. The first BBC match saw Everton beat Manchester United at Goodison Park, although when Kendall's team regained the Championship by winning at Norwich late in the season, the absence of a highlights programme meant that Pat Van Den Hauwe's significant goal was only seen on news bulletins.

If the balance of power had again shifted on Merseyside, new managers brought north London rivals Arsenal and Spurs back into the limelight with a neck-and-neck struggle for honours.

At Highbury, George Graham's first season saw Arsenal set a club record of 22 matches unbeaten, then defeat Liverpool in the Littlewoods Cup final. It was the BBC's turn to cover this final, and since Ian Rush had scored first for Liverpool, commentator Barry Davies was at last able to kill off the statistic which said Liverpool had never lost a game in which Rush scored.

At White Hart Lane, David Pleat introduced a five-man midfield which complemented lone striker Clive Allen (*see* 'Player of the Season', page 192) and had Tottenham on course for a treble. In the end, Spurs finished third in the league, lost an epic three-match Littlewoods Cup semi-final to Arsenal, and were beaten in extra-time in the FA Cup final, after twice taking the lead against Coventry.

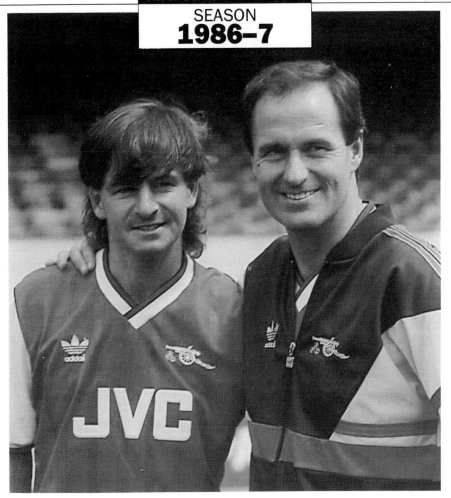

An Arsenal re-stocked. Sixteen years after playing in the double team, George Graham went back to Wembley as manager to lift the Littlewoods Cup thanks to two goals from Charlie Nicholas (left). Two championships followed in 1989 and 1991 as Graham bid to become the most successful Highbury manager since Herbert Chapman.

This was the only season in living memory when the BBC did not cover an FA Cup semi-final (ITV had both), but the BBC's *Match of the Day* cameras did capture the essence of the cup when rising upstarts Wimbledon put out Everton in the fifth round.

The following year, they would do even better.

21/9/86	**Everton** ....3 Sharp Heath Sheedy	**Manchester United** ....1 Robson	*Division One*
2/11/86	**West Ham United** ....1 Dickens	**Everton** 0	*Division One*
23/11/86	**Everton** 0	**Liverpool** 0	*Division One*
7/12/86	**Manchester United** ....3 Whiteside Davenport (2) (1 pen.)	**Tottenham Hotspur**..............3 Mabbutt Moran (o.g.) C. Allen	*Division One*
14/12/86	**Liverpool** ....3 Whelan Rush Nicol	**Chelsea** 0	*Division One*
4/1/87	**Tottenham Hotspur**..............1 M. Thomas	**Arsenal** ....2 Davis Adams	*Division One*
11/1/87	**Luton Town** 0	**Liverpool** 0	*FA Cup 3rd round*
31/1/87	**Manchester United** 0	**Coventry City** ....1 Houchen	*FA Cup 4th round*
	Wimbledon ....4 Fashanu (2) Blake (o.g.) Sayer	**Portsmouth**..........................0	*FA Cup 4th round*
	Bradford City 0	**Everton** ....1 Snodin	*FA Cup 4th round*
22/2/87	**Wimbledon** ....3 Hodges Fashanu Sayer	**Everton** ....1 Wilkinson	*FA Cup 5th round*
1/3/87	**Tottenham Hotspur**..............1 C. Allen	**Arsenal** ....2 (a.e.t.) Quinn Anderson	*Littlewoods Cup semi-final second leg*
8/3/87	**Watford**...........................2 Blissett Falco	**Everton** ....1 Heath	*Division One*
14/3/87	**Arsenal** ....1 Allinson	**Watford**.............................3 Barnes Blissett (2)	*FA Cup 6th round*
	Sheffield Wednesday ....1 Megson	**Coventry City** ....3 Regis Houchen (2)	*FA Cup 6th round*
5/4/87	**Arsenal** ....2 Nicholas (2)	**Liverpool** ....1 Rush	*Littlewoods Cup final*
16/5/87	**Coventry City** ....3 Bennett Houchen Mabbutt (o.g.)	**Tottenham Hotspur**.....2 (a.e.t.) C. Allen Mabbutt	*FA Cup final*

MATCH OF THE SEASON

Manchester United 3
Tottenham Hotspur 3
at Old Trafford,
Sunday 7 December 1986

Three years earlier, the BBC had selected this time-honoured fixture as their first-ever live League game. On that occasion the teams produced six goals. Only Manchester United and Spurs could be relied upon to serve up the same again.

Ever since the 60s, when these teams beat each other 5–1 in *Match of the Day*'s second season, this encounter had a cavalier ring about it. The personnel changed, but the entertainment value did not.

On this occasion, United were two up at half-time through Norman Whiteside and Peter Davenport. Their new manager, Alex Ferguson, who had taken over from Ron Atkinson, must have felt perfectly satisfied.

But in the second half, Spurs scored three times with a superb header from a corner by Gary Mabbutt, a bizarre, sliced own goal by Kevin Moran and then a brave finish by Clive Allen which earned him a broken nose.

United's third was a penalty by Davenport, which Clemence all but saved. A television audience of eight million were kept on the edge of their seats. Live football was here to stay.

The Great Entertainers. Manchester United and Tottenham Hotspur produced a series of *Match of the Day* classics over 25 years. The 3–3 draw at Old Trafford was shown 'live' on a Sunday afternoon

Manchester United: Turner, Sivebaeck, Duxbury, Moses, McGrath (sub. Stapleton), Moran, Robson, Strachan, Whiteside, Davenport, Olsen.
Scorers: Davenport (2) (1 pen.), Whiteside

Tottenham Hotspur: Clemence, P. Allen, M. Thomas, Roberts, Gough, Mabbutt, C. Allen, Galvin, Waddle, Hoddle, Ardiles (sub. D. Thomas).
Scorers: Mabbutt, Moran (o.g.), C. Allen

PLAYER OF THE SEASON
Clive Allen (Spurs)

When Clive Allen headed Chris Waddle's cross into the Coventry net with barely a minute gone in the FA Cup final, it was his 49th senior goal of the season. Thus, he went one better than Ian Rush three years earlier, and had he been allowed to count a hat-trick in a prestige friendly against Hamburg, the total would have been 52.

The landmark that meant the most to Allen and Spurs supporters was goal number 43, when he surpassed Jimmy Greaves's club record set in the 1962/3 season. Just for the record, Allen played in four more matches than Greaves.

Jimmy would have also been too polite to point out that four of Clive's goals were from the penalty spot, but bearing in mind how much tighter defences were 24 years on, there was no belittling Allen's towering achievement.

He scored three times at Villa Park on the opening day of the season, and never stopped scoring after that. The prompting and the openings came from the likes of Waddle, Hoddle and Ardiles.

The abrupt departure of David Pleat after just one season in charge led to far-reaching changes at Tottenham, and a year later Allen followed Glenn Hoddle into French football when he joined Bordeaux.

Allen later played for Manchester City, Chelsea and West Ham.

Was it a penalty? Watford's Steve Sims makes contact with Arsenal's Niall Quinn, and several Arsenal players stopped after seeing the linesman's flag. Referee Brian Stevens played on, and Luther Blissett scored for Watford

High drama at Highbury

The suspension of recorded highlights meant that Jimmy Hill's juicy Saturday night 'inquests' on events seen in *Match of the Day* were now a rare event. But on 14 March 1987, the programme made a brief return to its old slot to cover two matches in the FA Cup sixth round.

The tie between Arsenal and Watford at Highbury had connotations before a ball was kicked. The FA had appointed as referee Brian Stevens of Gloucestershire, who earlier in the season had sent off Watford keeper Tony Coton, in the League meeting between the two clubs at Highbury.

Watford's manager, Graham Taylor, said publicly that he thought it unwise for the same referee to be in charge for the Cup tie. Arsenal, in turn, felt Taylor's comments might influence events just as much as what had happened earlier.

Stevens kept the job, and for the greater part of the game met with nothing contentious. Ian Allinson put Arsenal ahead, but Watford's David Bardsley gave Kenny Sansom a harrowing afternoon, making goals for Luther Blissett and John Barnes.

So it was that Arsenal were trailing 1–2 late in the game, when Steve Sims challenged Niall Quinn in the Watford penalty area. There was contact between the two players, and Arsenal appealed that Quinn had been pushed.

Linesman Graham Crafter raised his yellow flag, but in a sea of colour it was hard to pick out. Referee Stevens followed the play as Watford broke clear, while several Arsenal players forgot the golden rule of playing to the whistle.

Blissett broke away, had his first shot saved by John Lukic, then netted the rebound. Infuriated Arsenal players drew the attention of Stevens to his colleague on the line, but after a consultation the goal was allowed to stand.

When the final whistle signalled Arsenal's exit from the FA Cup, there was an ugly scene on the touchline in which Arsenal's Steve Williams confronted Watford manager Graham Taylor. When all the fuss died down, Watford were through to the semi-final. And deservedly so. A re-examination of the video shows them to be clearly the better side, and the 'push' by Sims is barely discernible.

Mind you, there was hot debate in the pubs around Highbury that night. And many customers regained the habit of putting down their pint in time for *Match of the Day*.

EVEN BY LIVERPOOL'S standards, this was a remarkable season. Hurt by finishing the previous campaign empty-handed and losing Ian Rush to Juventus, they sent the First Division running for cover even before a ball was kicked by signing John Barnes and Peter Beardsley to link up with another recent acquisition John Aldridge. But it was the versatile Steve Nicol who stole the honours in the first live BBC match at St James' Park. He scored a hat-trick as Liverpool won 4–1 against a Newcastle side including the Brazilian import, Mirandinha, but missing the injured Paul Gascoigne.

Liverpool scored 28 goals in their first nine games, and equalled Leeds United's record of 29 First Division games unbeaten from the start of the season. Everton were the first side to beat them, but by now Liverpool's eyes were on their second 'double', having already won at Goodison Park in the fifth round of the FA Cup in front of the cameras.

As is often the case, the FA Cup had a mind of its own in 1988. Port Vale's victory over Spurs in the fourth round spoiled the start of Terry Venables's time at Tottenham, but Wimbledon's victory over Liverpool at Wembley belonged purely to football folklore.

When Dennis Wise scored their winning goal against Luton in the semi-final, Wimbledon celebrated like a Sunday side, and manager Bobby Gould had to push his players back on to the field.

Talking of Sundays, they remained the chosen day for televised football on both channels. But what nobody at the BBC realised then, was that *Match of the Day* was not to screen another league match for at least four years.

Heads you win, headbands you lose. Lawrie Sanchez (arms raised, left) has just scored for Wimbledon, and Gary Gillespie (No. 2) and Liverpool are on the other end of a monumental FA Cup final upset

20/9/87	**Newcastle United** ....**1** McDonald	**Liverpool** ....**4** Nicol (3) Aldridge	*Division One*
17/10/87	**Liverpool** ....**4** Johnston Aldridge (pen.) Barnes (2)	**Queens Park Rangers** **0**	*Division One*
1/11/87	**Liverpool** ....**2** McMahon Beardsley	**Everton** **0**	*Division One*
22/11/87	**Derby County** ....**2** Cross Gregory	**Chelsea** **0**	*Division One*
13/12/87	**Coventry City** **0**	**Arsenal** **0**	*Division One*
28/12/87	**Manchester United** ....**2** McClair (2) (1 pen.)	**Everton** ....**1** Watson	*Division One*
	Tottenham Hotspur ....**2** Waddle Fairclough	**West Ham United** ....**1** Hilton	*Division One*
	Wimbledon ....**3** Cork Wise Jones	**Arsenal** ....**1** Quinn	*Division One*
3/1/88	**Everton** ....**1** Clarke	**Nottingham Forest**...............**0**	*Division One*
10/1/88	**Ipswich Town** ....**1** Humes	**Manchester United** ....**2** D'Avray (o.g.) Anderson	*FA Cup 3rd round*
16/1/88	**Liverpool** ....**2** Aldridge Beardsley	**Arsenal** **0**	*Division One*
24/1/88	**Arsenal** ....**1** Quinn	**Manchester United** ....**2** Strachan McClair	*Division One*
30/1/88	**Manchester United** ....**2** Whiteside McClair	**Chelsea** **0**	*FA Cup 4th round*
	Port Vale ....**2** Walker Sproson	**Tottenham Hotspur**..............**1** Ruddock	*FA Cup 4th round*
	Leyton Orient......................**1** Juryeff	**Nottingham Forest**...............**2** Glover Plummer	*FA Cup 4th round*
21/2/88	**Everton** **0**	**Liverpool** ....**1** Houghton	*FA Cup 5th round*

28/2/88	**Luton Town** ....2 B. Stein Grimes	**Oxford United** 0	*Littlewoods Cup semi-final second leg*
6/3/88	**Arsenal** ....2 Smith Groves	**Tottenham Hotspur**..............1 C. Allen	*Division One*
12/3/88	**Arsenal** ....1 Rocastle	**Nottingham Forest**................2 Wilkinson Rice	*FA Cup 6th round*
	Wimbledon ....2 Young Fashanu	**Watford**..............................1 Allen	*FA Cup 6th round*
	Luton Town ....3 Wilson M. Stein Harford	**Portsmouth** ....1 Quinn	*FA Cup 6th round*
4/4/88	**Portsmouth** 0	**Nottingham Forest**...............1 Wilson	*Division One*
	Liverpool ....3 Beardsley Gillespie McMahon	**Manchester United** ....3 Robson (2) Strachan	*Division One*
9/4/88	**Liverpool** ....2 Aldridge (2) (1 pen.)	**Nottingham Forest**...............1 Clough	*FA Cup semi-final*
	Luton Town ....1 Harford	**Wimbledon** ....2 Fashanu (pen.) Wise	*FA Cup semi-final*
14/5/88	**Wimbledon** ....1 Sanchez	**Liverpool** 0	*FA Cup final*

MATCH OF THE SEASON
Liverpool 5
Nottingham Forest 0
at Anfield,
Wednesday 13 April 1988

Tom Finney said: 'It was one of the finest exhibitions of football I have seen in my life. I doubt whether it will ever be bettered for sheer entertainment.'

This was a huge compliment

Close to perfection. Ray Houghton scores one of the five goals in what was described as Liverpool's most complete performance in 30 years of televised success from one of football's finest, and no less than Liverpool deserved as they gave a 40,000 crowd and millions of BBC viewers a treat they would never forget.

Liverpool simply took Forest to pieces with a bewildering display of mature, one-touch football.

The purity of Liverpool's play was epitomised by their passing, like the sweet one-two which brought the first goal for Houghton, courtesy of Barnes. Aldridge got the second after a raking pass by Beardsley; Gillespie the third before Forest realised a corner had been taken; more magic from Barnes set up the fourth for Beardsley; Beardsley then combined with Spackman to carve out number five for Aldridge.

It was unquestionably the gala performance as Liverpool strode majestically to their 17th Championship.

Liverpool: Grobbelaar, Gillespie, Ablett, Nicol, Spackman, Hansen, Beardsley, Aldridge, Houghton (sub. Johnston), Barnes, McMahon (sub. Molby).
Scorers: Aldridge (2), Houghton, Beardsley, Gillespie

Nottingham Forest: Sutton, Chettle, Pearce, Walker (sub. Wassall), Foster, Wilson, Crosby, Webb, Clough, Glover, Rice

* This match does not appear in the statistics for the 1987–88 season because it was shown in *Sportsnight* not *Match of the Day*. However, the sheer quality of Liverpool's performance in front of BBC cameras demanded its inclusion.

PLAYER OF THE SEASON
John Barnes (Liverpool)

The colour of John Barnes's skin was never a sensitive issue on Merseyside once the Liverpool supporters saw the culture of his football. That moment came in his fifth League match at Anfield, against the hitherto First Division leaders, Queens Park Rangers. Barnes produced two individual goals of such breathtaking quality in front of the Kop, that Liverpool knew instantly they had purchased a rare jewel.

Barnes arrived from Watford in the wake of Ian Rush's departure to Italy. He gelled at once with Peter Beardsley and John Aldridge to form one of Liverpool's most prolific attacks.

When Barnes wasn't scoring goals, he was making them. His ability to glide effortlessly past opponents, his cunning crosses and explosive shooting, made such an impression on Liverpool fans that some chose to stand to the right of the goal so that they could better appreciate his line of attack.

They probably got a lot closer than some of Barnes's opponents. His professional peers voted him their Player of the Year, and the Football Writers' Association did likewise.

Black players made a huge impression on the game in the 80s. None made a bigger or better one than John Barnes.

THE SILVER JUBILEE OF *Match of the Day*, just like the programme's Coming of Age four years earlier, was overshadowed by a dreadful disaster. The ramifications and repercussions of Hillsborough, where 95 Liverpool fans lost their lives, were far-reaching, but at the time the sense of grief and personal loss made football meaningless.

The tragedy occurred in the first season of a new television arrangement, whereby ITV bought exclusive rights to Football League matches, and the BBC linked up with the new satellite channel, British Sky Broadcasting, to secure coverage of the FA Cup and England matches. There was no *Match of the Day* until November, when the programme returned with coverage of the first round proper of the FA Cup. Third and Fourth Division clubs received full camera coverage for the first time.

One or two were embarrassed by it. *Match of the Day – The Road to Wembley*, to give the programme its new title, tumbled across non-Leaguers Enfield, Kettering and Sutton putting paid to Leyton Orient, Bristol Rovers and Coventry (*see* 'Match of the Season', page 202).

And the shocks did not end there. Bradford City knocked out Tottenham, and Bournemouth came within a Luther Blissett miss of beating Manchester United.

Liverpool and Nottingham Forest met for the second year running in the semi-final at Hillsborough. In each of the preceding four rounds, the BBC had screened one match live on Sunday, but the FA wished to preserve the semi-final tradition and play both matches on Saturday afternoon. Thus it was that the grim truth of the Hillsborough disaster unfolded before a devastated *Grandstand* audience. It was left to *Match of the Day* in the evening to tell the whole, horrible story about what had happened at the Leppings Lane End.

Three weeks later, the replayed semi-final was shown live from

Old Trafford on a Sunday lunchtime. In a suitably muted atmosphere, Liverpool won 3–1 and went on to beat Everton in extra-time at Wembley.

The whole nation shared the mourning on Merseyside. It was a grim reflection on football in *Match of the Day*'s 25th season.

Football's blackest day. Fans who have escaped from the Leppings Lane terrace tell Liverpool's Steve Nicol the extent of the tragedy. Moments later the players left the pitch and it was subsequently learned that 95 Liverpool supporters had lost their lives in the crush behind the fences

20/8/88	**Liverpool** ....2 Aldridge (2)	**Wimbledon** ....1 Fashanu	*FA Charity Shield*
19/11/88	**Enfield** ....1 Furlong	**Leyton Orient**......................1 Ward	*FA Cup 1st round*
	Southport 0	**Port Vale** ....2 Sproson Riley	*FA Cup 1st round*
10/12/88	**Kettering Town** ....2 Cooke (2)	**Bristol Rovers**.....................1 Reece	*FA Cup 2nd round*
	Altrincham..........................0	**Halifax Town** ....3 W. Barr Allison (2)	*FA Cup 2nd round*
7/1/89	**Sutton United** ....2 Rains Hanlan	**Coventry City** ....1 Phillips	*FA Cup 3rd round*
	Bradford City ....1 Mitchell	**Tottenham Hotspur**..............0	*FA Cup 3rd round*
	West Bromwich Albion ....1 Anderson	**Everton** ....1 Sheedy (pen.)	*FA Cup 3rd round*
8/1/89	**West Ham United** ....2 Dickens Bould (o.g.)	**Arsenal** ....2 Merson (2)	*FA Cup 3rd round*
	Port Vale ....1 Webb	**Norwich City**.......................3 Townsend (2) Fleck	*FA Cup 3rd round*
23/1/89	**Manchester United** ....3 McClair (2) (1 pen.) Robson	**Queens Park Rangers** 0	*FA Cup 3rd round second replay*
28/1/89	**Norwich City**........................8 Putney Allen (4) Fleck (3)	**Sutton United** 0	*FA Cup 4th round*
	Charlton Athletic ....2 Williams Lee	**Kettering Town** ....1 Cooke	*FA Cup 4th round*
	Aston Villa 0	**Wimbledon** ....1 Jones	*FA Cup 4th round*
	Plymouth Argyle..................1 McCarthy	**Everton** ....1 Sheedy (pen.)	*FA Cup 4th round*
29/1/89	**Millwall**...............................0	**Liverpool** ....2 Rush Aldridge	*FA Cup 4th round*

18/2/89	**Hull City** 2	**Liverpool** 3	*FA Cup 5th round*
	Whitehurst	Barnes	
	Edwards	Aldridge (2)	
	Barnsley 0	**Everton** 1	*FA Cup 5th round*
		Sharp	
	AFC Bournemouth 1	**Manchester United** 1	*FA Cup 5th round*
	Aylott	Hughes	
	Wimbledon 3	**Grimsby Town** 1	*FA Cup 5th round*
	Fashanu	Alexander	
	Phelan		
	Wise		
	Norwich City 3	**Sheffield United** 2	*FA Cup 5th round*
	Thompson (o.g.)	Deane	
	Allen (pen.)	Agana	
	Gordon		
19/2/89	**Watford** 0	**Nottingham Forest** 3	*FA Cup 5th round*
		Webb	
		Chapman	
		Laws	
18/3/89	**Manchester United** 0	**Nottingham Forest** 1	*FA Cup 6th round*
		Parker	
	Liverpool 4	**Brentford** 0	*FA Cup 6th round*
	McMahon		
	Barnes		
	Beardsley (2)		
	West Ham United 0	**Norwich City** 0	*FA Cup 6th round*
19/3/89	**Everton** 1	**Wimbledon** 0	*FA Cup 6th round*
	McCall		
15/4/89	**Hillsborough disaster**		
7/5/89	**Liverpool** 3	**Nottingham Forest** 1	*FA Cup semi-final*
	Aldridge (2)	Webb	
	Laws (o.g.)		
20/5/89	**Liverpool** 3	**Everton** ....2 (a.e.t.)	*FA Cup final*
	Aldridge	McCall (2)	
	Rush (2)		

MATCH OF THE SEASON

Sutton United 2
Coventry City 1
(*FA Cup third round*)
at Ganders Green Lane,
Saturday 7 January 1989

Barrie Williams was not quoting his beloved Shakespeare that Saturday morning. He was cursing his players on a muddy recreation ground in suburban Surrey, because corner kicks they were practising were not working.

Three hours later, two of them worked flawlessly. Sutton United, of the GM Vauxhall Conference, became only the fifth non-League team to beat a First Division side in the FA Cup.

Their victims were Coventry City, winners of the trophy just 20 months earlier. It was boys' fiction stuff, with long-serving captain Tony Rains and bricklayer Matthew Hanlan scoring the goals from corners by Mickey Stephens.

Sutton enjoyed three glorious weeks in the limelight, before they came down to earth with a bump at Norwich in the fourth round. They lost 8–0 in front of the cameras, but they kept their dignity and their memories.

Sutton United: Roffey, Jones, Rains, Golley, Pratt, Rogers, Stephens, Dawson, Dennis, McKinnon, Hanlan.
Scorers: Rains, Hanlan

Coventry City: Orgizovic, Borrows, Phillips, Sedgley, Kilcline, Peake, Bennett, Speedie, Regis (sub. Houchen), McGrath, Smith.
Scorer: Phillips

A shock in suburbia. Sutton captain Tony Rains turns away after scoring their first goal against Coventry. It was an early coup for the re-titled *Match of the Day – The Road To Wembley*

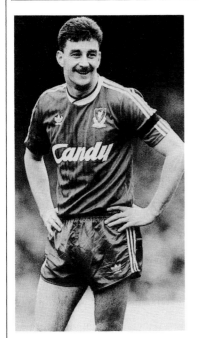

PLAYER OF THE SEASON
John Aldridge (Liverpool)

When Liverpool announced just two days before the start of the season that Ian Rush was coming back from Juventus, it was generally assumed that the man to make way for him would be John Aldridge.

But Aldridge, who had scored 29 goals in his first season at Anfield, had other ideas. He promptly got both goals in Liverpool's victory over Wimbledon in the Charity Shield, and equalled his figure of 29 for the season while Rush spent much of the time either injured or on the bench.

Match of the Day – The Road to Wembley showed that, if necessary, the pair could play together. They each got one of Liverpool's goals in the fourth round at Millwall, but it was Aldridge whose two goals got Liverpool out of trouble at Hull a round later.

In the replayed semi-final at Old Trafford, Aldridge scored twice to send Liverpool to Wembley, where he exorcised the ghost of his penalty miss a year earlier, by putting his side in front against Everton in their first attack.

After a spell in Spain, Aldridge returned to Merseyside with Tranmere Rovers in the 1991/2 season. Fittingly, he scored the 300th goal of his career in front of the *Match of the Day* cameras.

WHEN *Match of the Day – The Road to Wembley* returned in January to mark the start of the 90s, it had a ready-made story which ran and ran. That story featured Alex Ferguson and Manchester United.

When the draw was made for the FA Cup third round, United were lying an unpromising 15th in the First Division table and already out of the Littlewoods Cup. As the balls came out of the bag, Ferguson winced. They had to travel to Nottingham Forest.

The media build-up to the game turned it into 'Fergie's Last Stand', but United won with a goal by Mark Robins, and suddenly their FA Cup run became a roller-coaster ride.

In the fourth round, they won at Hereford with a Clayton Blackmore goal. Then it was away to Newcastle, where goals by Robins, Danny Wallace and Brian McClair put United into the quarter-finals. Ferguson's position had eased, but only partly, when McClair's goal brought victory at Sheffield United. There was still plenty of agony to endure in the semi-final against Oldham.

For the first time both semi-finals were televised live, and what a Sunday treat it turned out to be for BBC viewers.

At High Noon, Liverpool took on Steve Coppell's Crystal Palace and seemed to be coasting to Wembley thanks to Ian Rush's first-half goal. But the London side stormed back to win a thrilling match 4–3 after extra-time, Alan Pardew's winning header symptomatic of the way they exposed Liverpool's defence in the air.

'Follow that', said the fans at Villa Park, but Oldham and Manchester United did just that at Maine Road. They drew 3–3 after extra-time, with United winning the replay thanks to a goal by Robins.

At Wembley, Palace and United managed another 3–3 draw, making it a total of 19 goals in three matches for the BBC.

Oh yes, and Alex Ferguson won the cup and kept his job!

The Cup can make anyone famous. Crystal Palace's unsung Alan Pardew has just headed the winning goal against Liverpool in the semi-final at Villa Park. Palace won 4–3 in extra time

12/8/89	**Liverpool** .... **1** Beardsley	**Arsenal** **0**	*FA Charity Shield*
18/11/89	**Blackpool** .... **2** Eyres Garner	**Bolton Wanderers** .... **1** Crombie	*FA Cup 1st round*
	Kettering Town **0**	**Northampton Town** .... **1** Thomas	*FA Cup 1st round*
	Macclesfield Town .... **1** Burr	**Chester City** .... **1** Painter	*FA Cup 1st round*
9/12/89	**Whitley Bay** .... **2** Todd Robinson	**Preston North End** **0**	*FA Cup 2nd round*
	Colchester United **0**	**Birmingham City** .... **2** Gleghorn (2)	*FA Cup 2nd round*
6/1/90	**Blackburn Rovers** .... **2** Stapleton Sellars	**Aston Villa** .... **2** Olney Ormondroyd	*FA Cup 3rd round*
	Exeter City .... **1** Rowbotham	**Norwich City** .... **1** Fleck	*FA Cup 3rd round*
	Stoke City **0**	**Arsenal** .... **1** Quinn	*FA Cup 3rd round*
	Swansea City **0**	**Liverpool** **0**	*FA Cup 3rd round*
7/1/90	**Nottingham Forest** **0**	**Manchester United** .... **1** Robins	*FA Cup 3rd round*
27/1/90	**Arsenal** **0**	**Queens Park Rangers** **0**	*FA Cup 4th round*
	Bristol City .... **3** Turner (2) Gavin	**Chelsea** .... **1** K. Wilson	*FA Cup 4th round*
	West Bromwich Albion .... **1** Ford	**Charlton Athletic** **0**	*FA Cup 4th round*
28/1/90	**Norwich City** **0**	**Liverpool** **0**	*FA Cup 4th round*
	Hereford United **0**	**Manchester United** .... **1** Blackmore	*FA Cup 4th round*
	Sheffield Wednesday .... **1** Hirst	**Everton** .... **2** Whiteside (2)	*FA Cup 4th round*
17/2/90	**Oldham Athletic** .... **2** Ritchie (pen.) Palmer	**Everton** .... **2** Sharp Cottee	*FA Cup 5th round*
	Liverpool .... **3** Rush Beardsley Nicol	**Southampton** **0**	*FA Cup 5th round*
	West Bromwich Albion **0**	**Aston Villa** .... **2** Mountfield Daley	*FA Cup 5th round*

18/2/90	**Newcastle United** ....2 McGhee (pen.) Scott	**Manchester United** ....3 Robins Wallace McClair	*FA Cup 5th round*
	Blackpool ....2 Groves Eyres	**Queens Park Rangers** ....2 Clarke (2)	*FA Cup 5th round*
	Sheffield United ....2 Bradshaw Bryson	**Barnsley** ....2 Smith Cooper	*FA Cup 5th round*
10/3/90	**Oldham Athletic** ....2 Palmer Marshall (pen.)	**Everton** ....1 Cottee	*FA Cup 5th round second replay*
	Cambridge United 0	**Crystal Palace** ....1 Thomas	*FA Cup 6th round*
11/3/90	**Queens Park Rangers** ....2 Wilkins Barker	**Liverpool** ....2 Barnes Rush	*FA Cup 6th round*
	Sheffield United 0	**Manchester United** ....1 McClair	*FA Cup 6th round*
8/4/90	**Crystal Palace** ....4 Bright O'Reilly Gray Pardew	**Liverpool** ....3 (a.e.t.) Rush McMahon Barnes (pen.)	*FA Cup semi-final*
	Manchester United ....3 Robson Webb Wallace	**Oldham Athletic** ....3 (a.e.t.) Barrett Marshall Palmer	*FA Cup semi-final*
11/4/90	**Manchester United** ....2 McClair Robins	**Oldham Athletic** ....1 (a.e.t.) Ritchie	*FA Cup semi-final replay*
12/5/90	**Crystal Palace** ....3 O'Reilly Wright (2)	**Manchester United** .....3 (a.e.t.) Robson Hughes (2)	*FA Cup final*
17/5/90	**Crystal Palace** 0	**Manchester United** ....1 Martin	*FA Cup final replay*

MATCH OF THE SEASON

Whitley Bay 2
Preston North End 0
(*FA Cup 2nd round*)
at Hillheads Park,
Saturday 9 December 1989

The two semi-finals and the FA Cup final have all been well documented elsewhere, so the democracy of the competition is better served by recalling *Match of the Day*'s visit to the north-east, where one of the upsets that gives the Cup its true character occurred on an afternoon of biting winds on the Northumberland coast.

It was Preston who felt the chill. Proud Preston North End, the first winners of the Football League, and the first team to carry off the League and Cup double.

Whitley Bay, whose main ambition was to win promotion to the Premier Division of the HFS Loans League, had come to the nation's attention by winning at Fourth Division Scarborough in the first round.

Third Division Preston, managed by John McGrath, found the cramped ground and muddy conditions far from their liking. Defender Peter Robinson shot Whitley Bay ahead in the first half. The killer goal, from a sweeping move belonging to a higher grade of football, was struck by Kevin Todd, whose main claim to television fame before this was as the scorer of Newcastle's 'other' goal when Kevin Keegan scored four at Rotherham in 1982.

Whitley Bay: Dickson, Liddell, Teasdale, Robinson, Gowans, Johnson, Walker (sub. Haire), Dawson, Chandler (sub. Gamble), Todd, Pearson.
Scorers: Robinson, Todd

Preston: Kelly, Williams, Swann, Atkins, Joyce, Hughes, Mooney (sub. Flynn), Ellis, Bogie, Patterson, Harper

---

Coverage of the first and second rounds of the FA Cup brought a succession of teams from outside the Football League in front of the cameras. Whitley Bay's victory over Preston showed the gap between the part-timers and full professionals had narrowed in the *Match of the Day* era

PLAYER OF THE SEASON

Bryan Robson
(Manchester United)

When the England captain Bryan Robson went up the Wembley steps to receive the FA Cup after his club's 1–0 victory in the replay against Crystal Palace, he became the first captain to do so three times.

Robson had led United to their victory over Brighton in 1983 – scoring twice in the replay – and also collected a winners' medal and the trophy when his club defeated Everton in the 1985 final.

In 1990, on the eve of his departure to the World Cup in Italy, his contribution was just as emphatic. Robson scored in the first semi-final against Oldham at Maine Road, then headed United's equaliser at Wembley after Gary O'Reilly had put Palace in front.

The late 70s saw the young Robson first emerge on *Match of the Day* as a versatile member of Ron Atkinson's team at West Bromwich Albion, who qualified for Europe three years out of four. He joined Atkinson again at Manchester United in 1981 for a then record fee of £1.5 million, and for the next decade led United and England with a fearless disregard for his own well-being which earned him the nickname 'Captain Marvel'.

When United went to the top of the table above Leeds in January 1992, Robson was celebrating his 35th birthday. Earlier that season, he played his 90th and last match for England.

But another in the series of nagging injuries which were sent to try him, meant that Robson missed critical league matches as Manchester United faded in the Championship race and finished second to Leeds United.

BRIAN CLOUGH's managerial career had run just about concurrently with *Match of the Day*. In the programme's first season, injury brought his playing career to a premature end and he joined Hartlepool United as manager.

In his days at Derby, Clough became a high-profile figure on the BBC. His team produced some charming football, and his presence as an analyst brought a new dimension to football on television. Later, Clough 'defected' to ITV and to Nottingham Forest, where he had been manager for 16 years when he appeared on *Match of the Day – The Road to Wembley* in an interview after his team had drawn at Crystal Palace in the FA Cup third round.

The Forest–Palace saga dragged on. The replay was twice postponed through the weather, then the teams drew again at the City Ground, with Palace's John Salako equalising in the last minute with a chipped shot from all of 45 yards.

Finally, Forest got through. They needed another replay to dispose of Newcastle in the fourth round – Forest were two down in the first match – and by the time they beat Southampton in round five, again after a replay, the country started to believe that this could be Cloughie's year. He had never reached an FA Cup final as player or manager, but when Forest won at Norwich in the sixth round, the omens all pointed his way. Especially when West Ham had defender Tony Gale contentiously sent off early in the semi-final at Villa Park. Forest ran out comfortable winners and the Clough family – Nigel was at centre-forward – prepared for a day out at Wembley.

There was no happy ending, however. Forest were beaten by Spurs and Clough Senior was kept waiting for the only major trophy he had never won. But largely thanks to his presence and that of Paul Gascoigne, the BBC's FA Cup final audience of 15 million was the highest for many years.

Gary's glory. Despite having a penalty saved in the final, Tottenham's Gary Lineker won his first major medal in English football. He also became England captain under Graham Taylor

18/8/90	**Liverpool** ....1 Barnes (pen.)	**Manchester United** ....1 Blackmore	FA Charity Shield
17/11/90	**Witton Albion** ....1 Thomas	**Bolton Wanderers** ....2 Darby Comstive	FA Cup 1st round
	Aylesbury United 0	**Walsall** ....1 McDonald	FA Cup 1st round
	Telford United....................0	**Stoke City**..........................0	FA Cup 1st round
8/12/90	**Barnet** 0	**Northampton Town** 0	FA Cup 2nd round
	AFC Bournemouth ....1 Brooks	**Hayes** 0	FA Cup 2nd round
	Swansea City ....2 Connor Gilligan (pen.)	**Walsall** ....1 Hutchings	FA Cup 2nd round
5/1/91	**Blackburn Rovers** ....1 Garner	**Liverpool** ....1 Atkins (o.g.)	FA Cup 3rd round
	Blackpool 0	**Tottenham Hotspur**..............1 Stewart	FA Cup 3rd round
	Barnet 0	**Portsmouth** ....5 Aspinall Whittingham (3) Clarke	FA Cup 3rd round
6/1/91	**Crystal Palace** 0	**Nottingham Forest**..............0	FA Cup 3rd round
	Burnley 0	**Manchester City**..................1 Hendry	FA Cup 3rd round
7/1/91	**Manchester United** ....2 Hughes McClair	**Queens Park Rangers** ....1 Maddix	FA Cup 3rd round
21/1/91	**Nottingham Forest**...............2 Wilson Pearce	**Crystal Palace** ....2 (a.e.t.) Wright Salako	FA Cup 3rd round replay
26/1/91	**Tottenham Hotspur**..............4 Mabbutt Lineker Gascoigne (2)	**Oxford United** ....2 Foyle (2)	FA Cup 4th round
	Port Vale ....1 Beckford	**Manchester City**..................2 Quinn Allen	FA Cup 4th round
	Coventry City ....1 Kilcline	**Southampton** ....1 Shearer (pen.)	FA Cup 4th round
27/1/91	**Arsenal** 0	**Leeds United** 0	FA Cup 4th round
	Everton ....1 Sheedy	**Woking** 0	FA Cup 4th round

28/1/91	**Nottingham Forest**..........3 Parker (2) Crosby	**Crystal Palace** 0	*FA Cup 3rd round second replay*
16/2/91	**Leeds United** ....1 Chapman	**Arsenal** ....2 Merson Dixon	*FA Cup 4th round third replay*
	Notts County ....1 Lund	**Manchester City**..........0	*FA Cup 5th round*
	Portsmouth................1 Chamberlain	**Tottenham Hotspur**..........2 Gascoigne (2)	*FA Cup 5th round*
	West Ham United ....1 Quinn	**Crewe Alexandra** 0	*FA Cup 5th round*
17/2/91	**Liverpool** 0	**Everton** 0	*FA Cup 5th round*
18/2/91	**Nottingham Forest**..........3 Clough Hodge Parker	**Newcastle United** 0	*FA Cup 4th round replay*
	Norwich City................2 Fleck Gordon	**Manchester United** ....1 McClair	*FA Cup 5th round*
25/2/91	**Southampton** ....1 Ruddock	**Nottingham Forest**.........1 Hodge	*FA Cup 5th round*
4/3/91	**Nottingham Forest**.........3 Jemson (3) (1 pen.)	**Southampton** ....1 Rod Wallace	*FA Cup 5th round replay*
9/3/91	**Arsenal** ....2 Campbell Adams	**Cambridge United** ....1 Dublin	*FA Cup 6th round*
	Norwich City................0	**Nottingham Forest**.........1 Keane	*FA Cup 6th round*
10/3/91	**Tottenham Hotspur**.........2 Nayim Gascoigne	**Notts County** ....1 O'Riordan	*FA Cup 6th round*
11/3/91	**West Ham United** ....2 Foster Slater	**Everton** ....1 Watson	*FA Cup 6th round*
14/4/91	**Arsenal** ....1 Smith	**Tottenham Hotspur**..........3 Gascoigne Lineker (2)	*FA Cup semi-final*
	Nottingham Forest.........4 Crosby Keane Pearce Charles	**West Ham United** 0	*FA Cup semi-final*
18/5/91	**Nottingham Forest**.........1 Pearce	**Tottenham Hotspur**......2 (a.e.t.) Stewart Walker (o.g.)	*FA Cup final*

SEASON
1990–1

MATCH OF THE SEASON

**Blackburn Rovers 1
Liverpool 1
(*FA Cup third round*)
at Ewood Park,
Saturday 5 January 1991**

Liverpool, League champions and First Division leaders, were within a minute of an inglorious FA Cup exit. Blackburn Rovers, 19th in the Second Division, were leading 1–0 when the ball squirted out of play on the left flank of their defence.

An obliging ball-girl returned the ball to Steve Nicol, who threw it to Ray Houghton. His cross went over Gary Gillespie, who was baulked by a defender, and flew agonisingly off the foot of Blackburn right-back Mark Atkins into his own goal.

Such was the thin line between celebration and despair for Rovers. They scarcely had time to kick off before the final whistle went, condemning them to an unappetising replay at Anfield – and inevitable defeat.

It was a Cup-tie which bristled with incident. Ronnie Rosenthal missed two early chances for Liverpool; Simon Garner scored early in the second half for Blackburn. Kevin Moran of Blackburn and Glenn Hysen of Liverpool were sent off for professional fouls.

Atkins apart, most of the sympathy was reserved for Blackburn manager, Don Mackay. Early the following season he was dismissed – and his replacement was the man who had escaped in the dying seconds that day eight months earlier . . . Kenny Dalglish.

Blackburn Rovers: Mimms, Atkins, Duxbury, Reid, May, Moran, Gayle (sub. Johnrose), Miller, Stapleton, Garner, Sellars (sub. Shepstone).
Scorer: Garner

Liverpool: Grobbelaar, Hysen, Burrows, Nicol, Staunton (sub. Molby), Gillespie, Rosenthal, Houghton, Rush, Barnes, McMahon.
Scorer: Atkins (o.g.)

Breaking point? Tension on the face of Kenny Dalglish (right) as Liverpool trail at Ewood Park. Six weeks later, Dalglish resigned under personal stress. Ironically, he returned to the game in the 1991–92 season – as manager of Blackburn!

PLAYER OF THE SEASON
Paul Gascoigne
(Tottenham Hotspur)

His reckless tackle in the FA Cup final which led to his knee having to be virtually rebuilt will always haunt the World Cup hero who became known simply as 'Gazza'. He was probably even better known than Prime Minister John Major!

But Spurs fans prefer to remember the way that Gascoigne *got* the team to Wembley. Certainly, his manager Terry Venables, who became co-owner of the club after their Wembley success, had reason to look back on a major contribution from Gascoigne in every round.

From the moment he made the only goal at Blackpool for Paul Stewart in round three, Gazza seemed destined to prove that old adage that Spurs always win a Cup when the year ends in a one. In the fourth round, he scored two brilliant goals against Oxford, bettered only by the two he conjured up at Portsmouth, where Spurs trailed at half-time in round five.

In the quarter-final, Gascoigne settled a tight match against Notts County with the winning goal, then went into hospital for an operation to repair a hole in the wall of his stomach.

Five weeks later, he was back with the Goal of the Season. His free-kick against Arsenal in the semi-final at Wembley remains a towering testament to his unique personality.

MATCH OF THE DAY
SEASON
1991-2

A S MATCH OF THE DAY'S first season began with Liverpool back in 1964, so the 28th episode in the longest-running television football series ended with the same club at the centre of the screen.

The BBC reactivated their coverage of European club football by obtaining exclusive rights to Liverpool's matches in the UEFA Cup, following them to the quarter final. But it was in the FA Cup that the most successful club in the *Match of the Day* years served up unexpected drama.

Liverpool got to Wembley the hard way. After brushing aside Crewe with a John Barnes hat-trick, they were seen by BBC viewers to struggle against three Second Division sides. Bristol Rovers and Ipswich took them to replays and Portsmouth were within three minutes of victory in the semi-final at Highbury when Ronnie Whelan equalised.

It was after that match that Graeme Souness, in his first season as Liverpool manager, announced he was going into hospital for a triple heart by-pass operation. Five weeks later, Souness sat on the bench at Wembley under the scrutiny of the club doctor as well as hundreds of millions of television viewers around the world. They saw Liverpool beat another Second Division side, Sunderland, to win the FA Cup in their Centenary year.

The competition as a whole again lived up to its traditions and commanded considerable BBC audience figures. Quite apart from Wrexham (see 'Match of the Season'), Farnborough Town of the GM Vauxhall Conference pushed first division strugglers West Ham to a third round replay.

Viewers also saw the first penalty shoot-outs to settle FA Cup ties. None more agonising than that at Villa Park in the semi-final replay, when Jim Smith's Portsmouth were knocked out despite playing Liverpool for four hours without once being behind.

Heart-stopping stuff. Liverpool
manager Graeme Souness feels the
strain during the drawn FA Cup semi-
final against Portsmouth at Highbury.
Two days later, he was in hospital for
a triple heart by-pass operation

The season ended with England and Scotland preparing for the
European Championship finals in Sweden, but with the real
possibility of *Match of the Day* making a welcome return to the
BBC Saturday night schedule.

A joint bid for coverage of the new Premier League was initially
accepted from the BBC and BSkyB, with the satellite company
contributing the greater share of the £304 million offer over five
years. The plan would enable Sky to show 'live' matches on
Sunday afternoons and Monday evenings, with the BBC screening
highlights from two other games on Saturday night. ITV called
'foul' at this deal and tried for a High Court injunction, but the
application was rejected amidst much publicity.

| 10/8/91 | **Arsenal** ....0 | **Tottenham Hotspur**................0 | *FA Charity Shield* |

16/11/91	**Colchester United**................0	**Exeter City** 0	*FA Cup 1st round*
	Gretna 0	**Rochdale**..........................0	*FA Cup 1st round*
	Tranmere Rovers................3 Irons Aldridge (2)	**Runcorn** 0	*FA Cup 1st round*

7/12/91	**Enfield** ....1 Robinson	**Barnet** ....4 Carter (3) Bull	*FA Cup 2nd round*
	Bolton Wanderers ....3 Burke Reeves Philliskirk (pen.)	**Bradford City** ....1 Tinnion	*FA Cup 2nd round*
	York City..............................1 Hall	**Tranmere Rovers**................1 Morrissey	*FA Cup 2nd round*

4/1/92	**Wrexham**................................2 Thomas Watkin	**Arsenal** ....1 Smith	*FA Cup 3rd round*
	Middlesbrough ....2 Kernaghan Wilkinson	**Manchester City**....................1 Reid	*FA Cup 3rd round*
	Leicester City ....1 Smith	**Crystal Palace** 0	*FA Cup 3rd round*

| 5/1/92 | **Aston Villa** ....0 | **Tottenham Hotspur**................0 | *FA Cup 3rd round* |

| 6/1/92 | **Crewe Alexandra** ....0 | **Liverpool** 4
McManaman
Barnes (3) | *FA Cup 3rd round* |

| 14/1/92 | **Tottenham Hotspur**................0 | **Aston Villa** 1
Yorke | *FA Cup 3rd round replay* |
| | **West Ham United** 1
Morley | **Farnborough Town**................0 | *FA Cup 3rd round replay* |

| 15/1/92 | **Leeds United** ....0 | **Manchester United** 1
Hughes | *FA Cup 3rd round* |

25/1/92	**West Ham United** ....2 Dicks Morley	**Wrexham**............................2 Phillips L. Jones	*FA Cup 4th round*
	Leicester City ....1 Kitson	**Bristol City** ....2 Bent Dziekanowski	*FA Cup 4th round*
	Bolton Wanderers ....2 Walker Philliskirk (pen.)	**Brighton & Hove Albion**..........1 Meade	*FA Cup 4th round*

Date	Home	Score	Away	Score	Competition

26/1/92 **Chelsea** 1   **Everton** 0   *FA Cup 4th round*
Allen

27/1/92 **Southampton** 0   **Manchester United** 0   *FA Cup 4th round*

15/2/92 **Chelsea** 1   **Sheffield United** 0   *FA Cup 5th round*
Stuart

Sunderland 1   **West Ham United** 1   *FA Cup 5th round*
Byrne   Small

Nottingham Forest 4   **Bristol City** 1   *FA Cup 5th round*
Llewellyn (o.g.)   Dziekanowski
Clough
Pearce
Sheringham (pen.)

16/2/92 **Swindon Town** 1   **Aston Villa** 2   *FA Cup 5th round*
Mitchell   Yorke
Froggatt

Ipswich Town 0   **Liverpool** 0   *FA Cup 5th round*

Bolton Wanderers 2   **Southampton** 2   *FA Cup 5th round*
Walker   Hall (2)
Green

7/3/92 **Portsmouth** 1   **Nottingham Forest** 0   *FA Cup 6th round*
McLoughlin

Southampton 0   **Norwich City** 0   *FA Cup 6th round*

8/3/92 **Liverpool** 1   **Aston Villa** 0   *FA Cup 6th round*
Thomas

9/3/92 **Chelsea** 1   **Sunderland** 1   *FA Cup 6th round*
Allen   Byrne

5/4/92 **Liverpool** 1   **Portsmouth** .... 1 (a.e.t.)   *FA Cup semi-final*
Whelan   Anderton

Norwich City 0   **Sunderland** 1   *FA Cup semi-final*
Byrne

13/4/92 **Liverpool** 0   **Portsmouth** 0   *FA Cup semi-final replay*
(Liverpool won 3–1 on penalties)

9/5/92 **Liverpool** 2   **Sunderland** 0   *FA Cup final*
Thomas
Rush

17/5/92 **England** 1   **Brazil** 1   *Friendly*
Platt   Bebeto

3/6/92 **Finland** 1   **England** 2   *Friendly*
Hjelm (pen.)   Platt 2

Norway 0   **Scotland** 0   *Friendly*

MATCH OF THE SEASON

Wrexham 2 Arsenal 1
(*FA Cup third round*)
at the Racecourse Ground,
Saturday 4 January 1992

When the draw was made, this match had all the ingredients of a classic cup-tie. Wrexham had finished the previous season 92nd and last in the Football League, avoiding relegation only because there was no demotion to the GM Vauxhall Conference while the league increased its numbers. Arsenal had been crowned champions.

Admittedly, the crown was being worn a little uneasily by the time George Graham's illustrious outfit turned up in North Wales. Arsenal had been knocked out of the Rumbelows Cup by Coventry, rumbled in

Europe by Benfica, and were 16 points off the lead in the championship race.

But when Alan Smith put them in front just before half-time – just one of a string of chances they made in the first half – the Londoners looked home and dry against a Wrexham side made up of fast-fading veterans and promising youngsters.

With eight minutes to go, the score was still 1–0. Then David O'Leary was penalised for what seemed a fair challenge, and 37-year-old Mickey Thomas blasted the free-kick wide of David Seaman's right hand.

Two minutes later, Wrexham were ahead. As Tony Adams hesitated, 20-year-old Steve Watkin

squeezed his foot round the ball and sent it rolling past Seaman.

Arsenal desperately sought the equaliser. In the dying minutes, Jimmy Carter had the ball in the net, but a linesman's flag indicated an earlier, fractional offside against Paul Merson.

Wrexham, managed by Brian Flynn, coached by substitute Joey Jones, and inspired by two more former Welsh internationals, the itinerant Thomas and 36-year-old Gordon Davies, had pulled off a giantkilling coup to rank with the best.

It was probably the biggest cup shock of its kind since Herbert Chapman's Arsenal lost to third division Walsall nearly 60 years earlier.

Wrexham: O'Keefe, Thackeray, Hardy, Carey, Thomas, Sertori, Davies,Owen, Connolly, Watkin, Phillips.
Scorers: Thomas, Watkin

Arsenal: Seaman, Dixon, Winterburn, Hillier, O'Leary, Adams, Rocastle, Campbell (sub. Groves), Smith, Merson, Carter.
Scorer: Smith

Old enough to be his dad. Mickey Thomas (right) at the age of 37, celebrates with 20-year-old Steve Watkin after they had scored the goals which beat Arsenal.

Steve McManaman
(Liverpool)

Twenty-year-old Steve McManaman chose the FA Cup to announce his arrival on the English football scene and to salvage what by Liverpool's standards was a mediocre season. Yet when the 1991–92 campaign began, McManaman had not even started a first team match. Liverpool's horrendous catalogue of injuries when Graeme Souness took over meant he was catapulted from nowhere into the national spotlight.

BBC viewers had an early glimpse of the willowy figure who could play on either wing, when Liverpool eased their way back into European competition. But it was when the FA Cup got underway that the lad who supported Everton as a boy startled defenders with his close skill and proved himself a match winner.

In the third round, he scored against Crewe; in the fourth round, he rescued Liverpool in a replay against Bristol Rovers, scoring the equaliser and making the winner for Dean Saunders. In the fifth round, after Liverpool had trailed in extra time, he fired the winner against Ipswich.

When he was injured in the semi-final against Portsmouth at Highbury, it seemed McManaman's season was over. But five weeks later, following another injury to John Barnes, he returned to the side in the FA Cup final and made inroads through the Sunderland defence to swing the match in Liverpool's favour.

Twenty-eight years earlier, a Liverpool forward called Roger Hunt had scored the first goal on *Match of the Day*. As much as it is possible to predict anything in football, it seemed certain that one of his successors in the famous red shirt would be around to mark the programme's thirtieth anniversary.

NOTE

This list reflects the number of times clubs have been featured, home and away, in extended highlights coverage on *Match of the Day*. It does not include regional matches which were not seen nationwide.

Of the 93 clubs who competed in the four divisions of the Football League in the 1991–92 season, 86 have figured at least once on *Match of the Day*.

The seven teams whose names do not appear are Aldershot (wound up in 1992), Darlington, Doncaster Rovers, Hartlepool United, Maidstone United, Reading and Stockport County.

However, fans of these clubs may recall seeing short goal 'clips' from time to time, expecially in recent years when *Match of the Day – The Road To Wembley* has included a brief round-up of FA Cup ties not selected for main coverage.

#	Club	Apps	#	Club	Apps	#	Club	Apps
1	Liverpool	220	37	Portsmouth	21	74	Brentford	3
2	Manchester United	209		Swansea City	21		Kettering Town	3
3	Tottenham Hotspur	148	39	Bolton Wanderers	20		Sutton United	3
4	Arsenal	147		Notts County	20		Tranmere Rovers	3
5	Everton	139	41	Cardiff City	17	78	Bury	2
6	Leeds United	129	42	Charlton Athletic	16		Crewe Alexandra	2
7	Manchester City	123	43	Oxford United	15		Enfield	2
8	Chelsea	110		Wrexham	15		Halifax Town	2
9	West Ham United	109	45	Leyton Orient	14		Harlow Town	2
10	Ipswich Town	89	46	Millwall	13		Lincoln City	2
11	Nottingham Forest	87		Oldham Athletic	13		Southport	2
12	Southampton	82		Preston North End	13		Torquay United	2
13	Aston Villa	81		Swindon Town	13		Yeovil Town	2
14	Leicester City	76	50	Bristol Rovers	12	87	Altrincham	1
15	Derby County	75		Hull City	12		Aylesbury United	1
16	West Bromwich Albion	74		Wimbledon	12		Blyth Spartans	1
17	Wolverhampton Wanderers	73	53	Carlisle United	11		Boston United	1
18	Queens Park Rangers	72		Colchester United	11		Chester	1
19	Newcastle United	70		Plymouth Argyle	11		Chesterfield	1
20	Sunderland	58	56	Grimsby Town	9		Dagenham	1
21	Norwich City	57	57	AFC Bournemouth	8		Dartford	1
22	Coventry City	56		Huddersfield Town	8		Farnborough Town	1
23	Stoke City	53		Peterborough United	8		Gretna	1
24	Luton Town	49	60	Hereford United	7		Hayes	1
25	Birmingham City	47		Shrewsbury Town	7		Horwich RMI	1
26	Crystal Palace	44	62	Bradford City	6		Leatherhead	1
27	Sheffield Wednesday	43		Cambridge United	6		Macclesfield Town	1
	Watford	43		Rotherham United	6		Metropolitan Police	1
29	Sheffield United	40	65	Mansfield Town	5		Rochdale	1
30	Fulham	39		Northampton Town	5		Runcorn	1
31	Brighton and Hove Albion	37		York City	5		Scarborough	1
32	Burnley	35	68	Barnet	4		Scunthorpe United	1
33	Middlesbrough	32		Barnsley	4		Southend United	1
34	Bristol City	27		Exeter City	4		Telford United	1
35	Blackpool	24		Gillingham	4		Whitley Bay	1
36	Blackburn Rovers	23		Port Vale	4		Wigan Athletic	1
				Walsall	4		Witton Albion	1
							Woking	1

INDEX

Adams, Tony 220
Aldridge, John 174, 194, 198, 203
Allen, Clive 147, 188, 191, 192
Allison, Malcolm 28, 33, 90, 126
Anfield 8, 10, 14, 16, 40, 72, 97, 99, 107, 118, 148, 156–7, 166, 174, 175, 182, 197, 198, 203, 214
Antic, Raddy 164
Ardiles, Ossie 118, 119, 136, 192
Arsenal 10, 14–6, 34, 40, 47–8, 55, 63, 65, 73–5, 89–91, 99, 106, 109–10, 118, 125–6, 137, 147, 165, 166, 180–1, 188, 193, 215, 220
Astle, Jeff 55
Aston Villa 27, 82, 99, 110, 126, 136–7, 157, 167
Atkinson, Ron 10, 165, 191, 209

Ball, Alan 10, 29, 41, 73, 98
Barnes, John 193–94, 198, 216, 221
Baseball Ground 54, 99
BBC 8–10, 14–7, 21–2, 29, 33–4, 38, 40, 56, 65, 74–5, 90, 99, 106–8, 110, 116, 118–9, 125–6, 134–6, 147–8, 157, 166–7, 180–2, 186, 188–9, 191, 194, 198–9, 204, 210, 216, 221
Beardsley, Peter 172, 194, 198
Bell, Colin 33
Best, George 10–11, 15, 38, 47, 54, 64, 80–1, 99,107
Big Match, The 34
Birmingham City 72, 106, 118, 136
Blackburn Rovers 16, 165, 214
Blackpool 10, 47–8, 73, 82, 215
Blissett, Luther 193, 199
Bolton Wanderers 91, 97
Bond, John 136
Bowles, Stan 89–90
Bradford City 90, 165, 174–5, 199
Brady, Liam 125, 165
Brammall Lane 89, 99
Bremner, Billy 64, 81–2
Brighton & Hove Albion 83, 116, 165, 172, 209
Bristol City 135
Bristol Rovers 90, 116, 199, 216, 221
Brooking, Trevor 29

Brown, Sandy 40
Burkinshaw, Keith 116, 156
Busby, Sir Matt 23, 54

Callaghan, Ian 14
Carlisle United 73, 82
Carr, Willie 47
Catterick, Harry 73
Case, Jimmy 108, 134
Campbell, Bobby 125
Carrow Road 134
Celtic 45, 135, 166, 187
Charlton, Bobby 15–7, 21, 29, 38, 41, 54, 65
Charlton, Jack 34
Charlton Athletic 40–1, 174, 182
Channon, Mike 63, 98
Chelsea 10, 16, 22–3, 27, 38, 45–6, 56–7, 65, 73, 82, 90, 145, 147, 166, 182–3, 192
Chivers, Martin 80–1
City Ground 26, 210
Clarke, Allan 45, 55, 64
Clemence, Ray 72, 108, 134, 156, 191
Clough, Brian 41, 54, 82–3, 109, 117, 186, 210
Clough, Nigel 186, 210
Colchester United 47
Coppell, Steve 90, 204
Cormack, Peter 72
Corrigan, Joe 64
Cottee, Tony 182, 187
Coventry City 34, 47, 117, 135, 147, 166, 181, 192, 199, 202–3, 220
Cox, Arthur 145
Crawford, Ray 47
Crewe Alexandra 216, 221
Crooks, Garth 136, 146
Crystal Palace 90, 126, 147, 204–5, 209–10
Currie, Tony 89

Dalglish, Kenny 134–35, 173, 182–83, 214
Davenport, Peter 191
Davies, Barry 46, 55, 64, 188
Derby County 29, 41, 54, 81–3, 90, 99, 117, 126, 210
Docherty, Tommy 10, 16, 22–3, 27, 65, 81, 90

Earle, Steve 88–9
Elland Road 34, 55, 63
England 6, 14, 16–7, 21–2, 29, 39, 46, 65, 73–4, 89–91, 98, 118, 135, 148, 156–7, 167, 181, 186, 199, 209, 211, 216

European Championships 35, 38, 118, 126, 216
European Footballer of the Year 21, 107
European Cup 45, 97, 107–8, 110, 156, 166, 173
European Cup Winners Cup 174
Everton 26–8, 34, 40–1, 45, 47, 73, 99, 108–10, 118, 124, 126, 157, 166, 174–5, 181–3, 188–9, 194, 200, 203, 209, 221

FA Charity Shield 29, 82, 182, 203
FA Cup 8, 10, 16, 22, 26–7, 41, 45, 47, 54, 65, 72–4, 90–1, 98, 108–9, 125–6, 136, 146–7, 155–6, 165–6, 173–4, 181–2, 187, 189, 192–4, 198–9, 202, 204, 208–10, 214–7, 220–1
Fagan, Joe 166
Fairclough, David 98, 134
Fashanu, John 134
Fashanu, Justin 134
Ferguson, Alex 191, 204, 209
Filbert Street 88, 106, 155
Football Focus 34
Football League 118–9, 125, 127, 166, 199, 208, 220
Football Preview 34
Francis, Gerry 90–1
Fulham 10, 16–7, 74, 99

Ganders Green Lane 202
Gascoigne, Paul 194, 198, 210, 215, 221
Gemmill, Archie 54, 109
George, Ricky 56
Giles, Johnny 34, 45, 64, 99
Gillespie, Gary 194, 214
GM Vauxhall Conference 202, 216, 220
Goal of the Season 21, 65, 74, 82, 90, 108, 134
Goodison Park 29, 40, 65, 124, 157, 188, 194
Gould, Bobby 116, 194
Graham, George 10, 27, 47, 65, 80, 188–9, 220
Grandstand 34, 125
Gray, Andy 110, 126–7, 174
Gray, Eddie 34, 63
Greaves, Jimmy 16, 20–1, 23, 27, 33, 46, 173, 192
Greenwood, Ron 35, 39
Grobbelaar, Bruce 174

Hamilton, Bryan 108
Harvey, Colin 41
Hatton, Bob 72

Hector, Kevin 54
Hereford United 56, 181, 204
Heysel tragedy 174–5, 182
Highbury 106, 125, 136, 147, 188, 193, 217, 221
Hill, Jimmy 34, 74–5, 108, 118, 136, 182, 193
Hillsborough 90
Hillsborough tragedy 199
Hoddle, Glenn 89, 99, 146, 156, 192
Hollins, John 45, 90
Home International Championships 74
Houchen, Keith 180–1
Houghton, Ray 197–8, 214
Huddersfield Town 33, 165
Hughes, Emlyn 65, 98
Hunt, Roger 14–6, 221
Hurst, Geoff 16, 22, 39, 145
Husband, Jimmy 26, 99
Hutchinson, Ian 38
Hutchison, Tommy 146
Hysen, Glenn 214

Ipswich 65, 108–9, 118, 136, 181, 216, 221
ITV 7–8, 34, 40, 56, 75, 108, 118, 136, 157, 166, 182, 199, 210

Jennings, Pat 21, 29
John, Elton 119
Jones, Joey 108, 220
Jones, Mick 34–5, 45, 63

Keegan, Kevin 56, 65, 72, 74, 82, 98, 109, 157, 166, 172, 208
Keelan, Kevin 134
Keeley, Glenn 157
Kendall, Howard 41, 166, 174, 188
Kennedy, Alan 134, 136
Kennedy, Ray 47–8, 98
Kettering Town 199
Kidd, Brian 54, 64, 99–100
King, Andy 124–5
Knowles, Cyril 81
Knowles, Peter 41
Kop, The 156, 198

Latchford, Bob 72, 110, 149
Law, Denis 15, 21, 38, 54, 74, 135
Lawler, Chris 40
Lawrenson, Mark 175
Leatherhead 88–89
League Cup 26, 34, 40, 45, 81–2, 91, 109, 127, 136, 156
Lee, Colin 116, 145
Lee, Francis 33, 82

INDEX

Lee, Gordon 106, 108, 118, 125
Leeds United 16, 22, 34–5, 39, 45, 47, 55, 63–5, 74, 81–3, 116, 126, 148, 174, 194, 209
Leicester City 29, 34–5, 73, 88–9, 100, 106, 136, 155
Leitch, Sam 34
Leppings Lane End 199–200
Leyton Orient 199
Lindsay, Alec 72
Lineker, Gary 155–6,182, 211
Littlewoods Cup 188–9, 204
Liverpool 10, 14–6, 23, 40, 47, 56, 65–6, 72–74, 82, 90, 97–9, 107–110, 118–9, 124, 126, 134–6, 148, 156–7, 164–6, 173–4, 182–3, 188, 194, 197–200, 203–5, 214, 216–7, 221
Loftus Road 33, 126
LWT 34, 74
Lorimer, Peter 23, 45, 63–4
Lukic, John 193
Luton Town 99, 164, 173–4, 181, 187, 194
Lynam, Desmond 8
Lynex, Steve 155–6

Mabbutt, Gary 191
Macdonald, Malcolm 56–7, 91, 99, 106, 165
Mackay, Dave 54, 82, 99, 214
Maine Road 28, 33, 46, 100, 108, 118, 126, 164, 204, 209
Manchester City 22, 33, 39, 46, 64, 74, 99–100, 118, 126, 135–6, 146–9, 164, 174, 192
Manchester derby 126
Manchester United 10, 15–6, 20, 23, 27, 29, 33, 35, 38, 40, 47, 54, 56, 63–5, 73–4, 80–2, 90, 98–9, 109, 118, 125–6, 157, 165–6, 174, 186, 191, 199, 204, 209
Marsh, Rodney 33, 99
Matthews, Sir Stanley 21
McAvennie, Frank 182, 187
McCalliog, Jim 90
McClair, Brian 204
McDermott, Terry 108
McLintock, Frank 47, 90
McManaman, Steve 221
McMenemy, Lawrie 73, 90
McKenzie, Duncan 108
Mercer, Joe 28, 33, 74
Merson, Paul 220
Merseyside derby 40, 65, 108, 157

Middlesboro 136
Milk Cup 157, 165–6, 173–4
Millwall 88, 109, 203
Moore, Bobby 22, 39
Moore, Brian 34
Moran, Kevin 191, 214
Morley, Tony 137
Morrisey, Johnny 41
Mortimer, Dennis 137
Mountfield, Derek 181
Muhren, Arnold 118

Neal, Phil 97–8
Newcastle United 33, 40, 46, 56–7, 74, 91, 106–7, 126, 145, 157, 166, 172, 181, 194, 200, 214
Nicholas, Charlie 166, 188
Nicholson, Bill 54, 81–2, 136
Nicol, Steve 194, 200, 214
Norwich 39, 99, 134–6, 174, 188, 203, 210
Nottingham Forest 15–6, 26–7, 54, 56, 82–3, 109, 117–9, 126, 135–6, 186–7, 197–9, 204, 210
Notts County 126, 215

O'Farrell, Frank 56, 65
Oldham Athletic 174, 204, 209
Old Trafford 10, 20–1, 29, 45, 64–5, 82, 109, 165, 186, 191, 200, 203
O'Leary, David 125, 165, 220
On the Ball 34
Osgood, Peter 27, 38, 45, 65, 90
Oxford United 10, 166, 174, 215

Paisley, Bob 90, 97, 108, 126, 157–8
Pardew, Alan 204–5
Parkes, Phil 136
Parry, Alan 172
Perryman, Steve 46
Peters, Martin 16, 22, 39, 46, 65, 99
PFA 72
PFA Player of the Year 125, 198
Pleat, David 164, 188, 192
Port Vale 194
Portsmouth 27, 73, 98, 215–1, 221
Premier League 8, 216
Preston North End 208

Queen's Park Rangers 26, 33, 90–1, 126, 147, 198

Radford, John 47–8
Radford, Ronnie 56
Rains, Tony 202–3
Ramsey, Alf 39, 74
Revie, Don 16, 34–5, 55, 74, 81–2, 90
Rioch, Bruce 82, 108
Robinson, Peter 208
Robson, Bobby 16–17, 109, 136
Robson, Bryan 209
Robson, Bryan 'Pop' 99
Rogers, Don 40
Rosenthal, Ronnie 214
Rotherham United 157, 208
Roy of the Rovers 106
Royle, Joe 41, 99
Rumbelows Cup 220
Rush, Ian 157, 166, 173, 192, 194, 198, 203–4

Sabella, Alex 118
Sanchez, Lawrie 194
Sansom, Kenny 147, 193
Saunders, Ron 82, 137
Scotland 74, 81, 135, 187, 216
Sexton, Dave 38, 90
Shankly, Bill 14, 40–1, 65–6, 74, 82, 107, 148
Sharp, Graeme, 174–5
Sheffield United 63–4, 89, 118, 204
Sheffield Wednesday 16, 166
Shilton, Peter 29, 74, 97, 109, 117, 156
Sky TV 216
Smith, Jim 216
Souness, Graeme 216–17, 221
Southampton 63–4, 73, 90, 98, 107, 118, 157, 210
Spackman, Nigel 198
Sportsnight 9, 166
Sports Special 7
Stamford Bridge 23, 27, 38, 45, 65, 82, 108, 145
Stapleton, Frank 106, 125, 165
Stepney, Alex 29
Stiles, Nobby 16, 38
Stoke City 47, 73–4, 81, 89, 97–8, 117
Stokes, Bobby 98
Stokoe, Bob 82
Stoller, Barry 49
Storey-Moore, Ian 26–7
St James Park 40, 172, 194
Sunderland 33, 73, 82, 99, 126, 174, 216, 221
Sutton United 202–3
Swansea City 119, 148–9
Swindon Town 40, 54

Tambling, Bobby 27, 38
Taylor, Graham 6, 119, 148, 157, 167, 193, 211
Taylor, Peter 54, 109, 136
Thomas, Clive 108, 136
Tomaszewski, Jan 74
Toshack, John 65, 72, 98, 107, 119, 148
Tottenham Hotspur 15–6, 20, 21, 23, 27, 29, 33, 39, 46, 54, 80–2, 99, 109, 116, 118, 125, 136, 145–8, 156, 188, 191–2, 194, 199, 211, 215, 221
Tranmere Rovers 181, 203

UEFA Cup 65–6, 81, 90, 107, 136, 156, 216
Upton Park 22, 27, 39, 187

Venables, Terry 10, 27, 147, 194, 215
Villa Park 16, 22, 27, 82, 166, 173, 192, 204–5, 210, 216
Villa, Ricky 118–9, 136

Waddle, Chris 145, 172, 192
Wales 108
Wallington, Mark 88, 155
Walsh, Mickey 82
Watford 41, 119, 126, 148, 157, 166–7, 193, 198
Webb, David 38, 45, 90
Wembley 27, 40, 47, 74, 82, 98, 108–9, 127, 136, 157, 165–7, 174, 183, 189, 194, 200, 203–4, 209–10, 215–6, 221
West Brom 23, 26, 39, 55, 82, 99, 109, 118, 126, 209
West Ham 10, 22, 29, 34–5, 39–40, 46–7, 89, 98–9, 108, 136, 147, 182, 187, 192, 210, 216
Whelan, Ronnie 216
White Hart Lane 16, 20–1, 23, 46–7, 80–2, 116, 125, 146, 188
Whitley Bay 208
Williams, Steve 181, 193
Wimbledon 189, 194, 203
Woodcock, Tony 110
Wolstenholme, Kenneth 8, 14, 22
Wolverhampton Wanderers 41, 90, 109, 126–7, 135
Worthington, Frank 88–9
World Cup 22, 29, 39, 73–4, 81, 118, 157, 209, 215
Wrexham 110, 126, 216, 220